An Introduction to Genetic Algorithms

W9-BPP-050

Complex Adaptive Systems
John H. Holland, Christopher Langton, and Stewart W. Wilson, advisors

Adaptation in Natural and Artificial Systems: An Introductory Analysis with Applications in Biology, Control, and Artificial Intelligence, John H. Holland

Toward a Practice of Autonomous Systems: Proceedings of the First European Conference on Artificial Life, edited by Francisco J. Varela and Paul Bourgine

Genetic Programming: On the Programming of Computers by Means of Natural Selection, John R. Koza

From Animals to Animats 2: Proceedings of the Second International Conference on Simulation of Adaptive Behavior, edited by Jean-Arcady Meyer, Herbert L. Roitblat, and Stewart W. Wilson

Intelligent Behavior in Animals and Robots, David McFarland and Thomas Bösser

Advances in Genetic Programming, edited by Kenneth E. Kinnear, Jr.

Turtles, Termites, and Traffic Jams: Explorations in Massively Parallel Microworlds, Mitchell Resnick

From Animals to Animats 3: Proceedings of the Third International Conference on Simulation of Adaptive Behavior, edited by Dave Cliff, Philip Husbands, Jean-Arcady Meyer, and Stewart W. Wilson

Artificial Life IV: Proceedings of the Fourth International Workshop on the Synthesis and Simulation of Living Systems, edited by Rodney A. Brooks and Pattie Maes

Comparative Approaches to Cognitive Science, edited by Herbert L. Roitblat and Jean-Arcady Meyer

Artificial Life: An Overview, edited by Christopher G. Langton

Evolutionary Programming IV: Proceedings of the Fourth Annual Conference on Evolutionary Programming, edited by John R. McDonnell, Robert G. Reynolds, and David B. Fogel

An Introduction to Genetic Algorithms, Melanie Mitchell

An Introduction to Genetic Algorithms

Melanie Mitchell

A Bradford Book
The MIT Press
Cambridge, Massachusetts
London, England

First MIT Press paperback edition, 1998
© 1996 Massachusetts Institute of Technology

Set in Palatino by Windfall Software using ZzTEX.
Printed and bound in the United States of America.

Library of Congress Cataloging-in-Publication Data

Mitchell, Melanie.
 An introduction to genetic algorithms / Melanie Mitchell.
    p.   cm.
 "A Bradford book."
 Includes bibliographical references and index.
   ISBN 978-0-262-13316-6 (hc. : alk. paper) — 978-0-262-63185-3 (pb. : alk. paper)
   1. Genetics—Computer simulation. 2. Genetics—Mathematical
models. I. Title.
QH441.2.M55   1996
575.1′01′13—dc20   95-24489
                                                          CIP

20 19 18 17 16 15 14 13

Contents

Preface

This book introduces the rapidly growing field of genetic algorithms (GAs). Its purpose is to describe in depth some of the most interesting work in this field rather than to attempt a complete but less detailed survey. What is "most interesting" is, of course, very subjective; the choice of topics reflects my own interests, which lean toward machine learning, scientific modeling, and "artificial life" more than toward optimization and engineering. GAs have been widely explored in all these areas, but this book concentrates much more on the former than on the latter. This distinguishes it from other books on GAs, which focus mainly on optimization techniques and engineering applications.

In technology and science GAs have been used as adaptive algorithms for solving practical problems and as computational models of natural evolutionary systems. I will give equal space to these two roles, and I will also discuss their complementary aspects. In describing the applications and the modeling projects, I will venture beyond the strict boundaries of computer science into the worlds of dynamical systems theory, game theory, molecular biology, ecology, evolutionary biology, and population genetics. Such forays are a wonderful perquisite of GA research. Just as GAs are "general-purpose" search methods, GA researchers have to be generalists, willing to step out of their own discipline and learn something about a new one in order to pursue a promising application or model. Very often this is done in collaboration between scientists from different disciplines—computer scientists working with biologists using GAs to predict the structure of proteins or with political scientists modeling the evolution of cooperative behavior among nations. Such collaborations often lead to new insights in both fields. This interdisciplinary nature of GA research is one of the qualities that make it so valuable and so much fun. The field of GAs and the broader field of evolutionary computation are very young, and most of the important problems remain open. I hope that this book will communicate some of the excitement and the importance of this enterprise, and that it will provide enough information to enable scientists in a range of disciplines to become involved.

The first chapter introduces genetic algorithms and their terminology, sets the stage by describing two provocative GA applications in detail, and gives a brief introduction to the theory of GAs. Chapters 2 and 3 survey some of the most interesting GA applications in the fields of machine learning and scientific modeling. Chapter 4 describes several approaches to the theory of GAs, and chapter 5 discusses a number of important implementation issues that arise in the application of GAs. The last chapter poses some currently unanswered questions about GAs and surveys some prospects for the future of evolutionary computation in technology and in modeling. The appendices give a a selected list of general references on GAs and instructions on how to obtain information about GAs on the Internet.

This book is for anyone with a college-level scientific background who is interested in learning about or using genetic algorithms. Some knowledge of computer programming is assumed. No mathematics beyond algebra is used, except in chapter 4 (where calculus, vector algebra, and probability theory come into play). The book is meant to be accessible to scientists in any discipline, and it could be used as a text for graduate or upper-level undergraduate courses in which GAs are featured. For those who get hooked and want to explore the field in more depth, numerous pointers to the GA literature are given throughout the text and in the extensive bibliography. In addition, thought exercises and computer exercises are given at the end of each chapter.

Acknowledgments

I am very grateful to the following people for answering questions, for commenting on chapters, and for general moral support while I was writing this book: Dave Ackley, Bob Axelrod, Mark Bedau, Rik Belew, Lashon Booker, Ronda Butler-Villa, Jim Crutchfield, Raja Das, Doyne Farmer, Marc Feldman, William Finnoff, Stephanie Forrest, Bob French, Mark Galassi, Howard Gutowitz, Doug Hofstadter, John Holland, Greg Huber, Jeff Ihara, David Jefferson, George Johnson, Terry Jones, Hiroaki Kitano, Jim Levenick, Michael Littman, Dan McShea, Tom Meyer, Jack Mitchell, Norma Mitchell, David Moser, Una-May O'Reilly, Norman Packard, Richard Palmer, Rick Riolo, Jonathan Roughgarden, Steffen Schulze-Kremer, Jonathan Shapiro, Chuck Taylor, Peter Todd, and Stewart Wilson. I am also grateful to Betty Stanton, Harry Stanton, Teri Mendelsohn, and Paul Bethge for their help and patience on publishing and editorial matters. The Santa Fe Institute has provided an ideal environment for my research and writing. I especially want to thank Mike Simmons and Ginger Richardson for academic support and advice at SFI and Deborah Smith and Joleen Rocque-Frank for secretarial support. I am grateful for research funding from the Alfred P. Sloan Foundation (grant B1992-46), the National Science Foundation (grant IRI-9320200), and the Department of Energy (grant DE-FG03-94ER25231).

This book stems from a series of lectures I gave at the 1992 Santa Fe Institute Complex Systems Summer School. Many thanks to Dan Stein for inviting me to give these lectures, and to the 1992 Summer School students for their incisive questions and comments.

Finally, special thanks to John Holland for introducing me to genetic algorithms in the first place, for ongoing support and encouragement of my work, and for continuing to produce and share ideas and insights about complex adaptive systems.

An Introduction to Genetic Algorithms

1   Genetic Algorithms: An Overview

Science arises from the very human desire to understand and control the world. Over the course of history, we humans have gradually built up a grand edifice of knowledge that enables us to predict, to varying extents, the weather, the motions of the planets, solar and lunar eclipses, the courses of diseases, the rise and fall of economic growth, the stages of language development in children, and a vast panorama of other natural, social, and cultural phenomena. More recently we have even come to understand some fundamental limits to our abilities to predict. Over the eons we have developed increasingly complex means to control many aspects of our lives and our interactions with nature, and we have learned, often the hard way, the extent to which other aspects are uncontrollable.

The advent of electronic computers has arguably been the most revolutionary development in the history of science and technology. This ongoing revolution is profoundly increasing our ability to predict and control nature in ways that were barely conceived of even half a century ago. For many, the crowning achievements of this revolution will be the creation—in the form of computer programs—of new species of intelligent beings, and even of new forms of life.

The goals of creating artificial intelligence and artificial life can be traced back to the very beginnings of the computer age. The earliest computer scientists—Alan Turing, John von Neumann, Norbert Wiener, and others—were motivated in large part by visions of imbuing computer programs with intelligence, with the life-like ability to self-replicate, and with the adaptive capability to learn and to control their environments. These early pioneers of computer science were as much interested in biology and psychology as in electronics, and they looked to natural systems as guiding metaphors for how to achieve their visions. It should be no surprise, then, that from the earliest days computers were applied not only to calculating missile trajectories and deciphering military codes but also to modeling the brain, mimicking human learning, and simulating biological evolution. These biologically motivated computing activities have waxed and waned over the years, but since the early 1980s they have all undergone a resurgence in the computation research community. The first has grown into the field of neural networks, the second into machine learning, and the third into what is now called "evolutionary computation," of which genetic algorithms are the most prominent example.

1.1 A BRIEF HISTORY OF EVOLUTIONARY COMPUTATION

In the 1950s and the 1960s several computer scientists independently studied evolutionary systems with the idea that evolution could be used as an optimization tool for engineering problems. The idea in all these systems was to evolve a population of candidate solutions to a given problem, using operators inspired by natural genetic variation and natural selection.

In the 1960s, Rechenberg (1965, 1973) introduced "evolution strategies" (*Evolutionsstrategie* in the original German), a method he used to optimize real-valued parameters for devices such as airfoils. This idea was further developed by Schwefel (1975, 1977). The field of evolution strategies has remained an active area of research, mostly developing independently from the field of genetic algorithms (although recently the two communities have begun to interact). (For a short review of evolution strategies, see Bäck, Hoffmeister, and Schwefel 1991.) Fogel, Owens, and Walsh (1966) developed "evolutionary programming," a technique in which candidate solutions to given tasks were represented as finite-state machines, which were evolved by randomly mutating their state-transition diagrams and selecting the fittest. A somewhat broader formulation of evolutionary programming also remains an area of active research (see, for example, Fogel and Atmar 1993). Together, evolution strategies, evolutionary programming, and genetic algorithms form the backbone of the field of evolutionary computation.

Several other people working in the 1950s and the 1960s developed evolution-inspired algorithms for optimization and machine learning. Box (1957), Friedman (1959), Bledsoe (1961), Bremermann (1962), and Reed, Toombs, and Baricelli (1967) all worked in this area, though their work has been given little or none of the kind of attention or followup that evolution strategies, evolutionary programming, and genetic algorithms have seen. In addition, a number of evolutionary biologists used computers to simulate evolution for the purpose of controlled experiments (see, e.g., Baricelli 1957, 1962; Fraser 1957a,b; Martin and Cockerham 1960). Evolutionary computation was definitely in the air in the formative days of the electronic computer.

Genetic algorithms (GAs) were invented by John Holland in the 1960s and were developed by Holland and his students and colleagues at the University of Michigan in the 1960s and the 1970s. In contrast with evolution strategies and evolutionary programming, Holland's original goal was not to design algorithms to solve specific problems, but rather to formally study the phenomenon of adaptation as it occurs in nature and to develop ways in which the mechanisms of natural adaptation might be imported into computer systems. Holland's 1975 book *Adaptation in Natural and Artificial Systems* presented the genetic algorithm as an abstraction of biological evolution and gave a theoretical framework for adaptation under the GA. Holland's GA is a method for moving from one population of "chromosomes" (e.g., strings of ones and zeros, or "bits") to a new population by using a kind of "natural selection" together with the genetics-inspired operators of crossover, mutation, and inversion. Each chromosome consists of "genes" (e.g., bits), each gene being an instance of a particular "allele" (e.g., 0 or 1). The selection operator chooses those chromosomes in the population that will be allowed to reproduce, and on average the fitter chromosomes produce more offspring than the less fit ones. Crossover exchanges subparts of two chromosomes, roughly mimicking biological recombination between two single-chromosome ("haploid") organisms; mutation randomly changes the allele values of some locations in the chromosome; and inversion reverses the order of a contiguous section of the chromosome, thus rearranging the order in which genes are arrayed. (Here, as in most of the GA literature, "crossover" and "recombination" will mean the same thing.)

Holland's introduction of a population-based algorithm with crossover, inversion, and mutation was a major innovation. (Rechenberg's evolution strategies started with a "population" of two individuals, one parent and one offspring, the offspring being a mutated version of the parent; many-individual populations and crossover were not incorporated until later. Fogel, Owens, and Walsh's evolutionary programming likewise used only mutation to provide variation.) Moreover, Holland was the first to attempt to put computational evolution on a firm theoretical footing (see Holland 1975). Until recently this theoretical foundation, based on the notion of "schemas," was the basis of almost all subsequent theoretical work on genetic algorithms

In the last several years there has been widespread interaction among researchers studying various evolutionary computation methods, and the boundaries between GAs, evolution strategies, evolutionary programming, and other evolutionary approaches have broken down to some extent. Today, researchers often use the term "genetic algorithm" to describe something very far from Holland's original conception. In this book I adopt this flexibility. Most of the projects I will describe here were referred to by their originators as GAs; some were not, but they all have enough of a "family resemblance" that I include them under the rubric of genetic algorithms.

1.2 THE APPEAL OF EVOLUTION

Why use evolution as an inspiration for solving computational problems? To evolutionary-computation researchers, the mechanisms of evolution seem well suited for some of the most pressing computational problems in many fields. Many computational problems require searching through a huge number of possibilities for solutions. One example is the problem of computational protein engineering, in which an algorithm is sought that will search among the vast number of possible amino acid sequences for a protein with specified properties. Another example is searching for a set of rules or equations that will predict the ups and downs of a financial market, such as that for foreign currency. Such search problems can often benefit from an effective use of parallelism, in which many different possibilities are explored simultaneously in an efficient way. For example, in searching for proteins with specified properties, rather than evaluate one amino acid sequence at a time it would be much faster to evaluate many simultaneously. What is needed is both computational parallelism (i.e., many processors evaluating sequences at the same time) and an intelligent strategy for choosing the next set of sequences to evaluate.

Many computational problems require a computer program to be *adaptive*—to continue to perform well in a changing environment. This is typified by problems in robot control in which a robot has to perform a task in a variable environment, and by computer interfaces that must adapt to the idiosyncrasies of different users. Other problems require computer programs to be innovative—to construct something truly new and original, such as a new algorithm for accomplishing a computational task or even a new scientific discovery. Finally, many computational problems require complex solutions that are difficult to program by hand. A striking example is the problem of creating artificial intelligence. Early on, AI practitioners believed that it would be straightforward to encode the rules that would confer intelligence on a program; expert systems were one result of this early optimism. Nowadays, many AI researchers believe that the "rules" underlying intelligence are too complex for scientists to encode by hand in a "top-down" fashion. Instead they believe that the best route to artificial intelligence is through a "bottom-up" paradigm in which humans write only very simple rules, and complex behaviors such as intelligence emerge from the massively parallel application and interaction of these simple rules. Connectionism (i.e., the study of computer programs inspired by neural systems) is one example of this philosophy (see Smolensky 1988); evolutionary computation is another. In connectionism the rules are typically simple "neural" thresholding, activation spreading, and strengthening or weakening of connections; the hoped-for emergent behavior is sophisticated pattern recognition and learning. In evolutionary computation the rules are typically "natural selection" with variation due to crossover and/or mutation; the hoped-for emergent behavior is the design of high-quality solutions to difficult problems and the ability to adapt these solutions in the face of a changing environment.

Biological evolution is an appealing source of inspiration for addressing these problems. Evolution is, in effect, a method of searching among an enormous number of possibilities for "solutions." In biology the enormous set of possibilities is the set of possible genetic sequences, and the desired "solutions" are highly fit organisms—organisms well able to survive and reproduce in their environments. Evolution can also be seen as a method for *designing* innovative solutions to complex problems. For example, the mammalian immune system is a marvelous evolved solution to the problem of germs invading the body. Seen in this light, the mechanisms of evolution can inspire computational search methods. Of course the fitness of a biological organism depends on many factors—for example, how well it can weather the physical characteristics of its environment and how well it can compete with or cooperate with the other organisms around it. The fitness criteria continually change as creatures evolve, so evolution is searching a constantly changing set of possibilities. Searching for solutions in the face of changing conditions is precisely what is required for adaptive computer programs. Furthermore, evolution is a massively parallel search method: rather than work on one species at a time, evolution tests and changes millions of species in parallel. Finally, viewed from a high level the "rules" of evolution are remarkably simple: species evolve by means of random variation (via mutation, recombination, and other operators), followed by natural selection in which the fittest tend to survive and reproduce, thus propagating their genetic material to future generations. Yet these simple rules are thought to be responsible, in large part, for the extraordinary variety and complexity we see in the biosphere.

1.3 BIOLOGICAL TERMINOLOGY

At this point it is useful to formally introduce some of the biological terminology that will be used throughout the book. In the context of genetic algorithms, these biological terms are used in the spirit of analogy with real biology, though the entities they refer to are much simpler than the real biological ones.

All living organisms consist of cells, and each cell contains the same set of one or more *chromosomes*—strings of DNA—that serve as a "blueprint" for the organism. A chromosome can be conceptually divided into *genes*—functional blocks of DNA, each of which encodes a particular protein. Very roughly, one can think of a gene as encoding a *trait*, such as eye color. The different possible "settings" for a trait (e.g., blue, brown, hazel) are called *alleles*. Each gene is located at a particular *locus* (position) on the chromosome.

Many organisms have multiple chromosomes in each cell. The complete collection of genetic material (all chromosomes taken together) is called the organism's *genome*. The term *genotype* refers to the particular set of genes contained in a genome. Two individuals that have identical genomes are said to have the same genotype. The genotype gives rise, under fetal and later development, to the organism's *phenotype*—its physical and mental characteristics, such as eye color, height, brain size, and intelligence.

Organisms whose chromosomes are arrayed in pairs are called *diploid*; organisms whose chromosomes are unpaired are called *haploid*. In nature, most sexually reproducing species are diploid, including human beings, who each have 23 pairs of chromosomes in each somatic (non-germ) cell in the body. During sexual reproduction, *recombination* (or *crossover*) occurs: in each parent, genes are exchanged between each pair of chromosomes to form a *gamete* (a single chromosome), and then gametes from the two parents pair up to create a full set of diploid chromosomes. In haploid sexual reproduction, genes are exchanged between the two parents' single-strand chromosomes. Offspring are subject to *mutation,* in which single nucleotides (elementary bits of DNA) are changed from parent to offspring, the changes often resulting from copying errors. The *fitness* of an organism is typically defined as the probability that the organism will live to reproduce (*viability*) or as a function of the number of offspring the organism has (*fertility*).

In genetic algorithms, the term *chromosome* typically refers to a candidate solution to a problem, often encoded as a bit string. The "genes" are either single bits or short blocks of adjacent bits that encode a particular element of the candidate solution (e.g., in the context of multiparameter function optimization the bits encoding a particular parameter might be considered to be a gene). An allele in a bit string is either 0 or 1; for larger alphabets more alleles are possible at each locus. Crossover typically consists of exchanging genetic material between two single-chromosome haploid parents. Mutation consists of flipping the bit at a randomly chosen locus (or, for larger alphabets, replacing a the symbol at a randomly chosen locus with a randomly chosen new symbol).

Most applications of genetic algorithms employ haploid individuals, particularly, single-chromosome individuals. The genotype of an individual in a GA using bit strings is simply the configuration of bits in that individual's chromosome. Often there is no notion of "phenotype" in the context of GAs, although more recently many workers have experimented with GAs in which there is both a genotypic level and a phenotypic level (e.g., the bit-string encoding of a neural network and the neural network itself).

1.4 SEARCH SPACES AND FITNESS LANDSCAPES

The idea of searching among a collection of candidate solutions for a desired solution is so common in computer science that it has been given its own name: searching in a "search space." Here the term "search space" refers to some collection of candidate solutions to a problem and some notion of "distance" between candidate solutions. For an example, let us take one of the most important problems in computational bioengineering: the aforementioned problem of computational protein design. Suppose you want use a computer to search for a protein—a sequence of amino acids—that folds up to a particular three-dimensional shape so it can be used, say, to fight a specific virus. The search space is the collection of all possible protein sequences—an infinite set of possibilities. To constrain it, let us restrict the search to all possible sequences of length 100 or less—still a huge search space, since there are 20 possible amino acids at each position in the sequence. (How many possible sequences are there?) If we represent the 20 amino acids by letters of the alphabet, candidate solutions will look like this:

A G G M C G B L. . . .

We will define the distance between two sequences as the number of positions in which the letters at corresponding positions differ. For example, the distance between A G G M C G B L and M G G M C G B L is 1, and the distance between A G G M C G B L and L B M P A F G A is 8. An algorithm for searching this space is a method for choosing which candidate solutions to test at each stage of the search. In most cases the next candidate solution(s) to be tested will depend on the results of testing previous sequences; most useful algorithms assume that there will be some correlation between the quality of "neighboring" candidate solutions—those close in the space. Genetic algorithms assume that high-quality "parent" candidate solutions from different regions in the space can be combined via crossover to, on occasion, produce high-quality "offspring" candidate solutions.

Another important concept is that of "fitness landscape." Originally defined by the biologist Sewell Wright (1931) in the context of population genetics, a fitness landscape is a representation of the space of all possible genotypes along with their fitnesses.

Suppose, for the sake of simplicity, that each genotype is a bit string of length l, and that the distance between two genotypes is their "Hamming distance"—the number of locations at which corresponding bits differ. Also suppose that each genotype can be assigned a real-valued fitness. A fitness landscape can be pictured as an $(l + 1)$-dimensional plot in which each genotype is a point in l dimensions and its fitness is plotted along the $(l + 1)$st axis. A simple landscape for $l = 2$ is shown in figure 1.1. Such plots are called landscapes because the plot of fitness values can form "hills," "peaks," "valleys," and other features analogous to those of physical landscapes. Under Wright's formulation, evolution causes populations to move along landscapes in particular ways, and "adaptation" can be seen as the movement toward local peaks. (A "local peak," or "local optimum," is not necessarily the highest point in the landscape, but any small

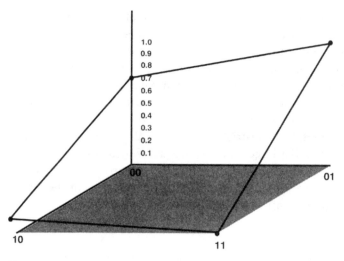

Figure 1.1 A simple fitness landscape for $l = 2$. Here $f(00) = 0.7$, $f(01) = 1.0$, $f(10) = 0.1$, and $f(11) = 0.0$.

movement away from it goes downward in fitness.) Likewise, in GAs the operators of crossover and mutation can be seen as ways of moving a population around on the landscape defined by the fitness function.

The idea of evolution moving populations around in unchanging landscapes is biologically unrealistic for several reasons. For example, an organism cannot be assigned a fitness value independent of the other organisms in its environment; thus, as the population changes, the fitnesses of particular genotypes will change as well. In other words, in the real world the "landscape" cannot be separated from the organisms that inhabit it. In spite of such caveats, the notion of fitness landscape has become central to the study of genetic algorithms, and it will come up in various guises throughout this book.

1.5 ELEMENTS OF GENETIC ALGORITHMS

It turns out that there is no rigorous definition of "genetic algorithm" accepted by all in the evolutionary-computation community that differentiates GAs from other evolutionary computation methods. However, it can be said that most methods called "GAs" have at least the following elements in common: populations of chromosomes, selection according to fitness, crossover to produce new offspring, and random mutation of new offspring. Inversion—Holland's fourth element of GAs—is rarely used in today's implementations, and its advantages, if any, are not well established. (Inversion will be discussed at length in chapter 5.)

The chromosomes in a GA population typically take the form of bit strings. Each locus in the chromosome has two possible alleles: 0 and 1.

Each chromosome can be thought of as a point in the search space of candidate solutions. The GA processes populations of chromosomes, successively replacing one such population with another. The GA most often requires a fitness function that assigns a score (fitness) to each chromosome in the current population. The fitness of a chromosome depends on how well that chromosome solves the problem at hand.

Examples of Fitness Functions

One common application of GAs is function optimization, where the goal is to find a set of parameter values that maximize, say, a complex multi-parameter function. As a simple example, one might want to maximize the real-valued one-dimensional function

$$f(y) = y + |\sin(32y)|, \quad 0 \le y < \pi$$

(Riolo 1992). Here the candidate solutions are values of y, which can be encoded as bit strings representing real numbers. The fitness calculation translates a given bit string x into a real number y and then evaluates the function at that value. The fitness of a string is the function value at that point.

As a non-numerical example, consider the problem of finding a sequence of 50 amino acids that will fold to a desired three-dimensional protein structure. A GA could be applied to this problem by searching a population of candidate solutions, each encoded as a 50-letter string such as

IHCCVASASDMIKPVFTVASYLKNWTKAKGPNFEICISGRTPYWDNFPGI,

where each letter represents one of 20 possible amino acids. One way to define the fitness of a candidate sequence is as the negative of the potential energy of the sequence with respect to the desired structure. The potential energy is a measure of how much physical resistance the sequence would put up if forced to be folded into the desired structure— the lower the potential energy, the higher the fitness. Of course one would not want to physically force every sequence in the population into the desired structure and measure its resistance—this would be very difficult, if not impossible. Instead, given a sequence and a desired structure (and knowing some of the relevant biophysics), one can estimate the potential energy by calculating some of the forces acting on each amino acid, so the whole fitness calculation can be done computationally.

These examples show two different contexts in which candidate solutions to a problem are encoded as abstract chromosomes encoded as strings of symbols, with fitness functions defined on the resulting space of strings. A genetic algorithm is a method for searching such fitness landscapes for highly fit strings.

GA Operators

The simplest form of genetic algorithm involves three types of operators: selection, crossover (single point), and mutation.

Selection This operator selects chromosomes in the population for reproduction. The fitter the chromosome, the more times it is likely to be selected to reproduce.

Crossover This operator randomly chooses a locus and exchanges the subsequences before and after that locus between two chromosomes to create two offspring. For example, the strings 10000100 and 11111111 could be crossed over after the third locus in each to produce the two offspring 10011111 and 11100100. The crossover operator roughly mimics biological recombination between two single-chromosome (haploid) organisms.

Mutation This operator randomly flips some of the bits in a chromosome. For example, the string 00000100 might be mutated in its second position to yield 01000100. Mutation can occur at each bit position in a string with some probability, usually very small (e.g., 0.001).

1.6   A SIMPLE GENETIC ALGORITHM

Given a clearly defined problem to be solved and a bit string representation for candidate solutions, a simple GA works as follows:

1. Start with a randomly generated population of n l-bit chromosomes (candidate solutions to a problem).

2. Calculate the fitness $f(x)$ of each chromosome x in the population.

3. Repeat the following steps until n offspring have been created:

a. Select a pair of parent chromosomes from the current population, the probability of selection being an increasing function of fitness. Selection is done "with replacement," meaning that the same chromosome can be selected more than once to become a parent.

b. With probability p_c (the "crossover probability" or "crossover rate"), cross over the pair at a randomly chosen point (chosen with uniform probability) to form two offspring. If no crossover takes place, form two offspring that are exact copies of their respective parents. (Note that here the crossover rate is defined to be the probability that two parents will cross over in a single point. There are also "multi-point crossover" versions of the GA in which the crossover rate for a pair of parents is the number of points at which a crossover takes place.)

c. Mutate the two offspring at each locus with probability p_m (the mutation probability or mutation rate), and place the resulting chromosomes in the new population.

If n is odd, one new population member can be discarded at random.

4. Replace the current population with the new population.

5. Go to step 2.

Each iteration of this process is called a *generation*. A GA is typically iterated for anywhere from 50 to 500 or more generations. The entire set of generations is called a *run*. At the end of a run there are often one or more highly fit chromosomes in the population. Since randomness plays a large role in each run, two runs with different random-number seeds will generally produce different detailed behaviors. GA researchers often report statistics (such as the best fitness found in a run and the generation at which the individual with that best fitness was discovered) averaged over many different runs of the GA on the same problem.

The simple procedure just described is the basis for most applications of GAs. There are a number of details to fill in, such as the size of the population and the probabilities of crossover and mutation, and the success of the algorithm often depends greatly on these details. There are also more complicated versions of GAs (e.g., GAs that work on representations other than strings or GAs that have different types of crossover and mutation operators). Many examples will be given in later chapters.

As a more detailed example of a simple GA, suppose that l (string length) is 8, that $f(x)$ is equal to the number of ones in bit string x (an extremely simple fitness function, used here only for illustrative purposes), that n (the population size) is 4, that $p_c = 0.7$, and that $p_m = 0.001$. (Like the fitness function, these values of l and n were chosen for simplicity. More typical values of l and n are in the range 50–1000. The values given for p_c and p_m are fairly typical.)

The initial (randomly generated) population might look like this:

Chromosome label	Chromosome string	Fitness
A	00000110	2
B	11101110	6
C	00100000	1
D	00110100	3

A common selection method in GAs is *fitness-proportionate selection*, in which the number of times an individual is expected to reproduce is equal to its fitness divided by the average of fitnesses in the population. (This is equivalent to what biologists call "viability selection.")

A simple method of implementing fitness-proportionate selection is "roulette-wheel sampling" (Goldberg 1989a), which is conceptually equivalent to giving each individual a slice of a circular roulette wheel equal in area to the individual's fitness. The roulette wheel is spun, the ball comes to rest on one wedge-shaped slice, and the corresponding individual is selected. In the $n = 4$ example above, the roulette wheel would be spun four times; the first two spins might choose chromosomes B and D to be parents, and the second two spins might choose chromosomes B and C to be parents. (The fact that A might not be selected is just the luck of the draw. If the roulette wheel were spun many times, the average results would be closer to the expected values.)

Once a pair of parents is selected, with probability p_c they cross over to form two offspring. If they do not cross over, then the offspring are exact copies of each parent. Suppose, in the example above, that parents B and D cross over after the first bit position to form offspring E $= 10110100$ and F $= 01101110$, and parents B and C do not cross over, instead forming offspring that are exact copies of B and C. Next, each offspring is subject to mutation at each locus with probability p_m. For example, suppose offspring E is mutated at the sixth locus to form E$'$ $= 10110000$, offspring F and C are not mutated at all, and offspring B is mutated at the first locus to form B$'$ $= 01101110$. The new population will be the following:

Chromosome label	Chromosome string	Fitness
E$'$	10110000	3
F	01101110	5
C	00100000	1
B$'$	01101110	5

Note that, in the new population, although the best string (the one with fitness 6) was lost, the average fitness rose from 12/4 to 14/4. Iterating this procedure will eventually result in a string with all ones.

1.7 GENETIC ALGORITHMS AND TRADITIONAL SEARCH METHODS

In the preceding sections I used the word "search" to describe what GAs do. It is important at this point to contrast this meaning of "search" with its other meanings in computer science.

There are at least three (overlapping) meanings of "search":

Search for stored data   Here the problem is to efficiently retrieve information stored in computer memory. Suppose you have a large database of names and addresses stored in some ordered way. What is the best way to search for the record corresponding to a given last name? "Binary search" is one method for efficiently finding the desired record. Knuth (1973) describes and analyzes many such search methods.

Search for paths to goals   Here the problem is to efficiently find a set of actions that will move from a given initial state to a given goal. This form of search is central to many approaches in artificial intelligence. A simple example—all too familiar to anyone who has taken a course in AI—is the "8-puzzle," illustrated in figure 1.2. A set of tiles numbered 1–8 are placed in a square, leaving one space empty. Sliding one of the adjacent tiles into the blank space is termed a "move." Figure 1.2a illustrates the problem of finding a set of moves from the initial state to the state in which all the tiles are in order. A partial search tree corresponding to this problem is illustrated in figure 1.2b. The "root" node represents the initial state, the nodes branching out from it represent all possible results of one move from that state, and so on down the tree. The search algorithms discussed in most AI contexts are methods for efficiently finding the best (here, the shortest) path in the tree from the initial state to the goal state. Typical algorithms are "depth-first search," "branch and bound," and "A*."

Search for solutions   This is a more general class of search than "search for paths to goals." The idea is to efficiently find a solution to a problem in a large space of candidate solutions. These are the kinds of search problems for which genetic algorithms are used.

There is clearly a big difference between the first kind of search and the second two. The first concerns problems in which one needs to find a piece of information (e.g., a telephone number) in a collection of explicitly stored information. In the second two, the information to be searched is not explicitly stored; rather, candidate solutions are created as the search process proceeds. For example, the AI search methods for solving the 8-puzzle do not begin with a complete search tree in which all the nodes are already stored in memory; for most problems of interest there are too many possible nodes in the tree to store them all. Rather, the search tree is elaborated step by step in a way that depends on the particular algorithm, and the goal is to find an optimal or high-quality solution by examining only a small portion of the tree. Likewise, when searching a space of candidate solutions with a GA, not all possible candidate solutions are created first and then evaluated; rather, the GA is a method for finding optimal or good solutions by examining only a small fraction of the possible candidates.

"Search for solutions" subsumes "search for paths to goals," since a path through a search tree can be encoded as a candidate solution. For the 8-puzzle, the candidate solutions could be lists of moves from the initial state to some other state (correct only if the final state is the goal state). However, many "search for paths to goals" problems are better solved by the AI tree-search techniques (in which partial solutions can be evaluated) than by GA or GA-like techniques (in which full candidate solutions must typically be generated before they can be evaluated).

However, the standard AI tree-search (or, more generally, graph-search) methods do not always apply. Not all problems require finding a path

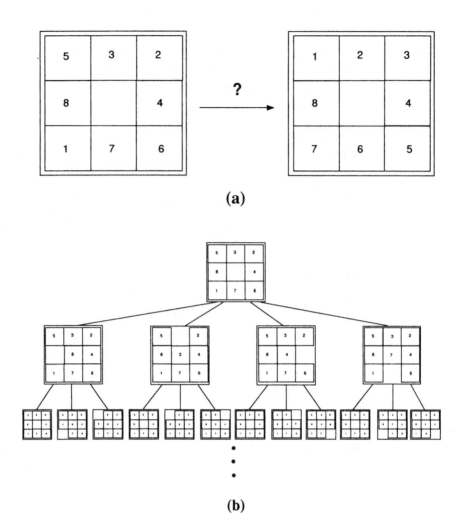

(a)

(b)

Figure 1.2 The 8-puzzle. (a) The problem is to find a sequence of moves that will go from the initial state to the state with the tiles in the correct order (the goal state). (b) A partial search tree for the 8-puzzle.

from an initial state to a goal. For example, predicting the three-dimensional structure of a protein from its amino acid sequence does not necessarily require knowing the sequence of physical moves by which a protein folds up into a 3D structure; it requires only that the final 3D configuration be predicted. Also, for many problems, including the protein-prediction problem, the configuration of the goal state is not known ahead of time.

The GA is a general method for solving "search for solutions" problems (as are the other evolution-inspired techniques, such as evolution strategies and evolutionary programming). Hill climbing, simulated annealing, and tabu search are examples of other general methods. Some of these are similar to "search for paths to goals" methods such as branch-and-bound and A*. For descriptions of these and other search methods see Winston 1992, Glover 1989 and 1990, and Kirkpatrick, Gelatt, and Vecchi 1983. "Steepest-ascent" hill climbing, for example, works as follows:

1. Choose a candidate solution (e.g., encoded as a bit string) at random. Call this string *current-string*.

2. Systematically mutate each bit in the string from left to right, one at a time, recording the fitnesses of the resulting one-bit mutants.

3. If any of the resulting one-bit mutants give a fitness increase, then set *current-string* to the one-bit mutant giving the highest fitness increase (the "steepest ascent").

4. If there is no fitness increase, then save *current-string* (a "hilltop") and go to step 1. Otherwise, go to step 2 with the new *current-string*.

5. When a set number of fitness-function evaluations has been performed, return the highest hilltop that was found.

In AI such general methods (methods that can work on a large variety of problems) are called "weak methods," to differentiate them from "strong methods" specially designed to work on particular problems. All the "search for solutions" methods (1) initially generate a set of candidate solutions (in the GA this is the initial population; in steepest-ascent hill climbing this is the initial string and all the one-bit mutants of it), (2) evaluate the candidate solutions according to some fitness criteria, (3) decide on the basis of this evaluation which candidates will be kept and which will be discarded, and (4) produce further variants by using some kind of operators on the surviving candidates.

The particular combination of elements in genetic algorithms—parallel population-based search with stochastic selection of many individuals, stochastic crossover and mutation—distinguishes them from other search methods. Many other search methods have some of these elements, but not this particular combination.

1.8   SOME APPLICATIONS OF GENETIC ALGORITHMS

The version of the genetic algorithm described above is very simple, but variations on the basic theme have been used in a large number of scientific and engineering problems and models. Some examples follow.

Optimization   GAs have been used in a wide variety of optimization tasks, including numerical optimization and such combinatorial optimization problems as circuit layout and job-shop scheduling.

Automatic programming GAs have been used to evolve computer programs for specific tasks, and to design other computational structures such as cellular automata and sorting networks.

Machine learning GAs have been used for many machine learning applications, including classification and prediction tasks, such as the prediction of weather or protein structure. GAs have also been used to evolve aspects of particular machine learning systems, such as weights for neural networks, rules for learning classifier systems or symbolic production systems, and sensors for robots.

Economics GAs have been used to model processes of innovation, the development of bidding strategies, and the emergence of economic markets.

Immune systems GAs have been used to model various aspects of natural immune systems, including somatic mutation during an individual's lifetime and the discovery of multi-gene families during evolutionary time.

Ecology GAs have been used to model ecological phenomena such as biological arms races, host-parasite coevolution, symbiosis, and resource flow.

Population genetics GAs have been used to study questions in population genetics, such as "Under what conditions will a gene for recombination be evolutionarily viable?"

Evolution and learning GAs have been used to study how individual learning and species evolution affect one another.

Social systems GAs have been used to study evolutionary aspects of social systems, such as the evolution of social behavior in insect colonies, and, more generally, the evolution of cooperation and communication in multi-agent systems.

This list is by no means exhaustive, but it gives the flavor of the kinds of things GAs have been used for, both in problem solving and in scientific contexts. Because of their success in these and other areas, interest in GAs has been growing rapidly in the last several years among researchers in many disciplines. The field of GAs has become a subdiscipline of computer science, with conferences, journals, and a scientific society.

1.9 TWO BRIEF EXAMPLES

As warmups to more extensive discussions of GA applications, here are brief examples of GAs in action on two particularly interesting projects.

Using GAs to Evolve Strategies for the Prisoner's Dilemma

The Prisoner's Dilemma, a simple two-person game invented by Merrill Flood and Melvin Dresher in the 1950s, has been studied extensively in game theory, economics, and political science because it can be seen as an idealized model for real-world phenomena such as arms races (Axelrod 1984; Axelrod and Dion 1988). It can be formulated as follows: Two individuals (call them Alice and Bob) are arrested for committing a crime together and are held in separate cells, with no communication possible between them. Alice is offered the following deal: If she confesses and agrees to testify against Bob, she will receive a suspended sentence with probation, and Bob will be put away for 5 years. However, if at the same time Bob confesses and agrees to testify against Alice, her testimony will be discredited, and each will receive 4 years for pleading guilty. Alice is told that Bob is being offered precisely the same deal. Both Alice and Bob know that if neither testify against the other they can be convicted only on a lesser charge for which they will each get 2 years in jail.

Should Alice "defect" against Bob and hope for the suspended sentence, risking a 4-year sentence if Bob defects? Or should she "cooperate" with Bob (even though they cannot communicate), in the hope that he will also cooperate so each will get only 2 years, thereby risking a defection by Bob that will send her away for 5 years?

The game can be described more abstractly. Each player independently decides which move to make—i.e., whether to cooperate or defect. A "game" consists of each player's making a decision (a "move"). The possible results of a single game are summarized in a payoff matrix like the one shown in figure 1.3. Here the goal is to get as many points (as opposed to as few years in prison) as possible. (In figure 1.3, the payoff in each case can be interpreted as 5 minus the number of years in prison.) If both players cooperate, each gets 3 points. If player A defects and player B cooperates, then player A gets 5 points and player B gets 0 points, and vice versa if the situation is reversed. If both players defect, each gets 1 point. What is the best strategy to use in order to maximize one's own payoff? If you suspect that your opponent is going to cooperate, then you should surely defect. If you suspect that your opponent is going to defect, then you should defect too. No matter what the other player does, it is always better to defect. The dilemma is that if both players defect each gets a worse score than if they cooperate. If the game is *iterated* (that is, if the two players play several games in a row), both players' always defecting will lead to a much lower total payoff than the players would get if they

	Cooperate	Defect
Cooperate	3, 3	0, 5
Defect	5, 0	1, 1

Player A is labeled on the left; Cooperate and Defect are the row labels.

Figure 1.3 The payoff matrix for the Prisoner's Dilemma (adapted from Axelrod 1987). The two numbers given in each box are the payoffs for players A and B in the given situation, with player A's payoff listed first in each pair.

cooperated. How can reciprocal cooperation be induced? This question takes on special significance when the notions of cooperating and defecting correspond to actions in, say, a real-world arms race (e.g., reducing or increasing one's arsenal).

Robert Axelrod of the University of Michigan has studied the Prisoner's Dilemma and related games extensively. His interest in determining what makes for a good strategy led him to organize two Prisoner's Dilemma tournaments (described in Axelrod 1984). He solicited strategies from researchers in a number of disciplines. Each participant submitted a computer program that implemented a particular strategy, and the various programs played iterated games with each other. During each game, each program remembered what move (i.e., cooperate or defect) both it and its opponent had made in each of the three previous games that they had played with each other, and its strategy was based on this memory. The programs were paired in a round-robin tournament in which each played with all the other programs over a number of games. The first tournament consisted of 14 different programs; the second consisted of 63 programs (including one that made random moves). Some of the strategies submitted were rather complicated, using techniques such as Markov processes and Bayesian inference to model the other players in order to determine the best move. However, in both tournaments the winner (the strategy with the highest average score) was the simplest of the submitted strategies: TIT FOR TAT. This strategy, submitted by Anatol Rapoport, cooperates in the first game and then, in subsequent games, does whatever the other player did in its move in the previous game with TIT FOR TAT. That is, it offers cooperation and reciprocates it. But if the other player defects, TIT FOR TAT punishes that defection with a defection of its own, and continues the punishment until the other player begins cooperating again.

After the two tournaments, Axelrod (1987) decided to see if a GA could evolve strategies to play this game successfully. The first issue was figuring out how to encode a strategy as a string. Here is how Axelrod's encoding worked. Suppose the memory of each player is one previous game. There are four possibilities for the previous game:

CC (case 1),

CD (case 2),

DC (case 3),

DD (case 4),

where *C* denotes "cooperate" and *D* denotes "defect." Case 1 is when both players cooperated in the previous game, case 2 is when player A cooperated and player B defected, and so on. A strategy is simply a rule that specifies an action in each of these cases. For example, TIT FOR TAT as played by player A is as follows:

If *CC* (case 1), then *C*.

If *CD* (case 2), then *D*.

If *DC* (case 3), then *C*.

If *DD* (case 4), then *D*.

If the cases are ordered in this canonical way, this strategy can be expressed compactly as the string *CDCD*. To use the string as a strategy, the player records the moves made in the previous game (e.g., *CD*), finds the case number i by looking up that case in a table of ordered cases like that given above (for *CD*, $i = 2$), and selects the letter in the ith position of the string as its move in the next game (for $i = 2$, the move is *D*).

Axelrod's tournaments involved strategies that remembered three previous games. There are 64 possibilities for the previous three games:

CC CC CC (case 1),

CC CC CD (case 2),

CC CC DC (case 3),

$$\vdots$$

DD DD DC (case 63),

DD DD DD (case 64).

Thus, a strategy can be encoded by a 64-letter string, e.g., *CDCCCDDCC CDD*. . . . Since using the strategy requires the results of the three previous games, Axelrod actually used a 70-letter string, where the six extra letters encoded three hypothetical previous games used by the strategy to decide how to move in the first actual game. Since each locus in the string has two possible alleles (*C* and *D*), the number of possible strategies is 2^{70}. The search space is thus far too big to be searched exhaustively.

In Axelrod's first experiment, the GA had a population of 20 such strategies. The fitness of a strategy in the population was determined as follows: Axelrod had found that eight of the human-generated strategies from the second tournament were representative of the entire set of strategies, in the sense that a given strategy's score playing with these eight was a good predictor of the strategy's score playing with all 63 entries. This set of eight strategies (which did *not* include TIT FOR TAT) served as the "environment" for the evolving strategies in the population. Each individual in the population played iterated games with each of the eight fixed strategies, and the individual's fitness was taken to be its average score over all the games it played.

Axelrod performed 40 different runs of 50 generations each, using different random-number seeds for each run. Most of the strategies that evolved were similar to TIT FOR TAT in that they reciprocated cooperation and punished defection (although not necessarily only on the basis of the immediately preceding move). However, the GA often found strategies that scored substantially higher than TIT FOR TAT. This is a striking result, especially in view of the fact that in a given run the GA is testing only $20 \times 50 = 1000$ individuals out of a huge search space of 2^{70} possible individuals.

It would be wrong to conclude that the GA discovered strategies that are "better" than any human-designed strategy. The performance of a strategy depends very much on its environment—that is, on the strategies with which it is playing. Here the environment was fixed—it consisted of eight human-designed strategies that did not change over the course of a run. The resulting fitness function is an example of a static (unchanging) fitness landscape. The highest-scoring strategies produced by the GA were designed to exploit specific weaknesses of several of the eight fixed strategies. It is not necessarily true that these high-scoring strategies would also score well in a different environment. TIT FOR TAT is a generalist, whereas the highest-scoring evolved strategies were more specialized to the given environment. Axelrod concluded that the GA is good at doing what evolution often does: developing highly specialized adaptations to specific characteristics of the environment.

To see the effects of a changing (as opposed to fixed) environment, Axelrod carried out another experiment in which the fitness of an individual was determined by allowing the individuals in the population to play with one another rather than with the fixed set of eight strategies. Now the environment changed from generation to generation because the opponents themselves were evolving. At every generation, each individual played iterated games with each of the 19 other members of the population and with itself, and its fitness was again taken to be its average score over all games. Here the fitness landscape was not static—it was a function of the particular individuals present in the population, and it changed as the population changed.

In this second set of experiments, Axelrod observed that the GA initially evolved uncooperative strategies. In the first few generations strategies that tended to cooperate did not find reciprocation among their fellow population members and thus tended to die out, but after about 10–20 generations the trend started to reverse: the GA discovered strategies that reciprocated cooperation and that punished defection (i.e., variants of TIT FOR TAT). These strategies did well with one another and were not completely defeated by less cooperative strategies, as were the initial cooperative strategies. Because the reciprocators scored above average, they spread in the population; this resulted in increasing cooperation and thus increasing fitness.

Axelrod's experiments illustrate how one might use a GA both to evolve solutions to an interesting problem and to model evolution and coevolution in an idealized way. One can think of many additional possible experiments, such as running the GA with the probability of crossover set to 0—that is, using only the selection and mutation operators (Axelrod 1987) or allowing a more open-ended kind of evolution in which the amount of memory available to a given strategy is allowed to increase or decrease (Lindgren 1992).

Hosts and Parasites: Using GAs to Evolve Sorting Networks

Designing algorithms for efficiently sorting collections of ordered elements is fundamental to computer science. Donald Knuth (1973) devoted more than half of a 700-page volume to this topic in his classic series *The Art of Computer Programming*. The goal of sorting is to place the elements in a data structure (e.g., a list or a tree) in some specified order (e.g., numerical or alphabetic) in minimal time. One particular approach to sorting described in Knuth's book is the *sorting network*, a parallelizable device for sorting lists with a fixed number n of elements. Figure 1.4 displays one such network (a "Batcher sort"—see Knuth 1973) that will sort lists of $n = 16$ elements (e_0–e_{15}). Each horizontal line represents one of the elements in the list, and each vertical arrow represents a comparison to be made between two elements. For example, the leftmost column of vertical arrows indicates that comparisons are to be made between e_0 and e_1, between e_2 and e_3, and so on. If the elements being compared are out of the desired order, they are swapped.

To sort a list of elements, one marches the list from left to right through the network, performing all the comparisons (and swaps, if necessary) specified in each vertical column before proceeding to the next. The comparisons in each vertical column are independent and can thus be performed in parallel. If the network is correct (as is the Batcher sort), any list will wind up perfectly sorted at the end. One goal of designing sorting networks is to make them correct *and* efficient (i.e., to minimize the number of comparisons).

An interesting theoretical problem is to determine the minimum number of comparisons necessary for a correct sorting network with a given n. In the 1960s there was a flurry of activity surrounding this problem for $n = 16$ (Knuth 1973; Hillis 1990, 1992). According to Hillis (1990), in 1962

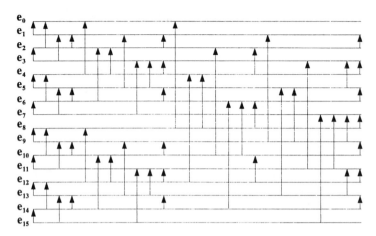

Figure 1.4 The "Batcher sort" $n = 16$ sorting network (adapted from Knuth 1973). Each horizontal line represents an element in the list, and each vertical arrow represents a comparison to be made between two elements. If the elements being compared are out of order, they are swapped. Comparisons in the same column can be made in parallel.

Bose and Nelson developed a general method of designing sorting networks that required 65 comparisons for $n = 16$, and they conjectured that this value was the minimum. In 1964 there were independent discoveries by Batcher and by Floyd and Knuth of a network requiring only 63 comparisons (the network illustrated in figure 1.4). This was again thought by some to be minimal, but in 1969 Shapiro constructed a network that required only 62 comparisons. At this point, it is unlikely that anyone was willing to make conjectures about the network's optimality—and a good thing too, since in that same year Green found a network requiring only 60 comparisons. This was an exciting time in the small field of $n = 16$ sorting-network design. Things seemed to quiet down after Green's discovery, though no proof of its optimality was given.

In the 1980s, W. Daniel Hillis (1990, 1992) took up the challenge again, though this time he was assisted by a genetic algorithm. In particular, Hillis presented the problem of designing an optimal $n = 16$ sorting network to a genetic algorithm operating on the massively parallel Connection Machine 2.

As in the Prisoner's Dilemma example, the first step here was to figure out a good way to encode a sorting network as a string. Hillis's encoding was fairly complicated and more biologically realistic than those used in most GA applications. Here is how it worked: A sorting network can be specified as an ordered list of pairs, such as

$(2, 5), (4, 2), (7, 14). \ldots$

These pairs represent the series of comparisons to be made ("first compare elements 2 and 5, and swap if necessary; next compare elements 4 and 2, and swap if necessary"). (Hillis's encoding did not specify which comparisons could be made in parallel, since he was trying only to minimize the total number of comparisons rather than to find the optimal *parallel* sorting network.) Sticking to the biological analogy, Hillis referred to ordered lists of pairs representing networks as "phenotypes." In Hillis's program, each phenotype consisted of 60–120 pairs, corresponding to networks with 60–120 comparisons. As in real genetics, the genetic algorithm worked not on phenotypes but on genotypes encoding the phenotypes.

The genotype of an individual in the GA population consisted of a set of chromosomes which could be decoded to form a phenotype. Hillis used diploid chromosomes (chromosomes in pairs) rather than the haploid chromosomes (single chromosomes) that are more typical in GA applications. As is illustrated in figure 1.5a, each individual consists of 15 pairs of 32-bit chromosomes. As is illustrated in figure 1.5b, each chromosome consists of eight 4-bit "codons." Each codon represents an integer between 0 and 15 giving a position in a 16-element list. Each adjacent pair of codons in a chromosome specifies a comparison between two list elements. Thus each chromosome encodes four comparisons. As is illustrated in figure 1.5c, each pair of chromosomes encodes between four and eight comparisons. The chromosome pair is aligned and "read off" from left to right. At each position, the codon pair in chromosome A is compared with the codon pair in chromosome B. If they encode the same pair of numbers (i.e., are "homozygous"), then only one pair of numbers is inserted in the phenotype; if they encode different pairs of numbers (i.e., are "heterozygous"), then both pairs are inserted in the phenotype. The 15 pairs of chromosomes are read off in this way in a fixed order to produce a phenotype with 60–120 comparisons. More homozygous positions appearing in each chromosome pair means fewer comparisons appearing in the resultant sorting network. The goal is for the GA to discover a minimal correct sorting network—to equal Green's network, the GA must discover an individual with all homozygous positions in its genotype that also yields a correct sorting network. Note that under Hillis's encoding the GA cannot discover a network with fewer than 60 comparisons.

In Hillis's experiments, the initial population consisted of a number of randomly generated genotypes, with one noteworthy provision: Hillis noted that most of the known minimal 16-element sorting networks begin with the same pattern of 32 comparisons, so he set the first eight chromosome pairs in each individual to (homozygously) encode these comparisons. This is an example of using knowledge about the problem domain (here, sorting networks) to help the GA get off the ground.

Most of the networks in a random initial population will not be correct networks—that is, they will not sort all input cases (lists of 16 numbers) correctly. Hillis's fitness measure gave partial credit: the fitness of a network was equal to the percentage of cases it sorted correctly. There are so many possible input cases that it was not practicable to test each network

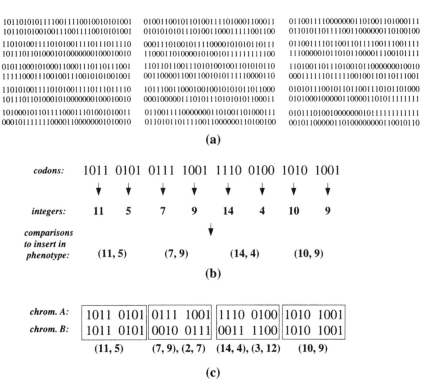

codons: 1011 0101 0111 1001 1110 0100 1010 1001

integers: 11   5   7   9   14   4   10   9

comparisons to insert in phenotype: (11, 5)   (7, 9)   (14, 4)   (10, 9)

(b)

chrom. A: 1011 0101 | 0111 1001 | 1110 0100 | 1010 1001
chrom. B: 1011 0101 | 0010 0111 | 0011 1100 | 1010 1001
           (11, 5)   (7, 9), (2, 7) (14, 4), (3, 12) (10, 9)

(c)

Figure 1.5 Details of the genotype representation of sorting networks used in Hillis's experiments. (a) An example of the genotype for an individual sorting network, consisting of 15 pairs of 32-bit chromosomes. (b) An example of the integers encoded by a single chromosome. The chromosome given here encodes the integers 11, 5, 7, 9, 14, 4, 10, and 9; each pair of adjacent integers is interpreted as a comparison. (c) An example of the comparisons encoded by a chromosome pair. The pair given here contains two homozygous positions and thus encodes a total of six comparisons to be inserted in the phenotype: (11, 5), (7, 9), (2, 7), (14, 4), (3, 12), and (10, 9).

exhaustively, so at each generation each network was tested on a sample of input cases chosen at random.

Hillis's GA was a considerably modified version of the simple GA described above. The individuals in the initial population were placed on a two-dimensional lattice; thus, unlike in the simple GA, there is a notion of spatial distance between two strings. The purpose of placing the population on a spatial lattice was to foster "speciation" in the population—Hillis hoped that different types of networks would arise at different spatial locations, rather than having the whole population converge to a set of very similar networks.

The fitness of each individual in the population was computed on a random sample of test cases. Then the half of the population with lower fitness was deleted, each lower-fitness individual being replaced on the grid with a copy of a surviving neighboring higher-fitness individual.

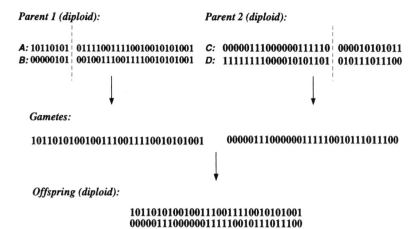

Figure 1.6 An illustration of diploid recombination as performed in Hillis's experiment. Here an individual's genotype consisted of 15 pairs of chromosomes (for the sake of clarity, only one pair for each parent is shown). A crossover point was chosen at random for each pair, and a gamete was formed by taking the codons before the crossover point in the first chromosome and the codons after the crossover point in the second chromosome. The 15 gametes from one parent were paired with the 15 gametes from the other parent to make a new individual. (Again for the sake of clarity, only one gamete pairing is shown.)

That is, each individual in the higher-fitness half of the population was allowed to reproduce once.

Next, individuals were paired with other individuals in their local spatial neighborhoods to produce offspring. Recombination in the context of diploid organisms is different from the simple haploid crossover described above. As figure 1.6 shows, when two individuals were paired, crossover took place within each chromosome pair inside each individual. For each of the 15 chromosome pairs, a crossover point was chosen at random, and a single "gamete" was formed by taking the codons before the crossover point from the first chromosome in the pair and the codons after the crossover point from the second chromosome in the pair. The result was 15 haploid gametes from each parent. Each of the 15 gametes from the first parent was then paired with one of the 15 gametes from the second parent to form a single diploid offspring. This procedure is roughly similar to sexual reproduction between diploid organisms in nature.

Such matings occurred until a new population had been formed. The individuals in the new population were then subject to mutation with $p_m = 0.001$. This entire process was iterated for a number of generations.

Since fitness depended only on network correctness, not on network size, what pressured the GA to find minimal networks? Hillis explained that there was an indirect pressure toward minimality, since, as in nature, homozygosity can protect crucial comparisons. If a crucial comparison is at a heterozygous position in its chromosome, then it can be lost under a crossover, whereas crucial comparisons at homozygous positions cannot be lost under crossover. For example, in figure 1.6, the leftmost comparison in chromosome B (i.e., the leftmost eight bits, which encode the comparison (0, 5)) is at a heterozygous position and is lost under this recombination (the gamete gets its leftmost comparison from chromosome A), but the rightmost comparison in chromosome A (10, 9) is at a homozygous position and is retained (though the gamete gets its rightmost comparison from chromosome B). In general, once a crucial comparison or set of comparisons is discovered, it is highly advantageous for them to be at homozygous positions. And the more homozygous positions, the smaller the resulting network.

In order to take advantage of the massive parallelism of the Connection Machine, Hillis used very large populations, ranging from 512 to about 1 million individuals. Each run lasted about 5000 generations. The smallest correct network found by the GA had 65 comparisons, the same as in Bose and Nelson's network but five more than in Green's network.

Hillis found this result disappointing—why didn't the GA do better? It appeared that the GA was getting stuck at local optima—local "hilltops" in the fitness landscape—rather than going to the globally highest hilltop. The GA found a number of moderately good (65-comparison) solutions, but it could not proceed further. One reason was that after early generations the randomly generated test cases used to compute the fitness of each individual were not challenging enough. The networks had found a strategy that worked, and the difficulty of the test cases was staying roughly the same. Thus, after the early generations there was no pressure on the networks to change their current suboptimal sorting strategy.

To solve this problem, Hillis took another hint from biology: the phenomenon of host-parasite (or predator-prey) coevolution. There are many examples in nature of organisms that evolve defenses to parasites that attack them only to have the parasites evolve ways to circumvent the defenses, which results in the hosts' evolving new defenses, and so on in an ever-rising spiral—a "biological arms race." In Hillis's analogy, the sorting networks could be viewed as hosts, and the test cases (lists of 16 numbers) could be viewed as parasites. Hillis modified the system so that a population of networks coevolved on the same grid as a population of parasites, where a parasite consisted of a set of 10–20 test cases. Both populations evolved under a GA. The fitness of a network was now determined by the parasite located at the network's grid location. The network's fitness was the percentage of test cases in the parasite that it sorted correctly. The fitness of the parasite was the percentage of its test cases that stumped the network (i.e., that the network sorted incorrectly).

The evolving population of test cases provided increasing challenges to the evolving population of networks. As the networks got better and better at sorting the test cases, the test cases got harder and harder, evolving to specifically target weaknesses in the networks. This forced the population of networks to keep changing—i.e., to keep discovering new sorting strategies—rather than staying stuck at the same suboptimal strategy. With coevolution, the GA discovered correct networks with only 61 comparisons—a real improvement over the best networks discovered without coevolution, but a frustrating single comparison away from rivaling Green's network.

Hillis's work is important because it introduces a new, potentially very useful GA technique inspired by coevolution in biology, and his results are a convincing example of the potential power of such biological inspiration. However, although the host-parasite idea is very appealing, its usefulness has not been established beyond Hillis's work, and it is not clear how generally it will be applicable or to what degree it will scale up to more difficult problems (e.g., larger sorting networks). Clearly more work must be done in this very interesting area.

1.10 HOW DO GENETIC ALGORITHMS WORK?

Although genetic algorithms are simple to describe and program, their behavior can be complicated, and many open questions exist about how they work and for what types of problems they are best suited. Much work has been done on the theoretical foundations of GAs (see, e.g., Holland 1975; Goldberg 1989a; Rawlins 1991; Whitley 1993b; Whitley and Vose 1995). Chapter 4 describes some of this work in detail. Here I give a brief overview of some of the fundamental concepts.

The traditional theory of GAs (first formulated in Holland 1975) assumes that, at a very general level of description, GAs work by discovering, emphasizing, and recombining good "building blocks" of solutions in a highly parallel fashion. The idea here is that good solutions tend to be made up of good building blocks—combinations of bit values that confer higher fitness on the strings in which they are present.

Holland (1975) introduced the notion of *schemas* (or *schemata*) to formalize the informal notion of "building blocks." A schema is a set of bit strings that can be described by a template made up of ones, zeros, and asterisks, the asterisks representing wild cards (or "don't cares"). For example, the schema $H = 1****1$ represents the set of all 6-bit strings that begin and end with 1. (In this section I use Goldberg's (1989a) notation, in which H stands for "hyperplane." H is used to denote schemas because schemas define hyperplanes—"planes" of various dimensions—in the l-dimensional space of length-l bit strings.) The strings that fit this template (e.g., 100111 and 110011) are said to be *instances* of H. The schema H is said to have two *defined* bits (non-asterisks) or, equivalently, to be of *order* 2. Its *defining length* (the distance between its outermost defined bits) is 5. Here I use the term "schema" to denote both a subset of strings represented by such a template and the template itself. In the following, the term's meaning should be clear from context.

Note that not every possible subset of the set of length-l bit strings can be described as a schema; in fact, the huge majority cannot. There are 2^l possible bit strings of length l, and thus 2^{2^l} possible subsets of strings, but there are only 3^l possible schemas. However, a central tenet of traditional GA theory is that schemas are—implicitly—the building blocks that the GA processes effectively under the operators of selection, mutation, and single-point crossover.

How does the GA process schemas? Any given bit string of length l is an instance of 2^l different schemas. For example, the string 11 is an instance of ∗∗ (all four possible bit strings of length 2), ∗1, 1∗, and 11 (the schema that contains only one string, 11). Thus, any given population of n strings contains instances of between 2^l and $n \times 2^l$ different schemas. If all the strings are identical, then there are instances of exactly 2^l different schemas; otherwise, the number is less than or equal to $n \times 2^l$. This means that, at a given generation, while the GA is explicitly evaluating the fitnesses of the n strings in the population, it is actually implicitly estimating the average fitness of a much larger number of schemas, where the average fitness of a schema is defined to be the average fitness of all possible instances of that schema. For example, in a randomly generated population of n strings, on average half the strings will be instances of $1 ∗ ∗ ∗ \cdots ∗$ and half will be instances of $0 ∗ ∗ ∗ \cdots ∗$. The evaluations of the approximately $n/2$ strings that are instances of $1 ∗ ∗ ∗ \cdots ∗$ give an estimate of the average fitness of that schema (this is an estimate because the instances evaluated in typical-size population are only a small sample of all possible instances). Just as schemas are not explicitly represented or evaluated by the GA, the estimates of schema average fitnesses are not calculated or stored explicitly by the GA. However, as will be seen below, the GA's behavior, in terms of the increase and decrease in numbers of instances of given schemas in the population, can be described as though it actually were calculating and storing these averages.

We can calculate the approximate dynamics of this increase and decrease in schema instances as follows. Let H be a schema with at least one instance present in the population at time t. Let $m(H, t)$ be the number of instances of H at time t, and let $\hat{u}(H, t)$ be the observed average fitness of H at time t (i.e., the average fitness of instances of H in the population at time t). We want to calculate $E(m(H, t + 1))$, the expected number of instances of H at time $t + 1$. Assume that selection is carried out as described earlier: the expected number of offspring of a string x is equal to $f(x)/\bar{f}(t)$, where $f(x)$ is the fitness of x and $\bar{f}(t)$ is the average fitness of the population at time t. Then, assuming x is in the population at time t, letting $x \in H$ denote "x is an instance of H," and (for now) ignoring the effects of crossover and mutation, we have

$$E(m(H, t+1)) = \sum_{x \in H} f(x)/\bar{f}(t)$$

$$= (\hat{u}(H, t)/\bar{f}(t))m(H, t) \qquad (1.1)$$

by definition, since $\hat{u}(H, t) = (\sum_{x \in H} f(x))/m(H, t)$ for x in the population at time t. Thus even though the GA does not calculate $\hat{u}(H, t)$ explicitly, the increases or decreases of schema instances in the population depend on this quantity.

Crossover and mutation can both destroy and create instances of H. For now let us include only the destructive effects of crossover and mutation—those that decrease the number of instances of H. Including these effects, we modify the right side of equation 1.1 to give a lower bound on $E(m(H, t+1))$. Let p_c be the probability that single-point crossover will be applied to a string, and suppose that an instance of schema H is picked to be a parent. Schema H is said to "survive" under single-point crossover if one of the offspring is also an instance of schema H. We can give a lower bound on the probability $S_c(H)$ that H will survive single-point crossover:

$$S_c(H) \geq 1 - p_c \left(\frac{d(H)}{l-1} \right),$$

where $d(H)$ is the defining length of H and l is the length of bit strings in the search space. That is, crossovers occurring within the defining length of H can destroy H (i.e., can produce offspring that are not instances of H), so we multiply the fraction of the string that H occupies by the crossover probability to obtain an upper bound on the probability that it will be destroyed. (The value is an upper bound because some crossovers inside a schema's defined positions will not destroy it, e.g., if two identical strings cross with each other.) Subtracting this value from 1 gives a lower bound on the probability of survival $S_c(H)$. In short, the probability of survival under crossover is higher for shorter schemas.

The disruptive effects of mutation can be quantified as follows: Let p_m be the probability of any bit being mutated. Then $S_m(H)$, the probability that schema H will survive under mutation of an instance of H, is equal to $(1 - p_m)^{o(H)}$, where $o(H)$ is the order of H (i.e., the number of defined bits in H). That is, for each bit, the probability that the bit will not be mutated is $1 - p_m$, so the probability that no defined bits of schema H will be mutated is this quantity multiplied by itself $o(H)$ times. In short, the probability of survival under mutation is higher for lower-order schemas.

These disruptive effects can be used to amend equation 1.1:

$$E(m(H, t+1)) \geq \frac{\hat{u}(H, t)}{\bar{f}(t)} m(H, t) \left(1 - p_c \frac{d(H)}{l-1} \right) [(1 - p_m)^{o(H)}]. \qquad (1.2)$$

This is known as the Schema Theorem (Holland 1975; see also Goldberg 1989a). It describes the growth of a schema from one generation to the next. The Schema Theorem is often interpreted as implying that short, low-order schemas whose average fitness remains above the mean will receive exponentially increasing numbers of samples (i.e., instances evaluated) over time, since the number of samples of those schemas that are not disrupted and remain above average in fitness increases by a factor of $\hat{u}(H, t)/\bar{f}(t)$ at each generation. (There are some caveats on this interpretation; they will be discussed in chapter 4.)

The Schema Theorem as stated in equation 1.2 is a lower bound, since it deals only with the destructive effects of crossover and mutation. However, crossover is believed to be a major source of the GA's power, with the ability to recombine instances of good schemas to form instances of equally good or better higher-order schemas. The supposition that this is the process by which GAs work is known as the Building Block Hypothesis (Goldberg 1989a). (For work on quantifying this "constructive" power of crossover, see Holland 1975, Thierens and Goldberg 1993, and Spears 1993.)

In evaluating a population of n strings, the GA is implicitly estimating the average fitnesses of all schemas that are present in the population, and increasing or decreasing their representation according to the Schema Theorem. This simultaneous implicit evaluation of large numbers of schemas in a population of n strings is known as *implicit parallelism* (Holland 1975). The effect of selection is to gradually bias the sampling procedure toward instances of schemas whose fitness is estimated to be above average. Over time, the estimate of a schema's average fitness should, in principle, become more and more accurate since the GA is sampling more and more instances of that schema. (Some counterexamples to this notion of increasing accuracy will be discussed in chapter 4.)

The Schema Theorem and the Building Block Hypothesis deal primarily with the roles of selection and crossover in GAs. What is the role of mutation? Holland (1975) proposed that mutation is what prevents the loss of diversity at a given bit position. For example, without mutation, every string in the population might come to have a one at the first bit position, and there would then be no way to obtain a string beginning with a zero. Mutation provides an "insurance policy" against such fixation.

The Schema Theorem given in equation 1.1 applies not only to schemas but to any subset of strings in the search space. The reason for specifically focusing on schemas is that they (in particular, short, high-average-fitness schemas) are a good description of the types of building blocks that are combined effectively by single-point crossover. A belief underlying this formulation of the GA is that schemas will be a good description of the relevant building blocks of a good solution. GA researchers have defined other types of crossover operators that deal with different types of building blocks, and have analyzed the generalized "schemas" that a given crossover operator effectively manipulates (Radcliffe 1991; Vose 1991).

The Schema Theorem and some of its purported implications for the behavior of GAs have recently been the subject of much critical discussion in the GA community. These criticisms and the new approaches to GA theory inspired by them will be reviewed in chapter 4.

THOUGHT EXERCISES

1. How many Prisoner's Dilemma strategies with a memory of three games are there that are behaviorally equivalent to TIT FOR TAT? What fraction is this of the total number of strategies with a memory of three games?

2. What is the total payoff after 10 games of TIT FOR TAT playing against (a) a strategy that always defects; (b) a strategy that always cooperates; (c) ANTI-TIT-FOR-TAT, a strategy that starts out by defecting and always does the opposite of what its opponent did on the last move? (d) What is the expected payoff of TIT FOR TAT against a strategy that makes random moves? (e) What are the total payoffs of each of these strategies in playing 10 games against TIT FOR TAT? (For the random strategy, what is its expected average payoff?)

3. How many possible sorting networks are there in the search space defined by Hillis's representation?

4. Prove that any string of length l is an instance of 2^l different schemas.

5. Define the fitness f of bit string x with $l = 4$ to be the integer represented by the binary number x. (e.g., $f(0011) = 3$, $f(1111) = 15$). What is the average fitness of the schema $1***$ under f? What is the average fitness of the schema $0***$ under f?

6. Define the fitness of bit string x to be the number of ones in x. Give a formula, in terms of l (the string length) and k, for the average fitness of a schema H that has k defined bits, all set to 1.

7. When is the union of two schemas also a schema? For example, $\{0*\} \bigcup \{1*\}$ is a schema $(**)$, but $\{01\} \bigcup \{10\}$ is not. When is the intersection of two schemas also a schema? What about the difference of two schemas?

8. Are there any cases in which a population of n l-bit strings contains *exactly* $n \times 2^l$ different schemas?

COMPUTER EXERCISES

(Asterisks indicate more difficult, longer-term projects.)

1. Implement a simple GA with fitness-proportionate selection, roulette-wheel sampling, population size 100, single-point crossover rate $p_c = 0.7$, and bitwise mutation rate $p_m = 0.001$. Try it on the following fitness function: $f(x) =$ number of ones in x, where x is a chromosome of length 20.

Perform 20 runs, and measure the average generation at which the string of all ones is discovered. Perform the same experiment with crossover turned off (i.e., $p_c = 0$). Do similar experiments, varying the mutation and crossover rates, to see how the variations affect the average time required for the GA to find the optimal string. If it turns out that mutation with crossover is better than mutation alone, why is that the case?

2. Implement a simple GA with fitness-proportionate selection, roulette-wheel sampling, population size 100, single-point crossover rate $p_c = 0.7$, and bitwise mutation rate $p_m = 0.001$. Try it on the fitness function $f(x) =$ the integer represented by the binary number x, where x is a chromosome of length 20. Run the GA for 100 generations and plot the fitness of the best individual found at each generation as well as the average fitness of the population at each generation. How do these plots change as you vary the population size, the crossover rate, and the mutation rate? What if you use only mutation (i.e., $p_c = 0$)?

3. Define ten schemas that are of particular interest for the fitness functions of computer exercises 1 and 2 (e.g., $1 * \cdots * $ and $0 * \cdots *$). When running the GA as in computer exercises 1 and 2, record at each generation how many instances there are in the population of each of these schemas. How well do the data agree with the predictions of the Schema Theorem?

4. Compare the GA's performance on the fitness functions of computer exercises 1 and 2 with that of steepest-ascent hill climbing (defined above) and with that of another simple hill-climbing method, "random-mutation hill climbing" (Forrest and Mitchell 1993b):

1. Start with a single randomly generated string. Calculate its fitness.
2. Randomly mutate one locus of the current string.
3. If the fitness of the mutated string is equal to or higher than the fitness of the original string, keep the mutated string. Otherwise keep the original string.
4. Go to step 2.

Iterate this algorithm for 10,000 steps (fitness-function evaluations). This is equal to the number of fitness-function evaluations performed by the GA in computer exercise 2 (with population size 100 run for 100 generations). Plot the best fitness found so far at every 100 evaluation steps (equivalent to one GA generation), averaged over 10 runs. Compare this with a plot of the GA's best fitness found so far as a function of generation. Which algorithm finds higher-fitness chromosomes? Which algorithm finds them faster? Comparisons like these are important if claims are to be made that a GA is a more effective search algorithm than other stochastic methods on a given problem.

*5. Implement a GA to search for strategies to play the Iterated Prisoner's Dilemma, in which the fitness of a strategy is its average score in playing

100 games with itself and with every other member of the population. Each strategy remembers the three previous turns with a given player. Use a population of 20 strategies, fitness-proportional selection, single-point crossover with $p_c = 0.7$, and mutation with $p_m = 0.001$.

a. See if you can replicate Axelrod's qualitative results: do at least 10 runs of 50 generations each and examine the results carefully to find out how the best-performing strategies work and how they change from generation to generation.

b. Turn off crossover (set $p_c = 0$) and see how this affects the average best fitness reached and the average number of generations to reach the best fitness. Before doing these experiments, it might be helpful to read Axelrod 1987.

c. Try varying the amount of memory of strategies in the population. For example, try a version in which each strategy remembers the four previous turns with each other player. How does this affect the GA's performance in finding high-quality strategies? (This is for the very ambitious.)

d. See what happens when noise is added—i.e., when on each move each strategy has a small probability (e.g., 0.05) of giving the opposite of its intended answer. What kind of strategies evolve in this case? (This is for the even more ambitious.)

* 6.

a. Implement a GA to search for strategies to play the Iterated Prisoner's Dilemma as in computer exercise 5a, except now let the fitness of a strategy be its score in 100 games with TIT FOR TAT. Can the GA evolve strategies to beat TIT FOR TAT?

b. Compare the GA's performance on finding strategies for the Iterated Prisoner's Dilemma with that of steepest-ascent hill climbing and with that of random-mutation hill climbing. Iterate the hill-climbing algorithms for 1000 steps (fitness-function evaluations). This is equal to the number of fitness-function evaluations performed by a GA with population size 20 run for 50 generations. Do an analysis similar to that described in computer exercise 4.

2 Genetic Algorithms in Problem Solving

Like other computational systems inspired by natural systems, genetic algorithms have been used in two ways: as techniques for solving technological problems, and as simplified scientific models that can answer questions about nature. This chapter gives several case studies of GAs as problem solvers; chapter 3 gives several case studies of GAs used as scientific models. Despite this seemingly clean split between engineering and scientific applications, it is often not clear on which side of the fence a particular project sits. For example, the work by Hillis described in chapter 1 above and the two other automatic-programming projects described below have produced results that, apart from their potential technological applications, may be of interest in evolutionary biology. Likewise, several of the "artificial life" projects described in chapter 3 have potential problem-solving applications. In short, the "clean split" between GAs for engineering and GAs for science is actually fuzzy, but this fuzziness—and its potential for useful feedback between problem-solving and scientific-modeling applications—is part of what makes GAs and other adaptive-computation methods particularly interesting.

2.1 EVOLVING COMPUTER PROGRAMS

Automatic programming—i.e., having computer programs automatically write computer programs—has a long history in the field of artificial intelligence. Many different approaches have been tried, but as yet no general method has been found for automatically producing the complex and robust programs needed for real applications.

Some early evolutionary computation techniques were aimed at automatic programming. The evolutionary programming approach of Fogel, Owens, and Walsh (1966) evolved simple programs in the form of finite-state machines. Early applications of genetic algorithms to simple automatic-programming tasks were performed by Cramer (1985) and by Fujiki and Dickinson (1987), among others. The recent resurgence of interest in automatic programming with genetic algorithms has been, in part, spurred by John Koza's work on evolving Lisp programs via "genetic programming."

The idea of evolving computer programs rather than writing them is very appealing to many. This is particularly true in the case of programs for massively parallel computers, as the difficulty of programming such computers is a major obstacle to their widespread use. Hillis's work on evolving efficient sorting networks is one example of automatic programming for parallel computers. My own work with Crutchfield, Das, and Hraber on evolving cellular automata to perform computations is an example of automatic programming for a very different type of parallel architecture.

Evolving Lisp Programs

John Koza (1992, 1994) has used a form of the genetic algorithm to evolve Lisp programs to perform various tasks. Koza claims that his method—"genetic programming" (GP)—has the potential to produce programs of the necessary complexity and robustness for general automatic programming. Programs in Lisp can easily be expressed in the form of a "parse tree," the object the GA will work on.

As a simple example, consider a program to compute the orbital period P of a planet given its average distance A from the Sun. Kepler's Third Law states that $P^2 = cA^3$, where c is a constant. Assume that P is expressed in units of Earth years and A is expressed in units of the Earth's average distance from the Sun, so $c = 1$. In FORTRAN such a program might be written as

```
PROGRAM ORBITAL_PERIOD
C       # Mars #
        A = 1.52
        P = SQRT(A * A * A)
        PRINT P
END ORBITAL_PERIOD
```

where ∗ is the multiplication operator and SQRT is the square-root operator. (The value for A for Mars is from Urey 1952.) In Lisp, this program could be written as

```
(defun orbital_period ()
        ; Mars ;
        (setf A 1.52)
        (sqrt (* A (* A A))))
```

In Lisp, operators precede their arguments: e.g., X ∗ Y is written (∗ X Y). The operator "setf" assigns its second argument (a value) to its first argument (a variable). The value of the last expression in the program is printed automatically.

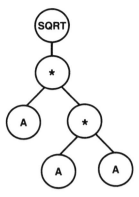

Figure 2.1 Parse tree for the Lisp expression (SQRT (∗ A (∗ A A))).

Assuming we know *A*, the important statement here is (SQRT (∗ A (∗ A A))). A simple task for automatic programming might be to automatically discover this expression, given only observed data for *P* and *A*.

Expressions such as (SQRT (∗ A (∗ A A))) can be expressed as parse trees, as shown in figure 2.1. In Koza's GP algorithm, a candidate solution is expressed as such a tree rather than as a bit string. Each tree consists of *functions* and *terminals*. In the tree shown in figure 2.1, SQRT is a function that takes one argument, ∗ is a function that takes two arguments, and *A* is a terminal. Notice that the argument to a function can be the result of another function—e.g., in the expression above one of the arguments to the top-level ∗ is (∗ A A).

Koza's algorithm is as follows:

1. Choose a set of possible functions and terminals for the program. The idea behind GP is, of course, to evolve programs that are difficult to write, and in general one does not know ahead of time precisely which functions and terminals will be needed in a successful program. Thus, the user of GP has to make an intelligent guess as to a reasonable set of functions and terminals for the problem at hand. For the orbital-period problem, the function set might be $\{+, \ -, \ *, \ /, \ \sqrt{}\}$ and the terminal set might simply consist of $\{A\}$, assuming the user knows that the expression will be an arithmetic function of *A*.

2. Generate an initial population of random trees (programs) using the set of possible functions and terminals. These random trees must be syntactically correct programs—the number of branches extending from each function node must equal the number of arguments taken by that function. Three programs from a possible randomly generated initial population are displayed in figure 2.2. Notice that the randomly generated programs can be of different sizes (i.e., can have different numbers of nodes and levels in the trees). In principle a randomly generated tree can be any

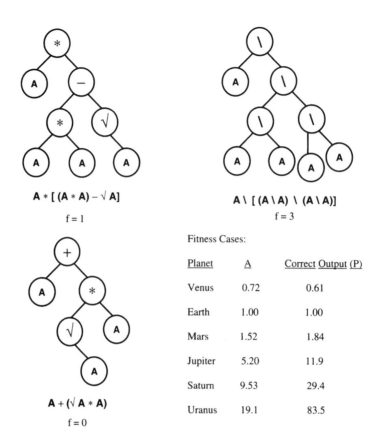

$A * [(A * A) - \sqrt{} A]$

$f = 1$

$A \backslash [(A \backslash A) \backslash (A \backslash A)]$

$f = 3$

$A + (\sqrt{} A * A)$

$f = 0$

Fitness Cases:

Planet	A	Correct Output (P)
Venus	0.72	0.61
Earth	1.00	1.00
Mars	1.52	1.84
Jupiter	5.20	11.9
Saturn	9.53	29.4
Uranus	19.1	83.5

Figure 2.2 Three programs from a possible randomly generated initial population for the orbital-period task. The expression represented by each tree is printed beneath the tree. Also printed is the fitness f (number of outputs within 20% of correct output) of each tree on the given set of fitness cases. A is given in units of Earth's semimajor axis of orbit; P is given in units of Earth years. (Planetary data from Urey 1952.)

size, but in practice Koza restricts the maximum size of the initially generated trees.

3. Calculate the fitness of each program in the population by running it on a set of "fitness cases" (a set of inputs for which the correct output is known). For the orbital-period example, the fitness cases might be a set of empirical measurements of P and A. The fitness of a program is a function of the number of fitness cases on which it performs correctly. Some fitness functions might give partial credit to a program for getting close to the correct output. For example, in the orbital-period task, we could define the fitness of a program to be the number of outputs that are within 20% of the correct value. Figure 2.2 displays the fitnesses of the three sample programs according to this fitness function on the given set of fitness cases. The randomly generated programs in the initial population are not likely to do very well; however, with a large enough population some of

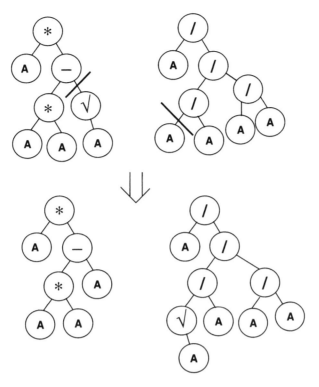

Figure 2.3 An example of crossover in the genetic programming algorithm. The two parents are shown at the top of the figure, the two offspring below. The crossover points are indicated by slashes in the parent trees.

them will do better than others by chance. This initial fitness differential provides a basis for "natural selection."

4. Apply selection, crossover, and mutation to the population to form a new population. In Koza's method, 10% of the trees in the population (chosen probabilistically in proportion to fitness) are copied without modification into the new population. The remaining 90% of the new population is formed by crossovers between parents selected (again probabilistically in proportion to fitness) from the current population. Crossover consists of choosing a random point in each parent and exchanging the subtrees beneath those points to produce two offspring. Figure 2.3 displays one possible crossover event. Notice that, in contrast to the simple GA, crossover here allows the size of a program to increase or decrease. Mutation might performed by choosing a random point in a tree and replacing the subtree beneath that point by a randomly generated subtree. Koza (1992) typically does not use a mutation operator in his applications; instead he uses initial populations that are presumably large enough to contain a sufficient diversity of building blocks so that crossover will be sufficient to put together a working program.

Figure 2.4 One initial state for the block-stacking problem (adapted from Koza 1992). The goal is to find a plan that will stack the blocks correctly (spelling "universal") from any initial state.

Steps 3 and 4 are repeated for some number of generations.

It may seem difficult to believe that this procedure would ever result in a correct program—the famous example of a monkey randomly hitting the keys on a typewriter and producing the works of Shakespeare comes to mind. But, surprising as it might seem, the GP technique has succeeded in evolving correct programs to solve a large number of simple (and some not-so-simple) problems in optimal control, planning, sequence induction, symbolic regression, image compression, robotics, and many other domains. One example (described in detail in Koza 1992) is the block-stacking problem illustrated in figure 2.4. The goal was to find a program that takes any initial configuration of blocks—some on a table, some in a stack—and places them in the stack in the correct order. Here the correct order spells out the word "universal." ("Toy" problems of this sort have been used extensively to develop and test planning methods in artificial intelligence.) The functions and terminals Koza used for this problem were a set of sensors and actions defined by Nilsson (1989). The terminals consisted of three sensors (available to a hypothetical robot to be controlled by the resulting program), each of which returns (i.e., provides the controlling Lisp program with) a piece of information:

CS ("current stack") returns the name of the top block of the stack. If the stack is empty, CS returns NIL (which means "false" in Lisp).

TB ("top correct block") returns the name of the topmost block on the stack such that it and all blocks below it are in the correct order. If there is no such block, TB returns NIL.

NN ("next needed") returns the name of the block needed immediately above TB in the goal "universal." If no more blocks are needed, this sensor returns NIL.

In addition to these terminals, there were five functions available to GP:

MS(x) ("move to stack") moves block x to the top of the stack if x is on the table, and returns x. (In Lisp, every function returns a value. The returned value is often ignored.)

MT(x) ("move to table") moves the block at the top of the stack to the table if block x is anywhere in the stack, and returns x.

DU(*expression1, expression2*) ("do until") evaluates *expression1* until *expression2* (a predicate) becomes TRUE.

NOT(*expression1*) returns TRUE if *expression1* is NIL; otherwise it returns NIL.

EQ(*expression1, expression2*) returns TRUE if *expression1* and *expression2* are equal (i.e., return the same value).

The programs in the population were generated from these two sets. The fitness of a given program was the number of sample fitness cases (initial configurations of blocks) for which the stack was correct after the program was run. Koza used 166 different fitness cases, carefully constructed to cover the various classes of possible initial configurations.

The initial population contained 300 randomly generated programs. Some examples (written in Lisp style rather than tree style) follow:

(EQ (MT CS) NN)
"Move the current top of stack to the table, and see if it is equal to the next needed." This clearly does not make any progress in stacking the blocks, and the program's fitness was 0.

(MS TB)
"Move the top correct block on the stack to the stack." This program does nothing, but doing nothing allowed it to get one fitness case correct: the case where all the blocks were already in the stack in the correct order. Thus, this program's fitness was 1.

(EQ (MS NN) (EQ (MS NN) (MS NN)))
"Move the next needed block to the stack three times." This program made some progress and got four fitness cases right, giving it fitness 4. (Here EQ serves merely as a control structure. Lisp evaluates the first expression, then evaluates the second expression, and then compares their value. EQ thus performs the desired task of executing the two expressions in sequence—we do not actually care whether their values are equal.)

By generation 5, the population contained some much more successful programs. The best one was (DU (MS NN) (NOT NN)) (i.e., "Move the next needed block to the stack until no more blocks are needed"). Here we have the basics of a reasonable plan. This program works in all cases in which the blocks in the stack are already in the correct order: the program moves the remaining blocks on the table into the stack in the correct order. There were ten such cases in the total set of 166, so this program's fitness was 10. Notice that this program uses a building block—(MS NN)—that was discovered in the first generation and found to be useful there.

In generation 10 a completely correct program (fitness 166) was discovered:

(EQ (DU (MT CS) (NOT CS)) (DU (MS NN) (NOT NN))).

This is an extension of the best program of generation 5. The program empties the stack onto the table and then moves the next needed block to the stack until no more blocks are needed. GP thus discovered a plan that works in all cases, although it is not very efficient. Koza (1992) discusses how to amend the fitness function to produce a more efficient program to do this task.

The block stacking example is typical of those found in Koza's books in that it is a relatively simple sample problem from a broad domain (planning). A correct program need not be very long. In addition, the necessary functions and terminals are given to the program at a fairly high level. For example, in the block stacking problem GP was given the high-level actions MS, MT, and so on; it did not have to discover them on its own. Could GP succeed at the block stacking task if it had to start out with lower-level primitives? O'Reilly and Oppacher (1992), using GP to evolve a sorting program, performed an experiment in which relatively low-level primitives (e.g., "if-less-than" and "swap") were defined separately rather than combined *a priori* into "if-less-than-then-swap". Under these conditions, GP achieved only limited success. This indicates a possible serious weakness of GP, since in most realistic applications the user will not know in advance what the appropriate high-level primitives should be; he or she is more likely to be able to define a larger set of lower-level primitives.

Genetic programming, as originally defined, includes no mechanism for automatically chunking parts of a program so they will not be split up under crossover, and no mechanism for automatically generating hierarchical structures (e.g., a main program with subroutines) that would facilitate the creation of new high-level primitives from built-in low-level primitives. These concerns are being addressed in more recent research. Koza (1992, 1994) has developed methods for encapsulation and automatic definition of functions. Angeline and Pollack (1992) and O'Reilly and Oppacher (1992) have proposed other methods for the encapsulation of useful subtrees.

Koza's GP technique is particularly interesting from the standpoint of evolutionary computation because it allows the size (and therefore the complexity) of candidate solutions to increase over evolution, rather than keeping it fixed as in the standard GA. However, the lack of sophisticated encapsulation mechanisms has so far limited the degree to which programs can usefully grow. In addition, there are other open questions about the capabilities of GP. Does it work well because the space of Lisp expressions is in some sense "dense" with correct programs for the relatively simple tasks Koza and other GP researchers have tried? This was given as one reason for the success of the artificial intelligence program AM (Lenat and Brown 1984), which evolved Lisp expressions to discover "interesting" conjectures in mathematics, such as the Goldbach conjecture (every even number is the sum of two primes). Koza refuted this hypothesis about GP by demonstrating how difficult it is to randomly generate a successful program to perform some of the tasks for which GP evolves successful programs. However, one could speculate that the space of Lisp expressions (with a given set of functions and terminals) is dense with useful intermediate-size building blocks for the tasks on which GP has been successful. GP's ability to find solutions quickly (e.g., within 10 generations using a population of 300) lends credence to this speculation.

GP also has not been compared systematically with other techniques that could search in the space of parse trees. For example, it would be interesting to know if a hill climbing technique could do as well as GP on the examples Koza gives. One test of this was reported by O'Reilly and Oppacher (1994a,b), who defined a mutation operator for parse trees and used it to compare GP with a simple hill-climbing technique similar to random-mutation hill climbing (see computer exercise 4 of chapter 1) and with simulated annealing (a more sophisticated hill-climbing technique). Comparisons were made on five problems, including the block stacking problem described above. On each of the five, simulated annealing either equaled or significantly outperformed GP in terms of the number of runs on which a correct solution was found and the average number of fitness-function evaluations needed to find a correct program. On two out of the five, the simple hill climber either equaled or exceeded the performance of GP.

Though five problems is not many for such a comparison in view of the number of problems on which GP has been tried, these results bring into question the claim (Koza 1992) that the crossover operator is a major contributor to GP's success. O'Reilly and Oppacher (1994a) speculate from their results that the parse-tree representation "may be a more fundamental asset to program induction than any particular search technique," and that "perhaps the concept of building blocks is irrelevant to GP." These speculations are well worth further investigation, and it is imperative to characterize the types of problems for which crossover is a useful operator and for which a GA will be likely to outperform gradient-ascent strategies such as hill climbing and simulated annealing. Some work toward those goals will be described in chapter 4.

Some other questions about GP:

Will the technique scale up to more complex problems for which larger programs are needed?

Will the technique work if the function and terminal sets are large?

How well do the evolved programs generalize to cases not in the set of fitness cases? In most of Koza's examples, the cases used to compute fitness are samples from a much larger set of possible fitness cases. GP very often finds a program that is correct on all the given fitness cases, but not enough has been reported on how well these programs do on the "out-of-sample" cases. We need to know the extent to which GP produces programs that generalize well after seeing only a small fraction of the possible fitness cases.

To what extent can programs be optimized for correctness, size, and efficiency at the same time?

Genetic programming's success on a wide range of problems should encourage future research addressing these questions. (For examples of more recent work on GP, see Kinnear 1994.)

Evolving Cellular Automata

A quite different example of automatic programming by genetic algorithms is found in work done by James Crutchfield, Rajarshi Das, Peter Hraber, and myself on evolving cellular automata to perform computations (Mitchell, Hraber, and Crutchfield 1993; Mitchell, Crutchfield, and Hraber 1994a; Crutchfield and Mitchell 1994; Das, Mitchell, and Crutchfield 1994). This project has elements of both problem solving and scientific modeling. One motivation is to understand how natural evolution creates systems in which "emergent computation" takes place—that is, in which the actions of simple components with limited information and communication give rise to coordinated global information processing. Insect colonies, economic systems, the immune system, and the brain have all been cited as examples of systems in which such emergent computation occurs (Forrest 1990; Langton 1992). However, it is not well understood *how* these natural systems perform computations. Another motivation is to find ways to engineer sophisticated emergent computation in decentralized multi-processor systems, using ideas from how natural decentralized systems compute. Such systems have many of the desirable properties for computer systems mentioned in chapter 1: they are sophisticated, robust, fast, and adaptable information processors. Using ideas from such systems to design new types of parallel computers might yield great progress in computer science.

One of the simplest systems in which emergent computation can be studied is a one-dimensional binary-state cellular automaton (CA)—a one-dimensional lattice of N two-state machines ("cells"), each of which changes its state as a function only of the current states in a local neighborhood. (The well-known "game of Life" (Berlekamp, Conway, and Guy 1982) is an example of a two-dimensional CA.) A one-dimensional CA is illustrated in figure 2.5. The lattice starts out with an initial configuration of cell states (zeros and ones) and this configuration changes in discrete time steps in which all cells are updated simultaneously according to the CA "rule" ϕ. (Here I use the term "state" to refer to a local state s_i—the value of the single cell at site i. The term "configuration" will refer to the pattern of local states over the entire lattice.)

A CA rule ϕ can be expressed as a lookup table ("rule table") that lists,

Rule table:

neighborhood: **000 001 010 011 100 101 110 111**
output bit: 0   0   0   1   0   1   1   1

Lattice:

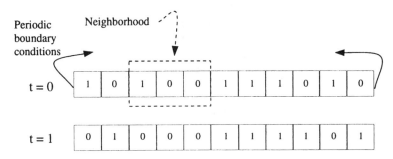

Figure 2.5 Illustration of a one-dimensional, binary-state, nearest-neighbor ($r = 1$) cellular automaton with $N = 11$. Both the lattice and the rule table for updating the lattice are illustrated. The lattice configuration is shown over one time step. The cellular automaton has periodic boundary conditions: the lattice is viewed as a circle, with the leftmost cell the right neighbor of the rightmost cell, and vice versa.

for each local neighborhood, the update state for the neighborhood's central cell. For a binary-state CA, the update states are referred to as the "output bits" of the rule table. In a one-dimensional CA, a neighborhood consists of a cell and its r ("radius") neighbors on either side. The CA illustrated in figure 2.5 has $r = 1$. It illustrates the "majority" rule: for each neighborhood of three adjacent cells, the new state is decided by a majority vote among the three cells. The CA illustrated in figure 2.5, like all those I will discuss here, has periodic boundary conditions: $s_i = s_{i+N}$. In figure 2.5 the lattice configuration is shown iterated over one time step.

Cellular automata have been studied extensively as mathematical objects, as models of natural systems, and as architectures for fast, reliable parallel computation. (For overviews of CA theory and applications, see Toffoli and Margolus 1987 and Wolfram 1986.) However, the difficulty of understanding the emergent behavior of CAs or of designing CAs to have desired behavior has up to now severely limited their use in science and engineering and for general computation. Our goal is to use GAs as a method for engineering CAs to perform computations.

Typically, a CA performing a computation means that the input to the computation is encoded as an initial configuration, the output is read off the configuration after some time step, and the intermediate steps that transform the input to the output are taken as the steps in the computation. The "program" emerges from the CA rule being obeyed by each cell. (Note that this use of CAs as computers differs from the impractical

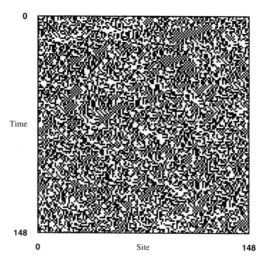

0

Time

148

0   Site   148

Figure 2.6 Space-time diagram for a randomly generated $r = 3$ cellular automaton, iterating on a randomly generated initial configuration. $N = 149$ sites are shown, with time increasing down the page. Here cells with state 0 are white and cells with state 1 are black. (This and the other space-time diagrams given here were generated using the program "la1d" written by James P. Crutchfield.)

though theoretically interesting method of constructing a universal Turing machine in a CA; see Mitchell, Crutchfield, and Hraber 1994b for a comparison of these two approaches.)

The behavior of one-dimensional CAs is often illustrated by a "space-time diagram"—a plot of lattice configurations over a range of time steps, with ones given as black cells and zeros given as white cells and with time increasing down the page. Figure 2.6 shows such a diagram for a binary-state $r = 3$ CA in which the rule table's output bits were filled in at random. It is shown iterating on a randomly generated initial configuration. Random-looking patterns, such as the one shown, are typical for the vast majority of CAs. To produce CAs that can perform sophisticated parallel computations, the genetic algorithm must evolve CAs in which the actions of the cells are not random-looking but are coordinated with one another so as to produce the desired result. This coordination must, of course, happen in the absence of any central processor or memory directing the coordination.

Some early work on evolving CAs with genetic algorithms was done by Norman Packard and his colleagues (Packard 1988; Richards, Meyer, and Packard 1990). John Koza (1992) also applied the GP paradigm to evolve CAs for simple random-number generation.

Our work builds on that of Packard (1988). As a preliminary project, we used a form of the GA to evolve one-dimensional, binary-state $r = 3$ CAs to perform a density-classification task. The goal is to find a CA that decides whether or not the initial configuration contains a majority of

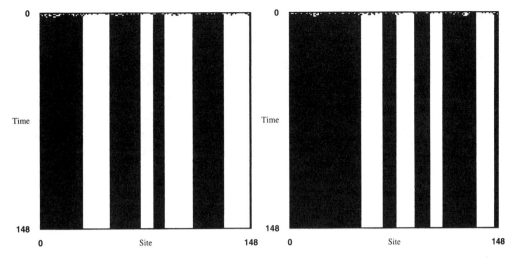

Figure 2.7 Space-time diagrams for the $r = 3$ majority rule. In the left diagram, $\rho_0 < \frac{1}{2}$; in the right diagram, $\rho_0 > \frac{1}{2}$.

ones (i.e., has high density). If it does, the whole lattice should eventually go to an unchanging configuration of all ones; all zeros otherwise. More formally, we call this task the "$\rho_c = \frac{1}{2}$" task. Here ρ denotes the density of ones in a binary-state CA configuration and ρ_c denotes a "critical" or threshold density for classification. Let ρ_0 denote the density of ones in the initial configuration (IC). If $\rho_0 > \rho_c$, then within M time steps the CA should go to the fixed-point configuration of all ones (i.e., all cells in state 1 for all subsequent t); otherwise, within M time steps it should go to the fixed-point configuration of all zeros. M is a parameter of the task that depends on the lattice size N.

It may occur to the reader that the majority rule mentioned above might be a good candidate for solving this task. Figure 2.7 gives space-time diagrams for the $r = 3$ majority rule (the output bit is decided by a majority vote of the bits in each seven-bit neighborhood) on two ICs, one with $\rho < \frac{1}{2}$ and one with $\rho > \frac{1}{2}$. As can be seen, local neighborhoods with majority ones map to regions of all ones and similarly for zeros, but when an all-ones region and an all-zeros region border each other, there is no way to decide between them, and both persist. Thus, the majority rule does not perform the $\rho_c = \frac{1}{2}$ task.

Designing an algorithm to perform the $\rho_c = \frac{1}{2}$ task is trivial for a system with a central controller or central storage of some kind, such as a standard computer with a counter register or a neural network in which all input units are connected to a central hidden unit. However, the task is nontrivial for a small-radius ($r \ll N$) CA, since a small-radius CA relies only on local interactions mediated by the cell neighborhoods. In fact, it can be proved that no finite-radius CA with periodic boundary conditions can perform this task perfectly across all lattice sizes, but even to perform this task well for a fixed lattice size requires more powerful computation than can be performed by a single cell or any linear combination of cells (such as the majority rule). Since the ones can be distributed throughout the CA lattice, the CA must transfer information over large distances ($\approx N$). To do this requires the global coordination of cells that are separated by large distances and that cannot communicate directly. How can this be done? Our interest was to see if the GA could devise one or more methods.

The chromosomes evolved by the GA were bit strings representing CA rule tables. Each chromosome consisted of the output bits of a rule table, listed in lexicographic order of neighborhood (as in figure 2.5). The chromosomes representing rules were thus of length $2^{2r+1} = 128$ (for binary $r = 3$ rules). The size of the rule space the GA searched was thus 2^{128}—far too large for any kind of exhaustive search.

In our main set of experiments, we set $N = 149$ (chosen to be reasonably large but not computationally intractable). The GA began with a population of 100 randomly generated chromosomes (generated with some initial biases—see Mitchell, Crutchfield, and Hraber 1994a, for details). The fitness of a rule in the population was calculated by (i) randomly choosing 100 ICs (initial configurations) that are uniformly distributed over $\rho \in [0.0, 1.0]$, with exactly half with $\rho < \rho_c$ and half with $\rho > \rho_c$, (ii) running the rule on each IC either until it arrives at a fixed point or for a maximum of approximately $2N$ time steps, and (iii) determining whether the final pattern is correct—i.e., N zeros for $\rho_0 < \rho_c$ and N ones for $\rho_0 > \rho_c$. The initial density, ρ_0, was never exactly $\frac{1}{2}$, since N was chosen to be odd. The rule's fitness, f_{100}, was the fraction of the 100 ICs on which the rule produced the correct final pattern. No partial credit was given for partially correct final configurations.

A few comments about the fitness function are in order. First, as was the case in Hillis's sorting-networks project, the number of possible input cases (2^{149} for $N = 149$) was far too large to test exhaustively. Instead, the GA sampled a different set of 100 ICs at each generation. In addition, the ICs were not sampled from an unbiased distribution (i.e., equal probability of a one or a zero at each site in the IC), but rather from a flat distribution across $\rho \in [0, 1]$ (i.e., ICs of each density from $\rho = 0$ to $\rho = 1$ were approximately equally represented). This flat distribution was used because the unbiased distribution is binomially distributed and thus very strongly peaked at $\rho = \frac{1}{2}$. The ICs selected from such a distribution will likely all have $\rho \approx \frac{1}{2}$, the hardest cases to classify. Using an unbiased sample made it too difficult for the GA to ever find any high-fitness CAs. (As will be discussed below, this biased distribution turns out to impede the GA in later generations: as increasingly fit rules are evolved, the IC sample becomes less and less challenging for the GA.)

Our version of the GA worked as follows. In each generation, (i) a new set of 100 ICs was generated, (ii) f_{100} was calculated for each rule in the population, (iii) the population was ranked in order of fitness, (iv) the 20 highest-fitness ("elite") rules were copied to the next generation without modification, and (v) the remaining 80 rules for the next generation were formed by single-point crossovers between randomly chosen pairs of elite rules. The parent rules were chosen from the elite with replacement—that is, an elite rule was permitted to be chosen any number of times. The offspring from each crossover were each mutated twice. This process was repeated for 100 generations for a single run of the GA. (More details of the implementation are given in Mitchell, Crutchfield, and Hraber 1994a.)

Note that this version of the GA differs from the simple GA in several ways. First, rather than selecting parents with probability proportional to fitness, the rules are ranked and selection is done at random from the top 20% of the population. Moreover, all of the top 20% are copied without modification to the next generation, and only the bottom 80% are replaced. This is similar to the selection method—called "$(\mu + \lambda)$"—used in some evolution strategies; see Bäck, Hoffmeister, and Schwefel 1991.

This version of the GA was the one used by Packard (1988), so we used it in our experiments attempting to replicate his work (Mitchell, Hraber, and Crutchfield 1993) and in our subsequent experiments. Selecting parents by rank rather than by absolute fitness prevents initially stronger individuals from quickly dominating the population and driving the genetic diversity down too early. Also, since testing a rule on 100 ICs provides only an approximate gauge of the true fitness, saving the top 20% of the rules was a good way of making a "first cut" and allowing rules that survive to be tested over more ICs. Since a new set of ICs was produced every generation, rules that were copied without modification were always retested on this new set. If a rule performed well and thus survived over a large number of generations, then it was likely to be a genuinely better rule than those that were not selected, since it was tested with a large set of ICs. An alternative method would be to test every rule in each generation on a much larger set of ICs, but this would waste computation time. Too much effort, for example, would go into testing very weak rules, which can safely be weeded out early using our method. As in most applications, evaluating the fitness function (here, iterating each CA) takes up most of the computation time.

Three hundred different runs were performed, each starting with a different random-number seed. On most runs the GA evolved a nonobvious but rather unsophisticated class of strategies. One example, a rule here called ϕ_a, is illustrated in figure 2.8a. This rule had $f_{100} \approx 0.9$ in the generation in which it was discovered (i.e., ϕ_a correctly classified 90% of the ICs in that generation). Its "strategy" is the following: Go to the fixed point of all zeros unless there is a sufficiently large block of adjacent (or almost adjacent) ones in the IC. If so, expand that block. (For this rule, "sufficiently large" is seven or more cells.) This strategy does a fairly good job of classifying low and high density under f_{100}: it relies on the appearance or

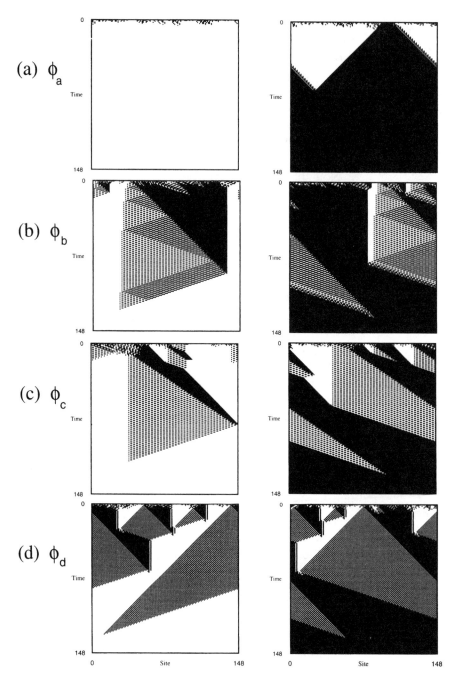

Figure 2.8 Space-time diagrams from four different rules discovered by the GA (adapted from Das, Mitchell, and Crutchfield 1994 by permission of the authors). The left diagrams have $\rho_0 < \frac{1}{2}$; the right diagrams have $\rho_0 > \frac{1}{2}$. All are correctly classified. Fitness increases from (a) to (d). The "gray" area in (d) is actually a checkerboard pattern of alternating zeros and ones.

absence of blocks of ones to be good predictors of ρ_0, since high-density ICs are statistically more likely to have blocks of adjacent ones than low-density ICs.

Similar strategies were evolved in most runs. On approximately half the runs, "expand ones" strategies were evolved, and on approximately half the runs, the opposite "expand zeros" strategies were evolved. These block-expanding strategies were initially surprising to us and even seemed clever, but they do not count as sophisticated examples of computation in CAs: all the computation is done locally in identifying and then expanding a "sufficiently large" block. There is no notion of global coordination or interesting information flow between distant cells—two things we claimed were necessary to perform well on the task.

In Mitchell, Crutchfield, and Hraber 1994a we analyzed the detailed mechanisms by which the GA evolved such block-expanding strategies. This analysis uncovered some quite interesting aspects of the GA, including a number of impediments that, on most runs, kept the GA from discovering better-performing rules. These included the GA's breaking the $\rho_c = \frac{1}{2}$ task's symmetries for short-term gains in fitness, as well as an "overfitting" to the fixed lattice size and the unchallenging nature of the samples of ICs. These impediments are discussed in detail in Mitchell, Crutchfield, and Hraber 1994a, but the last point merits some elaboration here.

The biased, flat distribution of ICs over $\rho \in [0, 1]$ helped the GA get a leg up in the early generations. We found that calculating fitness on an unbiased distribution of ICs made the problem too difficult for the GA early on—it was unable to find improvements to the rules in the initial population. However, the biased distribution became too easy for the improved CAs later in a run, and these ICs did not push the GA hard enough to find better solutions. Recall that the same problem plagued Hillis's GA until he introduced host-parasite coevolution. We are currently exploring a similar coevolution scheme to improve the GA's performance on this problem.

The weakness of ϕ_a and similar rules is clearly seen when they are tested using an unbiased distribution of ICs. We defined a rule ϕ's "unbiased performance" $\mathcal{P}_N(\phi)$ as the fraction of correct classifications produced by ϕ within approximately $2N$ time steps on 10,000 ICs on a lattice of length N, chosen from an unbiased distribution over ρ. As mentioned above, since the distribution is unbiased, the ICs are very likely to have $\rho \approx 0.5$. These are the very hardest cases to classify, so $\mathcal{P}_N(\phi)$ gives a lower bound on ϕ's overall performance.

Table 2.1 gives $\mathcal{P}_N(\phi)$ values for several different rules each for three values of N. The majority rule, unsurprisingly, has $\mathcal{P}_N = 0$ for all three values of N. The performance of ϕ_a (the block-expanding rule of figure 2.8a) decreases significantly as N is increased. This was true for all the block-expanding rules: the performance of these rules decreased dramatically

Table 2.1 Measured values of $\mathcal{P}_N$ at various values of N for six different $r = 3$ rules: the majority rule, four rules discovered by the GA in different runs (ϕ_a–ϕ_d), and the GKL rule. The subscripts for the rules discovered by the GA indicate the pair of space-time diagrams illustrating their behavior in figure 2.8. The standard deviation of $\mathcal{P}_{149}$, when calculated 100 times for the same rule, is approximately 0.004. The standard deviations for $\mathcal{P}_N$ for larger N are higher. (The actual lookup tables for these and other rules are given in Crutchfield and Mitchell 1994.)

CA	Symbol	$N = 149$	$N = 599$	$N = 999$
Majority	ϕ_{maj}	0.000	0.000	0.000
Expand 1-blocks	ϕ_a	0.652	0.515	0.503
Particle-based	ϕ_b	0.697	0.580	0.522
Particle-based	ϕ_c	0.742	0.718	0.701
Particle-based	ϕ_d	0.769	0.725	0.714
GKL	ϕ_{GKL}	0.816	0.766	0.757

for larger N, since the size of block to expand was tuned by the GA for $N = 149$.

Despite these various impediments and the unsophisticated rules evolved on most runs, on several different runs in our initial experiment the GA discovered rules with significantly higher performance and rather sophisticated strategies. The typical space-time behavior of three such rules (each from a different run) are illustrated in figure 2.8b–2.8d. Some $\mathcal{P}_N$ values for these three "particle-based" rules are given in table 2.1. As can be seen, $\mathcal{P}_N$ is significantly higher for these rules than for the typical block-expanding rule ϕ_a. In addition, the performances of the most highly fit rules remain relatively constant as N is increased, meaning that these rules can generalize better than can ϕ_a.

Why does ϕ_d, for example, perform relatively well on the $\rho_c = \frac{1}{2}$ task? In figure 2.8d it can be seen that, although the patterns eventually converge to fixed points, there is a transient phase during which spatial and temporal transfer of information about the density in local regions takes place. This local information interacts with other local information to produce the desired final state. Roughly, ϕ_d successively classifies "local" densities with a locality range that increases with time. In regions where there is some ambiguity, a "signal" is propagated. This is seen either as a checkerboard pattern propagated in both spatial directions or as a vertical black-to-white boundary. These signals indicate that the classification is to be made at a larger scale. (Such signals for resolving ambiguities are precisely what was lacking in the majority rule on this task.) Note that regions centered about each signal locally have $\rho = \frac{1}{2}$. The consequence is that the signal patterns can propagate, since the density of patterns with $\rho = \frac{1}{2}$ is neither increased nor decreased under the rule. The creation and interactions of these signals can be interpreted as the locus of the computation being performed by the CA—they form its emergent program.

The above explanation of how ϕ_d performs the $\rho_c = \frac{1}{2}$ task is an informal one obtained by careful scrutiny of many space-time patterns. Can we understand more rigorously how the rules evolved by the GA perform the desired computation? Understanding the results of GA evolution is a general problem—typically the GA is asked to find individuals that achieve high fitness but is not told how that high fitness is to be attained. One could say that this is analogous to the difficulty biologists have in understanding the products of natural evolution (e.g., us). We computational evolutionists have similar problems, since we do not specify what solution evolution is supposed to create; we ask only that it find some solution. In many cases, particularly in automatic-programming applications, it is difficult to understand exactly how an evolved high-fitness individual works. In genetic programming, for example, the evolved programs are often very long and complicated, with many irrelevant components attached to the core program performing the desired computation. It is usually a lot of work—and sometimes almost impossible—to figure out by hand what that core program is. The problem is even more difficult in the case of cellular automata, since the emergent "program" performed by a given CA is almost always impossible to extract from the bits of the rule table.

A more promising approach is to examine the space-time patterns created by the CA and to "reconstruct" from those patterns what the algorithm is. Crutchfield and Hanson have developed a general method for reconstructing and understanding the "intrinsic" computation embedded in space-time patterns in terms of "regular domains," "particles", and "particle interactions" (Hanson and Crutchfield, 1992; Crutchfield and Hanson 1993). This method is part of their "computational mechanics" framework for understanding computation in physical systems. A detailed discussion of computational mechanics and particle-based computation is beyond the scope of this chapter. Very briefly, for those familiar with formal language theory, regular domains are regions of space-time consisting of words in the same regular language—that is, they are regions that are computationally simple. Particles are localized boundaries between regular domains. In computational mechanics, particles are identified as information carriers, and collisions between particles are identified as the loci of important information processing. Particles and particle interactions form a high-level language for describing computation in spatially extended systems such as CAs. Figure 2.9 hints at this higher level of description: to produce it we filtered the regular domains from the space-time behavior of a GA-evolved CA to leave only the particles and their interactions, in terms of which the emergent algorithm of the CA can be understood.

The application of computational mechanics to the understanding of rules evolved by the GA is discussed further in Crutchfield and Mitchell 1994, in Das, Mitchell, and Crutchfield 1994, and in Das, Crutchfield, Mitchell, and Hanson 1995. In the last two papers, we used particles and

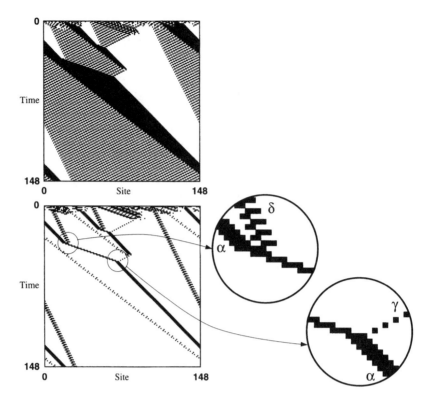

Figure 2.9 A space-time diagram of a GA-evolved rule for the $\rho_c = \frac{1}{2}$ task, and the same diagram with the regular domains filtered out, leaving only the particles and particle interactions (two of which are magnified). (Reprinted from Crutchfield and Mitchell 1994 by permission of the authors.)

particle interactions to describe the temporal stages by which highly fit rules were evolved by the GA.

Interestingly, it turns out that the behavior of the best rules discovered by the GA (such as ϕ_d) is very similar to the behavior of the well-known Gacs-Kurdyumov-Levin (GKL) rule (Gacs, Kurdyumov, and Levin, 1978; Gonzaga de Sá and Maes 1992). Figure 2.10 is a space-time diagram illustrating its typical behavior. The GKL rule (ϕ_{GKL}) was designed by hand to study reliable computation and phase transitions in one-dimensional spatially extended systems, but before we started our project it was also the rule with the best-known performance (for CAs with periodic boundary conditions) on the $\rho_c = \frac{1}{2}$ task. Its unbiased performance is given in the last row of table 2.1. The difference in performance between ϕ_d and ϕ_{GKL} is due to asymmetries in ϕ_d that are not present in ϕ_{GKL}. Further GA evolution of ϕ_d (using an increased number of ICs) has produced an improved version that approximately equals the performance of the ϕ_{GKL}. Rajarshi Das (personal communication) has gone further and, us-

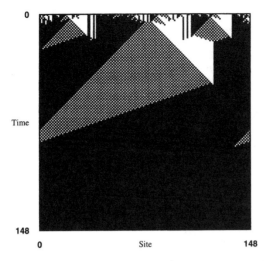

0

Time

148

0   Site   148

Figure 2.10   Space-time diagram for the GKL rule, with $\rho_0 > \frac{1}{2}$.

ing the aforementioned particle analysis, has designed by hand a rule that slightly outperforms ϕ_{GKL}.

The discovery of rules such as ϕ_b–ϕ_d is significant, since it is the first example of a GA's producing sophisticated emergent computation in decentralized, distributed systems such as CAs. It is encouraging for the prospect of using GAs to automatically evolve computation in more complex systems. Moreover, evolving CAs with GAs also gives us a tractable framework in which to study the mechanisms by which an evolutionary process might create complex coordinated behavior in natural decentralized distributed systems. For example, by studying the GA's behavior, we have already learned how evolution's breaking of symmetries can lead to suboptimal computational strategies; eventually we may be able to use such computer models to test ways in which such symmetry breaking might occur in natural evolution.

2.2   DATA ANALYSIS AND PREDICTION

A major impediment to scientific progress in many fields is the inability to make sense of the huge amounts of data that have been collected via experiment or computer simulation. In the fields of statistics and machine learning there have been major efforts to develop automatic methods for finding significant and interesting patterns in complex data, and for forecasting the future from such data; in general, however, the success of such efforts has been limited, and the automatic analysis of complex data remains an open problem. Data analysis and prediction can often be formulated as search problems—for example, a search for a model explaining the data, a search for prediction rules, or a search for a particular structure or scenario well predicted by the data. In this section I describe two projects in which a genetic algorithm is used to solve such search problems—one of predicting dynamical systems, and the other of predicting the structure of proteins.

Predicting Dynamical Systems

Norman Packard (1990) has developed a form of the GA to address this problem and has applied his method to several data analysis and prediction problems. The general problem can be stated as follows: A series of observations from some process (e.g., a physical system or a formal dynamical system) take the form of a set of pairs,

$$\{(\vec{x}^1, y^1), \ldots, (\vec{x}^N, y^N)\},$$

where $\vec{x}^i = (x_1^i, \ldots, x_n^i)$ are independent variables and y^i is a dependent variable ($1 \le i \le N$). For example, in a weather prediction task, the independent variables might be some set of features of today's weather (e.g., average humidity, average barometric pressure, low and high temperature, whether or not it rained), and the dependent variable might be a feature of tomorrow's weather (e.g., rain). In a stock market prediction task, the independent variables might be $\vec{x} = (x(t_1), x(t_2), \ldots, x(t_n))$, representing the values of the value of a particular stock (the "state variable") at successive time steps, and the dependent variable might be $y = x(t_{n+k})$, representing the value of the stock at some time in the future. (In these examples there is only one dependent variable y for each vector of independent variables $\vec{x}$; a more general form of the problem would allow a vector of dependent variables for each vector of indeperdent variables.)

Packard used a GA to search through the space of sets of conditions on the independent variables for those sets of conditions that give good predictions for the dependent variable. For example, in the stock market prediction task, an individual in the GA population might be a set of conditions such as

$C = \{(\$20 \le \text{Price of Xerox stock on day 1})$

$\wedge \ (\$25 \le \text{Price of Xerox stock on day 2} \le \$27)$

$\wedge \ (\$22 \le \text{Price of Xerox stock on day 3} \le \$25)\},$

where "$\wedge$" is the logical operator "AND". This individual represents all the sets of three days in which the given conditions were met (possibly the empty set if the conditions are never met). Such a condition set C thus specifies a particular subset of the data points (here, the set of all 3-day periods). Packard's goal was to use a GA to search for condition sets that are good predictors of *something*—in other words, to search for condition sets that specify subsets of data points whose dependent-variable values are close to being uniform. In the stock market example, if the GA found

Figure 2.11 Plot of a time series from Mackey-Glass equation with $\tau = 150$. Time is plotted on the horizontal axis; $x(t)$ is plotted on the vertical axis. (Reprinted from Martin Casdagli and Stephen Eubank, eds., *Nonlinear Modeling and Forecasting*; © 1992 Addison-Wesley Publishing Company, Inc. Reprinted by permission of the publisher.)

a condition set such that all the days satisfying that set were followed by days on which the price of Xerox stock rose to approximately $30, then we might be confident to predict that, if those conditions were satisfied today, Xerox stock will go up.

The fitness of each individual C is calculated by running all the data points $(\vec{x}, y)$ in the training set through C and, for each $\vec{x}$ that satisfies C, collecting the corresponding y. After this has been done, a measurement is made of the uniformity of the resulting values of y. If the y values are all close to a particular value v, then C is a candidate for a good predictor for y—that is, one can hope that a new $\vec{x}$ that satisfies C will also correspond to a y value close to v. On the other hand, if the y values are very different from one another, then $\vec{x}$ satisfying C does not seem to predict anything about the corresponding y value.

As an illustration of this approach, I will describe the work done by Thomas Meyer and Norman Packard (1992) on finding "regions of predictability" in time series generated by the Mackey-Glass equation, a chaotic dynamical system created as a model for blood flow (Mackey and Glass 1977):

$$\frac{dx}{dt} = \frac{ax(t - \tau)}{1 + [x(t - \tau)]^c} - bx(t).$$

Here $x(t)$ is the state variable, t is time in seconds, and a, b, c, and τ are constants. A time series from this system (with τ set to 150) is plotted in figure 2.11.

To form the data set, Meyer and Packard did the following: For each data point i, the independent variables $\vec{x}^i$ are 50 consecutive values of $x(t)$ (one per second):

$$\vec{x}^i = (x_1^i, x_2^i, \ldots, x_{50}^i).$$

The dependent variable for data point i, y^i, is the state variable t' time steps in the future: $y^i = x_{50 + t'}^i$. Each data point $(\vec{x}^i, y^i)$ is formed by iterating the Mackey-Glass equation with a different initial condition, where an initial condition consists of values for $\{x_{1-\tau}, \ldots, x_0\}$.

Meyer and Packard used the following as a fitness function:

$$f(C) = -\log_2\left(\frac{\sigma}{\sigma_0}\right) - \frac{\alpha}{N_C},$$

where σ is the standard deviation of the set of y's for data points satisfying C, σ_0 is the standard deviation of the distribution of y's over the entire data set, N_C is the number of data points satisfying condition C, and α is a constant. The first term of the fitness function measures the amount of information in the distribution of y's for points satisfying C, and the second term is a penalty term for poor statistics—if the number of points satisfying C is small, then the first term is less reliable, so C should have lower fitness. The constant α can be adjusted for each particular application.

Meyer and Packard used the following version of the GA:

1. Initialize the population with a random set of C's.

2. Calculate the fitness of each C.

3. Rank the population by fitness.

4. Discard some fraction of the lower-fitness individuals and replace them by new C's obtained by applying crossover and mutation to the remaining C's.

5. Go to step 2.

(Their selection method was, like that used in the cellular-automata project described above, similar to the "$(\mu + \lambda)$" method of evolution strategies.) Meyer and Packard used a form of crossover known in the GA literature as "uniform crossover" (Syswerda 1989). This operator takes two Cs and exchanges approximately half the "genes" (conditions). That is, at each gene position in parent A and parent B, a random decision is made whether that gene should go into offspring A or offspring B. An example follows:

Parent A: $\{(3.2 \leq x_6 \leq 5.5) \wedge (0.2 \leq x_8 \leq 4.8) \wedge (3.4 \leq x_9 \leq 9.9)\}$

Parent B: $\{(\mathbf{6.5} \leq \mathbf{x_2} \leq \mathbf{6.8}) \wedge (\mathbf{1.4} \leq \mathbf{x_4} \leq \mathbf{4.8}) \wedge (\mathbf{1.2} \leq \mathbf{x_9} \leq \mathbf{1.7})$
$\wedge (\mathbf{4.8} \leq \mathbf{x_{16}} \leq \mathbf{5.1})\}$

Offspring A: $\{(3.2 \leq x_6 \leq 5.5) \wedge (\mathbf{1.4} \leq \mathbf{x_4} \leq \mathbf{4.8}) \wedge (3.4 \leq x_9 \leq 9.9)\}$

Offspring B: $\{(\mathbf{6.5} \leq \mathbf{x_2} \leq \mathbf{6.8}) \wedge (0.2 \leq x_8 \leq 4.8) \wedge (\mathbf{1.2} \leq \mathbf{x_9} \leq \mathbf{1.7})$
$\wedge (\mathbf{4.8} \leq \mathbf{x_{16}} \leq \mathbf{5.1})\}$

Here offspring A has two genes from parent A and one gene from parent B. Offspring B has one gene from parent A and three genes from parent B.

In addition to crossover, four different mutation operators were used:

Add a new condition:

$$\{(3.2 \leq x_6 \leq 5.5) \wedge (0.2 \leq x_8 \leq 4.8)\}$$
$$\rightarrow \{(3.2 \leq x_6 \leq 5.5) \wedge (0.2 \leq x_8 \leq 4.8) \wedge (3.4 \leq x_9 \leq 9.9)\}$$

Delete a condition:

$$\{(3.2 \leq x_6 \leq 5.5) \wedge (0.2 \leq x_8 \leq 4.8) \wedge (3.4 \leq x_9 \leq 9.9)\}$$
$$\rightarrow \{(3.2 \leq x_6 \leq 5.5) \wedge (3.4 \leq x_9 \leq 9.9)\}$$

Broaden or shrink a range:

$$\{(3.2 \leq x_6 \leq 5.5) \wedge (0.2 \leq x_8 \leq 4.8)\}$$
$$\rightarrow \{(3.9 \leq x_6 \leq 4.8) \wedge (0.2 \leq x_8 \leq 4.8)\}$$

Shift a range up or down:

$$\{(3.2 \leq x_6 \leq 5.5) \wedge (0.2 \leq x_8 \leq 4.8)\}$$
$$\rightarrow \{(3.2 \leq x_6 \leq 5.5) \wedge (1.2 \leq x_8 \leq 5.8)\}$$

The results of running the GA using these data from the $\tau = 150$ time series with $t' = 150$ are illustrated in figures 2.12 and 2.13. Figure 2.12 gives the four highest-fitness condition sets found by the GA, and figure 2.13 shows the four results of those condition sets. Each of the four plots in figure 2.13 shows the trajectories corresponding to data points $(\vec{x}^i, y^i)$ that satisfied the condition set. The leftmost white region is the initial 50 time steps during which the data were taken. The vertical lines in that region represent the various conditions on $\vec{x}$ given in the condition set. For example, in plot a the leftmost vertical line represents a condition on x_{20} (this set of trajectories is plotted starting at time step 20), and the rightmost vertical line in that region represents a condition on x_{49}. The shaded region represents the period of time between time steps 50 and 200, and the rightmost vertical line marks time step 200 (the point at which the y^i observation was made). Notice that in each of these plots the values of y^i fall into a very narrow range, which means that the GA was successful in finding subsets of the data for which it is possible to make highly accurate predictions. (Other results along the same lines are reported in Meyer 1992.)

These results are very striking, but some questions immediately arise. First and most important, do the discovered conditions yield correct predictions for data points outside the training set (i.e., the set of data points used to calculate fitness), or do they merely describe chance statistical fluctuations in the data that were learned by the GA? Meyer and Packard performed a number of "out of sample" tests with data points outside the training set that satisfied the evolved condition sets and found that the results were robust—the y^i values for these data points also tended to be in the narrow range (Thomas Meyer, personal communication).

$$C_a = \left\{ \begin{array}{llll} (x_{20} > 1.122) & \wedge & (x_{25} < 1.330) & \wedge & (x_{26} > 1.168) & \wedge \\ (x_{35} < 1.342) & \wedge & (x_{41} > 1.304) & \wedge & (x_{49} > 1.262) & \end{array} \right\} \rightarrow y = 0.18 \pm 0.014$$

$$C_b = \left\{ \begin{array}{llll} (x_{25} < 1.330) & \wedge & (x_{26} > 1.177) & \wedge & (x_{31} > 1.127) & \wedge \\ (x_{38} < 1.156) & \wedge & (x_{40} < 1.256) & \wedge & (x_{46} > 1.194) & \wedge \\ (x_{47} < 1.311) & \wedge & (x_{49} > 1.070) & & & \end{array} \right\} \rightarrow y = 0.27 \pm 0.019$$

$$C_c = \left\{ \begin{array}{llll} (x_{24} > 0.992) & \wedge & (x_{29} < 1.150) & \wedge & (x_{30} > 1.020) & \wedge \\ (x_{34} < 1.090) & \wedge & (x_{40} < 0.951) & \wedge & (x_{42} > 0.599) & \wedge \\ (x_{45} > 0.591) & \wedge & (x_{49} < 0.763) & \wedge & (x_{50} > 0.576) & \end{array} \right\} \rightarrow y = 1.22 \pm 0.024$$

$$C_d = \left\{ \begin{array}{llll} (x_{19} < 0.967) & \wedge & (x_{22} < 1.049) & \wedge & (x_{26} > 0.487) & \wedge \\ (x_{29} < 1.066) & \wedge & (x_{33} > 0.416) & \wedge & (x_{34} < 1.008) & \wedge \\ (x_{37} < 1.331) & \wedge & (x_{40} < 0.941) & \wedge & (x_{41} > 0.654) & \wedge \\ (x_{42} > 0.262) & \wedge & (x_{48} > 0.639) & \wedge & (x_{49} < 0.814) & \end{array} \right\} \rightarrow y = 1.34 \pm 0.034$$

Figure 2.12 The four highest-fitness condition sets found by the GA for the Mackey-Glass system with $\tau = 150$. (Adapted from Meyer and Packard 1992.)

Exactly how is the GA solving the problem? What are the schemas that are being processed? What is the role of crossover in finding a good solution? Uniform crossover of the type used here has very different properties than single-point crossover, and its use makes it harder to figure out what schemas are being recombined. Meyer (personal communication) found that turning crossover off and relying solely on the four mutation operators did not make a big difference in the GA's performance; as in the case of genetic programming, this raises the question of whether the GA is the best method for this task. An interesting extension of this work would be to perform control experiments comparing the performance of the GA with that of other search methods such as hill climbing.

To what extent are the results restricted by the fact that only certain conditions are allowed (i.e., conditions that are conjunctions of ranges on independent variables)? Packard (1990) proposed a more general form for conditions that also allows disjunctions ($\vee$'s); an example might be

$$\{[(3.2 \le x_6 \le 5.5) \vee (1.1 \le x_6 \le 2.5)] \wedge [0.2 \le x_8 \le 4.8]\},$$

where we are given two nonoverlapping choices for the conditions on x_6. A further generalization proposed by Packard would be to allow disjunctions between sets of conditions.

To what extent will this method succeed on other types of prediction tasks? Packard (1990) proposes applying this method to tasks such as weather prediction, financial market prediction, speech recognition, and visual pattern recognition. Interestingly, in 1991 Packard left the Physics Department at the University of Illinois to help form a company to predict financial markets (Prediction Company, in Santa Fe, New Mexico). As I

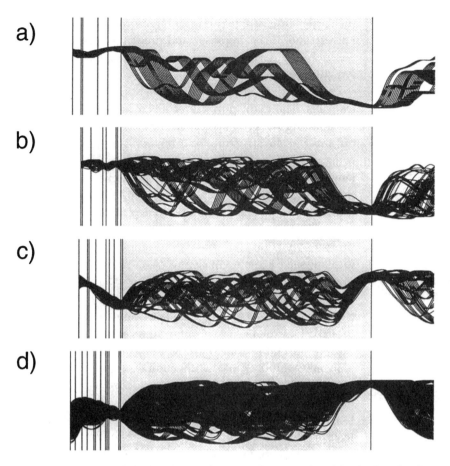

Figure 2.13 Results of the four highest-fitness condition sets found by the GA. (See figure 2.12.) Each plot shows trajectories of data points that satisfied that condition set. The leftmost white region is the initial 50 time steps during which data were taken. The vertical lines in that region represent the various conditions on $\vec{x}$ given in the condition set. The vertical line on the right-hand side represents the time at which the prediction is to be made. Note how the trajectories narrow at that region, indicating that the GA has found conditions for good predictability. (Reprinted from Martin Casdagli and Stephen Eubank (eds.), *Nonlinear Modeling and Forecasting*; © 1992 Addison-Wesley Publishing Company, Inc. Reprinted by permission of the publisher.)

write this (mid 1995), the company has not yet gone public with their results, but stay tuned.

Predicting Protein Structure

One of the most promising and rapidly growing areas of GA application is data analysis and prediction in molecular biology. GAs have been used for, among other things, interpreting nuclear magnetic resonance data to determine the structure of DNA (Lucasius and Kateman 1989), finding the correct ordering for an unordered group of DNA fragments (Parsons, Forrest, and Burks, in press), and predicting protein structure. Here I will describe one particular project in which a GA was used to predict the structure of a protein.

Proteins are the fundamental functional building blocks of all biological cells. The main purpose of DNA in a cell is to encode instructions for building up proteins out of amino acids; the proteins in turn carry out most of the structural and metabolic functions of the cell. A protein is made up of a sequence of amino acids connected by peptide bonds. The length of the sequence varies from protein to protein but is typically on the order of 100 amino acids. Owing to electrostatic and other physical forces, the sequence "folds up" to a particular three-dimensional structure. It is this three-dimensional structure that primarily determines the protein's function. The three-dimensional structure of a Crambin protein (a plant-seed protein consisting of 46 amino acids) is illustrated in figure 2.14. The three-dimensional structure of a protein is determined by the particular sequence of its amino acids, but it is not currently known precisely how a given sequence leads to a given structure. In fact, being able to predict a protein's structure from its amino acid sequence is one of the most important unsolved problems of molecular biology and biophysics. Not only would a successful prediction algorithm be a tremendous advance in the understanding of the biochemical mechanisms of proteins, but, since such an algorithm could conceivably be used to *design* proteins to carry out specific functions, it would have profound, far-reaching effects on biotechnology and the treatment of disease.

Recently there has been considerable effort toward developing methods such as GAs and neural networks for automatically predicting protein structures (see, for example, Hunter, Searls, and Shavlik 1993). The relatively simple GA prediction project of Steffen Schulze-Kremer (1992) illustrates one way in which GAs can be used on this task; it also illustrates some potential pitfalls.

Schulze-Kremer took the amino acid sequence of the Crambin protein and used a GA to search in the space of possible structures for one that would fit well with Crambin's amino acid sequence. The most straightforward way to describe the structure of a protein is to list the three-dimensional coordinates of each amino acid, or even each atom. In principle, a GA could use such a representation, evolving vectors of coordinates to find one that resulted in a plausible structure. But, because of a number of difficulties with that representation (e.g., the usual crossover and mutation operators would be too likely to create physically impossible structures), Schulze-Kremer instead described protein structures using "torsion angles"—roughly, the angles made by the peptide bonds connecting amino acids and the angles made by bonds in an amino acid's "side chain." (See Dickerson and Geis 1969 for an overview of how three-dimensional protein structure is measured.) Schulze-Kremer used 10 tor-

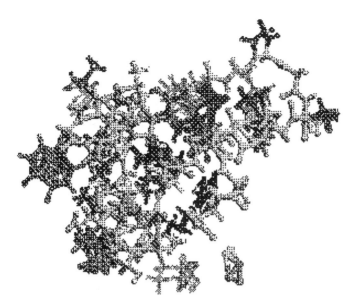

Figure 2.14 A representation of the three-dimensional structure of a Crambin protein. (From the "PDB at a Glance" page at the World Wide Web URL http://www.nih.gov /molecular_modeling/pdb_at_a_glance.)

sion angles to describe each of the N (46 in the case of Crambin) amino acids in the sequence for a given protein. This collection of N sets of 10 torsion angles completely defines the three-dimensional structure of the protein. A chromosome, representing a candidate structure with N amino acids, thus contains N sets of ten real numbers. This representation is illustrated in figure 2.15.

The next step is to define a fitness function over the space of chromosomes. The goal is to find a structure that has low potential energy for the given sequence of amino acids. This goal is based on the assumption that a sequence of amino acids will fold to a minimal-energy state, where energy is a function of physical and chemical properties of the individual amino acids and their spatial interactions (e.g., electrostatic pair interactions between atoms in two spatially adjacent amino acids). If a complete description of the relevant forces were known and solvable, then in principle the minimum-energy structure could be calculated. However, in practice this problem is intractable, and biologists instead develop approximate models to describe the potential energy of a structure. These models are essentially intelligent guesses as to what the most relevant forces will be. Schulze-Kremer's initial experiments used a highly simplified model in which the potential energy of a structure was assumed to be a function of only the torsion angles, electrostatic pair interactions between atoms, and van der Waals pair interactions between atoms (Schulze-Kremer 1992). The goal was for the GA to find a structure (defined in terms of torsion angles) that minimized torsion angles

amino acid 1	amino acid 2	⋯	amino acid 46
φ: 66.3°	φ: -27.2°		
ψ: 45.2°	ψ: 23.1°		.
ω: 180.0°	ω: 180.0°		.
χ^{1}: -22.7°	χ^{1}: 111.4°		.
χ^{2}: 127.1°	χ^{2}: 120.2°		
χ^{3}: -100.0°	χ^{3}: -22.1°		
χ^{4}: 32.2°	χ^{4}: 32.2°		
χ^{5}: -125.9°	χ^{5}: -87.3°		
χ^{6}: 55.4°	χ^{6}: -95.2°		
χ^{7}: 76.6°	χ^{7}: -54.1°		

chromosome:

[66.3 45.2 180.0 -22.7 127.1 -100.0 32.2 -125.9 55.4 76.6] [-27.2 23.1 …] … […]

Figure 2.15 An illustration of the representation for protein structure used in Schulze-Kremer's experiments. Each of the N amino acids in the sequence is represented by 10 torsion angles: ϕ, ψ, ω, and χ^{1}–χ^{7}. (See Schulze-Kremer 1992 for details of what these angles represent.) A chromosome is a list of these N sets of 10 angles. Crossover points are chosen only at amino acid boundaries.

this simplified potential-energy function for the amino acid sequence of Crambin.

In Schulze-Kremer's GA, crossover was either two-point (i.e., performed at two points along the chromosome rather than at one point) or uniform (i.e., rather than taking contiguous segments from each parent to form the offspring, each "gene" is chosen from one or the other parent, with a 50% probability for each parent). Here a "gene" consisted of a group of 10 torsion angles; crossover points were chosen only at amino acid boundaries. Two mutation operators designed to work on real numbers rather than on bits were used: the first replaced a randomly chosen torsion angle with a new value randomly chosen from the 10 most frequently occurring angle values for that particular bond, and the second incremented or decremented a randomly chosen torsion angle by a small amount.

The GA started on a randomly generated initial population of ten structures and ran for 1000 generations. At each generation the fitness was calculated (here, high fitness means low potential energy), the population was sorted by fitness, and a number of the highest-fitness individuals were selected to be parents for the next generation (this is, again, a form of rank selection). Offspring were created via crossover and mutation. A scheme was used in which the probabilities of the different mutation and crossover operators increased or decreased over the course of the run.

In designing this scheme, Schulze-Kremer relied on his intuitions about which operators were likely to be most useful at which stages of the run.

The GA's search produced a number of structures with quite low potential energy—in fact, much lower than that of the actual structure for Crambin! Unfortunately, however, none of the generated individuals was structurally similar to Crambin. The snag was that it was too easy for the GA to find low-energy structures under the simplified potential energy function; that is, the fitness function was not sufficiently constrained to force the GA to find the actual target structure. The fact that Schulze-Kremer's initial experiments were not very successful demonstrates how important it is to get the fitness function right—here, by getting the potential-energy model right (a difficult biophysical problem), or at least getting a good enough approximation to lead the GA in the right direction.

Schulze-Kremer's experiments are a first step in the process of "getting it right." I predict that fairly soon GAs and other machine learning methods will help biologists make real breakthroughs in protein folding and in other areas of molecular biology. I'll even venture to predict that this type of application will be much more profitable (both scientifically and financially) than using GAs to predict financial markets.

2.3 EVOLVING NEURAL NETWORKS

Neural networks are biologically motivated approaches to machine learning, inspired by ideas from neuroscience. Recently some efforts have been made to use genetic algorithms to evolve aspects of neural networks.

In its simplest "feedforward" form (figure 2.16), a neural network is a collection of connected activatable units ("neurons") in which the connections are weighted, usually with real-valued weights. The network is presented with an activation pattern on its input units, such a set of numbers representing features of an image to be classified (e.g., the pixels in an image of a handwritten letter of the alphabet). Activation spreads in a forward direction from the input units through one or more layers of middle ("hidden") units to the output units over the weighted connections. Typically, the activation coming into a unit from other units is multiplied by the weights on the links over which it spreads, and then is added together with other incoming activation. The result is typically thresholded (i.e., the unit "turns on" if the resulting activation is above that unit's threshold). This process is meant to roughly mimic the way activation spreads through networks of neurons in the brain. In a feedforward network, activation spreads only in a forward direction, from the input layer through the hidden layers to the output layer. Many people have also experimented with "recurrent" networks, in which there are feedback connections as well as feedforward connections between layers.

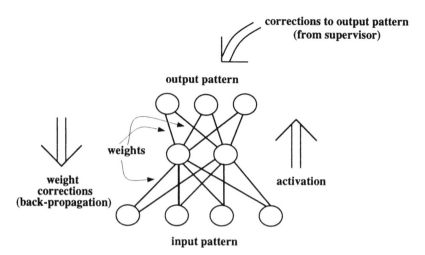

corrections to output pattern
(from supervisor)

output pattern

weights

weight
corrections
(back-propagation)

activation

input pattern

Figure 2.16 A schematic diagram of a simple feedforward neural network and the back-propagation process by which weight values are adjusted.

After activation has spread through a feedforward network, the resulting activation pattern on the output units encodes the network's "answer" to the input (e.g., a classification of the input pattern as the letter A). In most applications, the network learns a correct mapping between input and output patterns via a learning algorithm. Typically the weights are initially set to small random values. Then a set of training inputs is presented sequentially to the network. In the back-propagation learning procedure (Rumelhart, Hinton, and Williams 1986), after each input has propagated through the network and an output has been produced, a "teacher" compares the activation value at each output unit with the correct values, and the weights in the network are adjusted in order to reduce the difference between the network's output and the correct output. Each iteration of this procedure is called a "training cycle," and a complete pass of training cycles through the set of training inputs is called a "training epoch." (Typically many training epochs are needed for a network to learn to successfully classify a given set of training inputs.) This type of procedure is known as "supervised learning," since a teacher supervises the learning by providing correct output values to guide the learning process. In "unsupervised learning" there is no teacher, and the learning system must learn on its own using less detailed (and sometimes less reliable) environmental feedback on its performance. (For overviews of neural networks and their applications, see Rumelhart et al. 1986, McClelland et al. 1986, and Hertz, Krogh, and Palmer 1991.)

There are many ways to apply GAs to neural networks. Some aspects that can be evolved are the weights in a fixed network, the network architecture (i.e., the number of units and their interconnections can change), and the learning rule used by the network. Here I will describe four different projects, each of which uses a genetic algorithm to evolve one of these aspects. (Two approaches to evolving network architecture will be described.) (For a collection of papers on various combinations of genetic algorithms and neural networks, see Whitley and Schaffer 1992.)

Evolving Weights in a Fixed Network

David Montana and Lawrence Davis (1989) took the first approach—evolving the weights in a fixed network. That is, Montana and Davis were using the GA *instead* of back-propagation as a way of finding a good set of weights for a fixed set of connections. Several problems associated with the back-propagation algorithm (e.g., the tendency to get stuck at local optima in weight space, or the unavailability of a "teacher" to supervise learning in some tasks) often make it desirable to find alternative weight-training schemes.

Montana and Davis were interested in using neural networks to classify underwater sonic "lofargrams" (similar to spectrograms) into two classes: "interesting" and "not interesting." The overall goal was to "detect and reason about interesting signals in the midst of the wide variety of acoustic noise and interference which exist in the ocean." The networks were to be trained from a database containing lofargrams and classifications made by experts as to whether or not a given lofargram is "interesting." Each network had four input units, representing four parameters used by an expert system that performed the same classification. Each network had one output unit and two layers of hidden units (the first with seven units and the second with ten units). The networks were fully connected feed-forward networks—that is, each unit was connected to every unit in the next higher layer. In total there were 108 weighted connections between units. In addition, there were 18 weighted connections between the non-input units and a "threshold unit" whose outgoing links implemented the thresholding for each of the non-input units, for a total of 126 weights to evolve.

The GA was used as follows. Each chromosome was a list (or "vector") of 126 weights. Figure 2.17 shows (for a much smaller network) how the encoding was done: the weights were read off the network in a fixed order (from left to right and from top to bottom) and placed in a list. Notice that each "gene" in the chromosome is a real number rather than a bit. To calculate the fitness of a given chromosome, the weights in the chromosome were assigned to the links in the corresponding network, the network was run on the training set (here 236 examples from the database of lofargrams), and the sum of the squares of the errors (collected over all the training cycles) was returned. Here, an "error" was the difference between the desired output activation value and the actual output activation value. Low error meant high fitness.

Network:

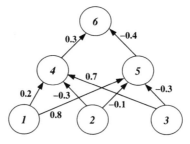

Chromosome: (0.3 −0.4 0.2 0.8 −0.3 −0.1 0.7 −0.3)

Figure 2.17 Illustration of Montana and Davis's encoding of network weights into a list that serves as a chromosome for the GA. The units in the network are numbered for later reference. The real-valued numbers on the links are the weights.

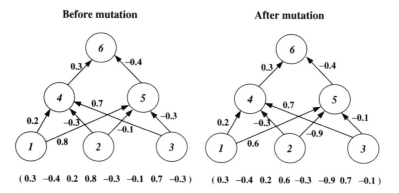

Before mutation

After mutation

(0.3 −0.4 0.2 0.8 −0.3 −0.1 0.7 −0.3)   (0.3 −0.4 0.2 0.6 −0.3 −0.9 0.7 −0.1)

Figure 2.18 Illustration of Montana and Davis's mutation method. Here the weights on incoming links to unit 5 are mutated.

An initial population of 50 weight vectors was chosen randomly, with each weight being between −1.0 and +1.0. Montana and Davis tried a number of different genetic operators in various experiments. The mutation and crossover operators they used for their comparison of the GA with back-propagation are illustrated in figures 2.18 and 2.19. The mutation operator selects n non-input units and, for each incoming link to those units, adds a random value between −1.0 and +1.0 to the weight on the link. The crossover operator takes two parent weight vectors and, for each non-input unit in the offspring vector, selects one of the parents at random and copies the weights on the incoming links from that parent to the offspring. Notice that only one offspring is created.

The performance of a GA using these operators was compared with the performance of a back-propagation algorithm. The GA had a population of 50 weight vectors, and a rank-selection method was used. The GA was allowed to run for 200 generations (i.e., 10,000 network evaluations). The back-propagation algorithm was allowed to run for 5000 iterations, where one iteration is a complete epoch (a complete pass through the training data). Montana and Davis reasoned that two network evalua-

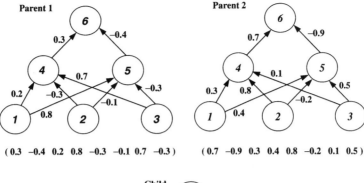

(0.3 −0.4 0.2 0.8 −0.3 −0.1 0.7 −0.3)   (0.7 −0.9 0.3 0.4 0.8 −0.2 0.1 0.5)

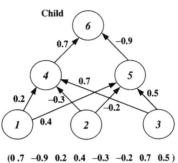

(0.7 −0.9 0.2 0.4 −0.3 −0.2 0.7 0.5)

Figure 2.19 Illustration of Montana and Davis's crossover method. The offspring is created as follows: for each non-input unit, a parent is chosen at random and the weights on the incoming links to that unit are copied from the chosen parent. In the child network shown here, the incoming links to unit 4 come from parent 1 and the incoming links to units 5 and 6 come from parent 2.

tions under the GA are equivalent to one back-propagation iteration, since back-propagation on a given training example consists of two parts— the forward propagation of activation (and the calculation of errors at the output units) and the backward error propagation (and adjusting of the weights). The GA performs only the first part. Since the second part requires more computation, two GA evaluations takes less than half the computation of a single back-propagation iteration.

The results of the comparison are displayed in figure 2.20. Here one back-propagation iteration is plotted for every two GA evaluations. The x axis gives the number of iterations, and the y axis gives the best evaluation (lowest sum of squares of errors) found by that time. It can be seen that the GA significantly outperforms back-propagation on this task, obtaining better weight vectors more quickly.

This experiment shows that in some situations the GA is a better training method for networks than simple back-propagation. This does not mean that the GA will outperform back-propagation in all cases. It is also possible that enhancements of back-propagation might help it overcome some of the problems that prevented it from performing as well as the GA in this experiment. Schaffer, Whitley, and Eshelman (1992) point out

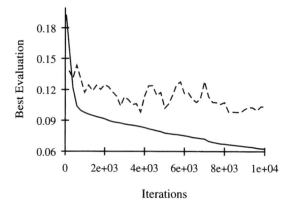

Figure 2.20 Montana and Davis's results comparing the performance of the GA with back-propagation. The figure plots the best evaluation (lower is better) found by a given iteration. Solid line: genetic algorithm. Broken line: back-propagation. (Reprinted from *Proceedings of the International Joint Conference on Artificial Intelligence;* © 1989 Morgan Kaufmann Publishers, Inc. Reprinted by permission of the publisher.)

that the GA has not been found to outperform the best weight-adjustment methods (e.g., "quickprop") on supervised learning tasks, but they predict that the GA will be most useful in finding weights in tasks where back-propagation and its relatives cannot be used, such as in unsupervised learning tasks, in which the error at each output unit is not available to the learning system, or in situations in which only sparse reinforcement is available. This is often the case for "neurocontrol" tasks, in which neural networks are used to control complicated systems such as robots navigating in unfamiliar environments.

Evolving Network Architectures

Montana and Davis's GA evolved the weights in a fixed network. As in most neural network applications, the architecture of the network—the number of units and their interconnections—is decided ahead of time by the programmer by guesswork, often aided by some heuristics (e.g., "more hidden units are required for more difficult problems") and by trial and error. Neural network researchers know all too well that the particular architecture chosen can determine the success or failure of the application, so they would like very much to be able to automatically optimize the procedure of designing an architecture for a particular application. Many believe that GAs are well suited for this task. There have been several efforts along these lines, most of which fall into one of two categories: direct encoding and grammatical encoding. Under direct encoding, a network architecture is directly encoded into a GA chromosome. Under grammatical encoding, the GA does not evolve network architec-

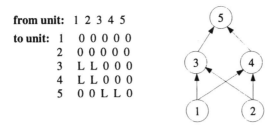

from unit: 1 2 3 4 5

to unit: 1   0 0 0 0 0
        2   0 0 0 0 0
        3   L L 0 0 0
        4   L L 0 0 0
        5   0 0 L L 0

chromosome: 0 0 0 0 0 0 0 0 0 0 1 1 0 0 0 1 1 0 0 0 0 0 1 1 0

Figure 2.21 An illustration of Miller, Todd, and Hegde's representation scheme. Each entry in the matrix represents the type of connection on the link between the "from unit" (column) and the "to unit" (row). The rows of the matrix are strung together to make the bit-string encoding of the network, given at the bottom of the figure. The resulting network is shown at the right. (Adapted from Miller, Todd, and Hegde 1989.)

tures; rather, it evolves grammars that can be used to develop network architectures.

Direct Encoding

The method of direct encoding is illustrated in work done by Geoffrey Miller, Peter Todd, and Shailesh Hegde (1989), who restricted their initial project to feedforward networks with a fixed number of units for which the GA was to evolve the connection topology. As is shown in figure 2.21, the connection topology was represented by an $N \times N$ matrix (5×5 in figure 2.21) in which each entry encodes the type of connection from the "from unit" to the "to unit." The entries in the connectivity matrix were either "0" (meaning no connection) or "L" (meaning a "learnable" connection—i.e., one for which the weight can be changed through learning). Figure 2.21 also shows how the connectivity matrix was transformed into a chromosome for the GA ("0" corresponds to 0 and "L" to 1) and how the bit string was decoded into a network. Connections that were specified to be learnable were initialized with small random weights. Since Miller, Todd, and Hegde restricted these networks to be feedforward, any connections to input units or feedback connections specified in the chromosome were ignored.

Miller, Todd, and Hegde used a simple fitness-proportionate selection method and mutation (bits in the string were flipped with some low probability). Their crossover operator randomly chose a row index and swapped the corresponding rows between the two parents to create two offspring. The intuition behind that operator was similar to that behind Montana and Davis's crossover operator—each row represented all the incoming connections to a single unit, and this set was thought to be a functional building block of the network. The fitness of a chromosome was calculated in the same way as in Montana and Davis's project: for a given problem, the network was trained on a training set for a certain number of epochs, using back-propagation to modify the weights. The fitness of the chromosome was the sum of the squares of the errors on the training set at the last epoch. Again, low error translated to high fitness.

Miller, Todd, and Hegde tried their GA on three tasks:

XOR: The single output unit should turn on (i.e., its activation should be above a set threshold) if the exclusive-or of the initial values (1 = on and 0 = off) of the two input units is 1.

Four Quadrant: The real-valued activations (between 0.0 and 1.0) of the two input units represent the coordinates of a point in a unit square. All inputs representing points in the lower left and upper right quadrants of the square should produce an activation of 0.0 on the single output unit, and all other points should produce an output activation of 1.0.

Encoder/Decoder (Pattern Copying): The output units (equal in number to the input units) should copy the initial pattern on the input units. This would be trivial, except that the number of hidden units is smaller than the number of input units, so some encoding and decoding must be done.

These are all relatively easy problems for multi-layer neural networks to learn to solve under back-propagation. The networks had different numbers of units for different tasks (ranging from 5 units for the XOR task to 20 units for the encoder/decoder task); the goal was to see if the GA could discover a good connection topology for each task. For each run the population size was 50, the crossover rate was 0.6, and the mutation rate was 0.005. In all three tasks, the GA was easily able to find networks that readily learned to map inputs to outputs over the training set with little error. However, the three tasks were too easy to be a rigorous test of this method—it remains to be seen if this method can scale up to more complex tasks that require much larger networks with many more interconnections. I chose the project of Miller, Todd, and Hegde to illustrate this approach because of its simplicity. For several examples of more sophisticated approaches to evolving network architectures using direct encoding, see Whitley and Schaffer 1992.

Grammatical Encoding
The method of grammatical encoding can be illustrated by the work of Hiroaki Kitano (1990), who points out that direct-encoding approachs become increasingly difficult to use as the size of the desired network increases. As the network's size grows, the size of the required chromosome increases quickly, which leads to problems both in performance (how high a fitness can be obtained) and in efficiency (how long it takes to obtain high fitness). In addition, since direct-encoding methods explicitly represent each connection in the network, repeated or nested structures

cannot be represented efficiently, even though these are common for some problems.

The solution pursued by Kitano and others is to encode networks as grammars; the GA evolves the grammars, but the fitness is tested only after a "development" step in which a network develops from the grammar. That is, the "genotype" is a grammar, and the "phenotype" is a network derived from that grammar.

A grammar is a set of rules that can be applied to produce a set of structures (e.g., sentences in a natural language, programs in a computer language, neural network architectures). A simple example is the following grammar:

$$S \rightarrow aSb,$$

$$S \rightarrow \epsilon.$$

Here S is the start symbol and a nonterminal, a and b are terminals, and ϵ is the empty-string terminal. ($S \rightarrow \epsilon$ means that S can be replaced by the empty string.) To construct a structure from this grammar, start with S, and replace it by one of the allowed replacements given by the right-hand sides (e.g., $S \rightarrow aSb$). Now take the resulting structure and replace any nonterminal (here S) by one of its allowed replacements (e.g., $aSb \rightarrow aaSbb$). Continue in this way until no nonterminals are left (e.g., $aaSbb \rightarrow aabb$, using $S \rightarrow \epsilon$). It can easily be shown that the set of structures that can be produced by this grammar are exactly the strings $a^n b^n$ consisting of the same number of as and bs with all the as on the left and all the bs on the right.

Kitano applied this general idea to the development of neural networks using a type of grammar called a "graph-generation grammar," a simple example of which is given in figure 2.22a. Here the right-hand side of each rule is a 2×2 matrix rather than a one-dimensional string. Capital letters are nonterminals, and lower-case letters are terminals. Each lower-case letter from a through p represents one of the 16 possible 2×2 arrays of ones and zeros. In contrast to the grammar for $a^n b^n$ given above, each nonterminal in this particular grammar has exactly one right-hand side, so there is only one structure that can be formed from this grammar: the 8×8 matrix shown in figure 2.22b. This matrix can be interpreted as a connection matrix for a neural network: a 1 in row i and column i means that unit i is present in the network and a 1 in row i and column j, $i \neq j$, means that there is a connection from unit i to unit j. (In Kitano's experiments, connections to or from nonexistent units and recurrent connections were ignored.) The result is the network shown in figure 2.22c, which, with appropriate weights, computes the Boolean function XOR.

Kitano's goal was to have a GA evolve such grammars. Figure 2.23 illustrates a chromosome encoding the grammar given in figure 2.22a. The chromosome is divided up into separate rules, each of which consists of five loci. The first locus is the left-hand side of the rule; the second

$$S \rightarrow \begin{matrix} A & B \\ C & D \end{matrix} \quad A \rightarrow \begin{matrix} c & p \\ a & c \end{matrix} \quad B \rightarrow \begin{matrix} a & a \\ a & e \end{matrix} \quad C \rightarrow \begin{matrix} a & a \\ a & a \end{matrix} \quad D \rightarrow \begin{matrix} a & a \\ a & b \end{matrix}$$

$$a \rightarrow \begin{matrix} 0 & 0 \\ 0 & 0 \end{matrix} \quad b \rightarrow \begin{matrix} 0 & 0 \\ 0 & 1 \end{matrix} \quad c \rightarrow \begin{matrix} 1 & 0 \\ 0 & 1 \end{matrix} \quad e \rightarrow \begin{matrix} 0 & 1 \\ 0 & 1 \end{matrix} \quad p \rightarrow \begin{matrix} 1 & 1 \\ 1 & 1 \end{matrix}$$

(a)

$$S \Rightarrow \begin{matrix} A & B \\ C & D \end{matrix} \Rightarrow \begin{matrix} c & p & a & a \\ a & c & a & e \\ a & a & a & a \\ a & a & a & b \end{matrix} \Rightarrow \begin{matrix} 1 & 0 & 1 & 1 & 0 & 0 & 0 & 0 \\ 0 & 1 & 1 & 1 & 0 & 0 & 0 & 0 \\ 0 & 0 & 1 & 0 & 0 & 0 & 0 & 1 \\ 0 & 0 & 0 & 1 & 0 & 0 & 0 & 1 \\ 0 & 0 & 0 & 0 & 0 & 0 & 0 & 0 \\ 0 & 0 & 0 & 0 & 0 & 0 & 0 & 0 \\ 0 & 0 & 0 & 0 & 0 & 0 & 0 & 0 \\ 0 & 0 & 0 & 0 & 0 & 0 & 0 & 1 \end{matrix}$$

(b)

(c)

Figure 2.22 Illustration of the use of Kitano's "graph generation grammar" to produce a network to solve the XOR problem. (a) Grammatical rules. (b) A connection matrix is produced from the grammar. (c) The resulting network. (Adapted from Kitano 1990.)

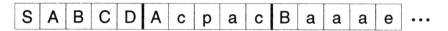

Figure 2.23 Illustration of a chromosome encoding a grammar.

through fifth loci are the four symbols in the matrix on the right-hand side of the rule. The possible alleles at each locus are the symbols $A–Z$ and $a–p$. The first locus of the chromosome is fixed to be the start symbol, S; at least one rule taking S into a 2×2 matrix is necessary to get started in building a network from a grammar. All other symbols are chosen at random. A network is built applying the grammar rules encoded in the chromosome for a predetermined number of iterations. (The rules that take $a–p$ to the 16 2×2 matrices of zeros and ones are fixed and are not represented in the chromosome.) In the simple version used by Kitano, if a nonterminal (e.g., A) appears on the left-hand side in two or more different rules, only the first such rule is included in the grammar (Hiroaki Kitano, personal communication).

The fitness of a grammar was calculated by constructing a network from the grammar, using back-propagation with a set of training inputs to train the resulting network to perform a simple task, and then, after training, measuring the sum of the squares of the errors made by the network on either the training set or a separate test set. (This is similar to the fitness measure used by Montana and Davis and by Miller, Todd, and Hegde.) The GA used fitness-proportionate selection, multi-point crossover (crossover was performed at one or more points along the chromosome), and mutation. A mutation consisted of replacing one symbol in the chromosome with a randomly chosen symbol from the $A-Z$ and $a-p$ alphabets. Kitano used what he called "adaptive mutation": the probability of mutation of an offspring depended on the Hamming distance (number of mismatches) between the two parents. High distance resulted in low mutation, and vice versa. In this way, the GA tended to respond to loss of diversity in the population by selectively raising the mutation rate.

Kitano (1990) performed a series of experiments on evolving networks for simple "encoder/decoder" problems to compare the grammatical and direct encoding approaches. He found that, on these relatively simple problems, the performance of a GA using the grammatical encoding method consistently surpassed that of a GA using the direct encoding method, both in the correctness of the resulting neural networks and in the speed with which they were found by the GA. An example of Kitano's results is given in figure 2.24, which plots the error rate of the best network in the population (averaged over 20 runs) versus generation. In the grammatical encoding runs, the GA found networks with lower error rate, and found the best networks more quickly, than in the direct encoding runs. Kitano also discovered that the performance of the GA scaled much better with network size when grammatical encoding was used—performance decreased very quickly with network size when direct encoding was used, but stayed much more constant with grammatical encoding.

What accounts for the grammatical encoding method's apparent superiority? Kitano argues that the grammatical encoding method can easily create "regular," repeated patterns of connectivity, and that this is a result of the repeated patterns that naturally come from repeatedly applying grammatical rules. We would expect grammatical encoding approaches to perform well on problems requiring this kind of regularity. Grammatical encoding also has the advantage of requiring shorter chromosomes, since the GA works on the instructions for building the network (the grammar) rather than on the network structure itself. For complex networks, the latter could be huge and intractable for any search algorithm.

Although these attributes might lend an advantage in general to the grammatical encoding method, it is not clear that they accounted for the grammatical encoding method's superiority in the experiments reported by Kitano (1990). The encoder/decoder problem is one of the simplest

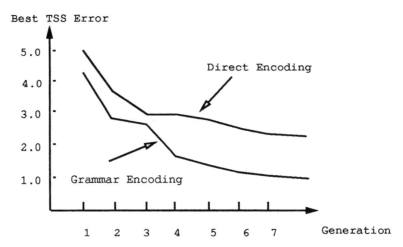

Figure 2.24 Results from Kitano's experiment comparing the direct and grammatical encoding methods. Total sum squared (TSS) error for the average best individual (over 20 runs) is plotted against generation. (Low TSS is desired.) (Reprinted from Kitano 1990 by permission of the publisher. © 1990 *Complex Systems*.)

problems for neural networks; moreover, it is interesting only if the number of hidden units is smaller than the number of input units. This was enforced in Kitano's experiments with direct encoding but not in his experiments with grammatical encoding. It is possible that the advantage of grammatical encoding in these experiments was simply due to the GA's finding network topologies that make the problem trivial; the comparison is thus unfair, since this route was not available to the particular direct encoding approach being compared.

Kitano's idea of evolving grammars is intriguing, and his informal arguments are plausible reasons to believe that the grammatical encoding method (or extensions of it) will work well on the kinds of problems on which complex neural networks could be needed. However, the particular experiments used to support the arguments are not convincing, since the problems may have been too simple. An extension of Kitano's initial work, in which the evolution of network architecture and the setting of weights are integrated, is reported in Kitano 1994. More ambitious approaches to grammatical encoding have been tried by Gruau (1992) and Belew (1993).

Evolving a Learning Rule

David Chalmers (1990) took the idea of applying genetic algorithms to neural networks in a different direction: he used GAs to evolve a good learning rule for neural networks. Chalmers limited his initial study to fully connected feedforward networks with input and output layers only, no hidden layers. In general a learning rule is used during the training procedure for modifying network weights in response to the network's performance on the training data. At each training cycle, one training pair is given to the network, which then produces an output. At this point the learning rule is invoked to modify weights. A learning rule for a single-layer, fully connected feedforward network might use the following local information for a given training cycle to modify the weight on the link from input unit i to output unit j:

a_i: the activation of input unit i

o_j: the activation of output unit j

t_j: the training signal (i.e., correct activation, provided by a teacher) on output unit j

w_{ij}: the current weight on the link from i to j.

The change to make in weight w_{ij}, Δw_{ij}, is a function of these values:

$$\Delta w_{ij} = f(a_i, o_j, t_j, w_{ij}).$$

The chromosomes in the GA population encoded such functions.

Chalmers made the assumption that the learning rule should be a linear function of these variables and all their pairwise products. That is, the general form of the learning rule was

$$\Delta w_{ij} = k_0(k_1 w_{ij} + k_2 a_i + k_3 o_j + k_4 t_j + k_5 w_{ij} a_i + k_6 w_{ij} o_j$$
$$+ k_7 w_{ij} t_j + k_8 a_i o_j + k_9 a_i t_j + k_{10} o_j t_j).$$

The k_m ($1 \leq m \leq 10$) are constant coefficients, and k_0 is a scale parameter that affects how much the weights can change on any one cycle. (k_0 is called the "learning rate.") Chalmers's assumption about the form of the learning rule came in part from the fact that a known good learning rule for such networks—the "Widrow-Hoff" or "delta" rule—has the form

$$\Delta w_{ij} = \eta(t_j o_j - a_i o_j)$$

(Rumelhart et al. 1986), where η is a constant representing the learning rate. One goal of Chalmers's work was to see if the GA could evolve a rule that performs as well as the delta rule.

The task of the GA was to evolve values for the k_m's. The chromosome encoding for the set of k_m's is illustrated in figure 2.25. The scale parameter k_0 is encoded as five bits, with the zeroth bit encoding the sign (1 encoding + and 0 encoding −) and the first through fourth bits encoding an integer n: $k_0 = 0$ if $n = 0$; otherwise $|k_0| = 2^{n-9}$. Thus k_0 can take on the values 0, $\pm 1/256$, $\pm 1/128$, ..., ± 32, ± 64. The other coefficients k_m are encoded by three bits each, with the zeroth bit encoding the sign and the

Genome encoding:

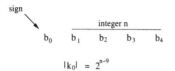

k_0 **encoded by 5 bits:**

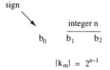

$$|k_0| = 2^{n-9}$$

Other k's encoded by 3 bits each:

sign

integer n

$b_0 \quad b_1 \quad b_2$

$$|k_m| = 2^{n-1}$$

Figure 2.25 Illustration of the method for encoding the k_ms in Chalmers's system.

first and second bits encoding an integer n. For $i = 1 \ldots 10$, $k_m = 0$ if $n = 0$; otherwise $|k_m| = 2^{n-1}$.

It is known that single-layer networks can learn only those classes of input-output mappings that are "linearly separable" (Rumelhart et al. 1986). As an "environment" for the evolving learning rules, Chalmers used 30 different linearly separable mappings to be learned via the learning rules. The mappings always had a single output unit and between two and seven input units.

The fitness of each chromosome (learning rule) was determined as follows. A subset of 20 mappings was selected from the full set of 30 mappings. For each mapping, 12 training examples were selected. For each of these mappings, a network was created with the appropriate number of input units for the given mapping (each network had one output unit). The network's weights were initialized randomly. The network was run on the training set for some number of epochs (typically 10), using the learning rule specified by the chromosome. The performance of the learning rule on a given mapping was a function of the network's error on the training set, with low error meaning high performance. The overall fitness of the learning rule was a function of the average error of the 20 networks over the chosen subset of 20 mappings—low average error translated to high fitness. This fitness was then transformed to be a percentage, where a high percentage meant high fitness.

Using this fitness measure, the GA was run on a population of 40 learning rules, with two-point crossover and standard mutation. The crossover rate was 0.8 and the mutation rate was 0.01. Typically, over 1000 generations, the fitness of the best learning rules in the population rose from between 40% and 60% in the initial generation (indicating no significant learning ability) to between 80% and 98%, with a mean (over several runs) of about 92%. The fitness of the delta rule is around 98%, and on one out of a total of ten runs the GA discovered this rule. On three of the ten runs, the GA discovered slight variations of this rule with lower fitness.

These results show that, given a somewhat constrained representation, the GA was able to evolve a successful learning rule for simple single-layer networks. The extent to which this method can find learning rules for more complex networks (including networks with hidden units) remains an open question, but these results are a first step in that direction. Chalmers suggested that it is unlikely that evolutionary methods will discover learning methods that are more powerful than back-propagation, but he speculated that the GA might be a powerful method for discovering learning rules for unsupervised learning paradigms (e.g., reinforcement learning) or for new classes of network architectures (e.g., recurrent networks).

Chalmers also performed a study of the generality of the evolved learning rules. He tested each of the best evolved rules on the ten mappings that had not been used in the fitness calculation for that rule (the "test set"). The mean fitness of the best rules on the original mappings was 92%, and Chalmers found that the mean fitness of these rules on the test set was 91.9%. In short, the evolved rules were quite general.

Chalmers then looked at the question of how diverse the environment has to be to produce general rules. He repeated the original experiment, varying the number of mappings in each original environment between 1 and 20. A rule's *evolutionary fitness* is the fitness obtained by testing a rule on its original environment. A rule's *test fitness* is the fitness obtained by testing a rule on ten additional tasks not in the original environment. Chalmers then measured these two quantities as a function of the number of tasks in the original environment. The results are shown in figure 2.26. The two curves are the mean evolutionary fitness and the mean test fitness for rules that were tested in an environment with the given number of tasks. This plot shows that while the evolutionary fitness stays roughly constant for different numbers of environmental tasks, the test fitness increases sharply with the number of tasks, leveling off somewhere between 10 and 20 tasks. The conclusion is that the evolution of a general learning rule requires a diverse environment of tasks. (In this case of simple single-layer networks, the necessary degree of diversity is fairly small.)

THOUGHT EXERCISES

1. Using the function set {AND, OR, NOT} and the terminal set $\{s^{-1}, s^0, s^{+1}\}$, construct a parse tree (or Lisp expression) that encodes the $r = 1$ majority-rule CA, where s^i denotes the state of the neighborhood site i sites away from the central cell (with $-$ indicating distance to the

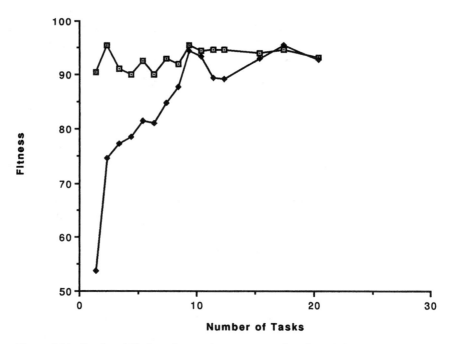

Figure 2.26 Results of Chalmers's experiments testing the effect of diversity of environment on generalization ability. The plot gives the evolutionary fitness (squares) and test fitness (diamonds) as a function of the number of tasks in the environment. (Reprinted from D. S. Touretzky et al. (eds.), *Proceedings of the 1990 Connectionist Models Summer School*. Reprinted by permission of the publisher. © 1990 Morgan Kaufmann.)

left and + indicating distance to the right). AND and OR each take two arguments, and NOT takes one argument.

2. Assume that "MUTATE-TREE(TREE)" is a function that replaces a subtree in TREE by a randomly generated subtree. Using this function, write pseudo code for a steepest-ascent hill climbing algorithm that searches the space of GP parse trees, starting from a randomly chosen parse tree. Do the same for random-mutation hill climbing.

3. Write a formula for the number of CA rules of radius r.

4. Follow the same procedure as in figure 2.23 to construct the network given by the grammar displayed in figure 2.27.

5. Design a grammar that will produce the network architecture given in figure 2.28.

$$S \rightarrow \begin{matrix} A & B \\ C & D \end{matrix} \quad A \rightarrow \begin{matrix} c & p \\ a & c \end{matrix} \quad B \rightarrow \begin{matrix} c & a \\ g & e \end{matrix} \quad C \rightarrow \begin{matrix} a & a \\ b & a \end{matrix} \quad D \rightarrow \begin{matrix} f & e \\ a & b \end{matrix}$$

$$a \rightarrow \begin{matrix} 0 & 0 \\ 0 & 0 \end{matrix} \quad b \rightarrow \begin{matrix} 0 & 0 \\ 0 & 1 \end{matrix} \quad c \rightarrow \begin{matrix} 1 & 0 \\ 0 & 1 \end{matrix} \quad e \rightarrow \begin{matrix} 0 & 1 \\ 0 & 1 \end{matrix} \quad f \rightarrow \begin{matrix} 1 & 1 \\ 0 & 1 \end{matrix}$$

$$g \rightarrow \begin{matrix} 0 & 0 \\ 1 & 0 \end{matrix} \quad p \rightarrow \begin{matrix} 1 & 1 \\ 1 & 1 \end{matrix}$$

Figure 2.27 Grammar for thought exercise 4.

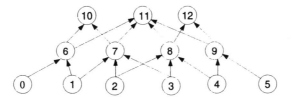

Figure 2.28 Network for thought exercise 5.

COMPUTER EXERCISES

1. Implement a genetic programming algorithm and use it to solve the "6-multiplexer" problem (Koza 1992). In this problem there are six Boolean-valued terminals, $\{a_0, a_1, d_0, d_1, d_2, d_3\}$, and four functions, $\{$AND, OR, NOT, IF$\}$. The first three functions are the usual logical operators, taking two, two, and one argument respectively, and the IF function takes three arguments. (IF X Y Z) evaluates its first argument X. If X is true, the second argument Y is evaluated; otherwise the third argument Z is evaluated. The problem is to find a program that will return the value of the d terminal that is addressed by the two a terminals. E.g., if $a_0 = 0$ and $a_1 = 1$, the address is 01 and the answer is the value of d_1. Likewise, if $a_0 = 1$ and $a_1 = 1$, the address is 11 and the answer is the value of d_3. Experiment with different initial conditions, crossover rates, and population sizes. (Start with a population size of 300.) The fitness of a program should be the fraction of correct answers over all 2^6 possible fitness cases (i.e., values of the six terminals).

2. Perform the same experiment as in computer exercise 1, but add some "distractors" to the function and terminal sets—extra functions and terminals not necessary for the solution. How does this affect the performance of GP on this problem?

3. Perform the same experiment as in computer exercise 1, but for each fitness calculation use a random sample of 10 of the 2^6 possible fitness

cases rather than the entire set (use a new random sample for each fitness calculation). How does this affect the performance of GP on this problem?

4. Implement a random search procedure to search for parse trees for the 6-multiplexer problem: at each time step, generate a new random parse tree (with the maximum tree size fixed ahead of time) and calculate its fitness. Compare the rate at which the best fitness found so far (plotted every 300 time steps—equivalent to one GP generation in computer exercise 1) increases with that under GP.

5. Implement a random-mutation hill-climbing procedure to search for parse trees for the 6-multiplexer problem (see thought exercise 2). Compare its performance with that of GP and the random search method of computer exercise 4.

6. Modify the fitness function used in computer exercise 1 to reward programs for small size as well as for correct performance. Test this new fitness function using your GP procedure. Can GP find correct but smaller programs by this method?

*7. Repeat the experiments of Crutchfield, Mitchell, Das, and Hraber on evolving $r = 3$ CAs to solve the $\rho_c = \frac{1}{2}$ problem. (This will also require writing a program to simulate cellular automata.)

*8. Compare the results of the experiment in computer exercise 7 with that of using random-mutation hill climbing to search for CA lookup tables to solve the $\rho_c = \frac{1}{2}$ problem. (See Mitchell, Crutchfield, and Hraber 1994a for their comparison.)

*9. Perform the same experiment as in computer exercise 7, but use GP on parse-tree representations of CAs (see thought exercise 1). (This will require writing a program to translate between parse tree representations and CA lookup tables that you can give to your CA simulator.) Compare the results of your experiments with the results you obtained in computer exercise 7 using lookup-table encodings.

*10. Figure 2.29 gives a 19-unit neural network architecture for the "encoder/decoder" problem. The problem is to find a set of weights so that the network will perform the mapping given in table 2.2—that is, for each given input activation pattern, the network should copy the pattern onto its output units. Since there are fewer hidden units than input and output units, the network must learn to encode and then decode the input via the hidden units. Each hidden unit j and each output unit j has a *threshold* σ_j. If the incoming activation is greater than or equal to σ_j, the activation of the unit is set to 1; otherwise it is set to 0. At the first time step, the input units are activated according to the input activation pattern (e.g., 10000000). Then activation spreads from the input units to the hidden

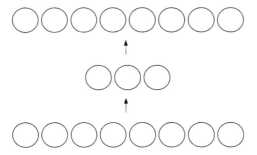

Figure 2.29 Network for computer exercise 10. The arrows indicate that each input node is connected to each hidden node, and each hidden node is connected to each output node.

Table 2.2 Table for computer exercise 10.

Input Pattern	Output Pattern
10000000	10000000
01000000	01000000
00100000	00100000
00010000	00010000
00001000	00001000
00000100	00000100
00000010	00000010
00000001	00000001

units. The incoming activation of each hidden unit j is given by $\sum_i a_i w_{i,j}$, where a_i is the activation of input unit i and $w_{i,j}$ is the weight on the link from unit i to unit j. After the hidden units have been activated, they in turn activate the output units via the same procedure. Use Montana and Davis's method to evolve weights $w_{i,j}$ $(0 \leq w_{i,j} \leq 1)$ and thresholds σ_j $(0 \leq \sigma_j \leq 1)$ to solve this problem. Put the $w_{i,j}$ values and the σ_j values on the same chromosome. (The σ_j values are ignored by the input nodes, which are always set to 0 or 1.) The fitness of a chromosome is the average sum of the squares of the errors (differences between the output and input patterns at each position) over the entire training set. How well does the GA succeed? For the very ambitious reader: Compare the performance of the GA with that of back-propagation (Rumelhart, Hinton, and Williams 1986a) in the same way that Montana and Davis did. (This exercise is intended for those already familiar with neural networks.)

3 Genetic Algorithms in Scientific Models

Genetic algorithms have been for the most part techniques applied by computer scientists and engineers to solve practical problems. However, John Holland's original work on the subject was meant not only to develop adaptive computer systems for problem solving but also to shed light, via computer models, on the mechanisms of natural evolution.

The idea of using computer models to study evolution is still relatively new and is not widely accepted in the evolutionary biology community. Traditionally, biologists have used several approaches to understanding evolution, including the following:

Examining the fossil record to determine how evolution has proceeded over geological time.

Examining existing biological systems in their natural habitats in order to understand the evolutionary forces at work in the process of adaptation. This includes both understanding the role of genetic mechanisms (such as geographical effects on mating) and understanding the function of various physical and behavioral characteristics of organisms so as to infer the selective forces responsible for the evolution of these adaptations.

Performing laboratory experiments in which evolution over many generations in a population of relatively simple organisms is studied and controlled. Many such experiments involve fruit flies (*Drosophila*) because their life span and their reproductive cycle are short enough that experimenters can observe natural selection over many generations in a reasonable amount of time.

Studying evolution at the molecular level by looking at how DNA and RNA change over time under particular genetic mechanisms, or by determining how different evolutionarily related species compare at the level of DNA so as to reconstruct "phylogenies" (evolutionary family histories of related species).

Developing mathematical models of evolution in the form of equations (representing properties of genotypes and phenotypes and their evolution) that can be solved (analytically or numerically) or approximated.

These are the types of methods that have produced the bulk of our current understanding of natural evolution. However, such methods have a number of inherent limitations. The observed fossil record is almost certainly incomplete, and what is there is often hard to interpret; in many cases what is surmised from fossils is intelligent guesswork. It is hard, if not impossible, to do controlled experiments on biological systems in nature, and evolutionary time scales are most often far too long for scientists to directly observe how biological systems change. Evolution in systems such as *Drosophila* can be observed to a limited extent, but many of the important questions in evolution (How does speciation take place? How did multicellular organisms come into being? Why did sex evolve?) cannot be answered by merely studying evolution in *Drosophila*. The molecular level is often ambiguous—for example, it is not clear what it is that individual pieces of DNA encode, or how they work together to produce phenotypic traits, or even which pieces do the encoding and which are "junk DNA" (noncoding regions of the chromosome). Finally, to be solvable, mathematical models of evolution must be simplified greatly, and it is not obvious that the simple models provide insight into real evolution.

The invention of computers has permitted a new approach to studying evolution and other natural systems: simulation. A computer program can simulate the evolution of populations of organisms over millions of simulated generations, and such simulations can potentially be used to test theories about the biggest open questions in evolution. Simulation experiments can do what traditional methods typically cannot: experiments can be controlled, they can be repeated to see how the modification of certain parameters changes the behavior of the simulation, and they can be run for many simulated generations. Such computer simulations are said to be "microanalytic" or "agent based." They differ from the more standard use of computers in evolutionary theory to solve mathematical models (typically systems of differential equations) that capture only the global dynamics of an evolving system. Instead, they simulate each component of the evolving system and its local interactions; the global dynamics emerges from these simulated local dynamics. This "microanalytic" strategy is the hallmark of artificial life models.

Computer simulations have many limitations as models of real-world phenomena. Most often, they must drastically simplify reality in order to be computationally tractable and for the results to be understandable. As with the even simpler purely mathematical models, it is not clear that the results will apply to more realistic systems. On the other hand, more realistic models take a long time to simulate, and they suffer from the same problem we often face in direct studies of nature: they produce huge amounts of data that are often very hard to interpret.

Such questions dog every kind of scientific model, computational or otherwise, and to date most biologists have not been convinced that computer simulations can teach them much. However, with the increasing power (and decreasing cost) of computers, and given the clear limitations of simple analytically solvable models of evolution, more researchers are looking seriously at what simulation can uncover. Genetic algorithms are one obvious method for microanalytic simulation of evolutionary systems. Their use in this arena is also growing as a result of the rising interest among computer scientists in building computational models of biological processes. Here I describe several computer modeling efforts, undertaken mainly by computer scientists, and aimed at answering questions such as: How can learning during a lifetime affect the evolution of a species? What is the evolutionary effect of sexual selection? What is the relative density of different species over time in a given ecosystem? How are evolution and adaptation to be measured in an observed system?

3.1 MODELING INTERACTIONS BETWEEN LEARNING AND EVOLUTION

Many people have drawn analogies between learning and evolution as two adaptive processes, one taking place during the lifetime of an organism and the other taking place over the evolutionary history of life on Earth. To what extent do these processes interact? In particular, can learning that occurs over the course of an individual's lifetime guide the evolution of that individual's species to any extent? These are major questions in evolutionary psychology. Genetic algorithms, often in combination with neural networks, have been used to address these questions. Here I describe two systems designed to model interactions between learning and evolution, and in particular the "Baldwin effect."

The Baldwin Effect

The well-known "Lamarckian hypothesis" states that traits acquired during the lifetime of an organism can be transmitted genetically to the organism's offspring. Lamarck's hypothesis is generally interpreted as referring to acquired physical traits (such as physical defects due to environmental toxins), but something learned during an organism's lifetime also can be thought of as a type of acquired trait. Thus, a Lamarckian view might hold that learned knowledge can guide evolution directly by being passed on genetically to the next generation. However, because of overwhelming evidence against it, the Lamarckian hypothesis has been rejected by virtually all biologists. It is very hard to imagine a direct mechanism for "reverse transcription" of acquired traits into a genetic code.

Does this mean that learning can have no effect on evolution? In spite of the rejection of Lamarckianism, the perhaps surprising answer seems to be that learning (or, more generally, phenotypic plasticity) can indeed have significant effects on evolution, though in less direct ways than Lamarck suggested. One proposal for a non-Lamarckian mechanism was made by J. M. Baldwin (1896), who pointed out that if learning helps survival then the organisms best able to learn will have the most offspring, thus increasing the frequency of the genes responsible for learning. And if the environment remains relatively fixed, so that the best things to learn remain constant, this can lead, via selection, to a genetic encoding of a trait that originally had to be learned. (Note that Baldwin's proposal was published long before the detailed mechanisms of genetic inheritance were known.) For example, an organism that has the capacity to learn that a particular plant is poisonous will be more likely to survive (by learning not to eat the plant) than organisms that are unable to learn this information, and thus will be more likely to produce offspring that also have this learning capacity. Evolutionary variation will have a chance to work on this line of offspring, allowing for the possibility that the trait—avoiding the poisonous plant—will be discovered genetically rather than learned anew each generation. Having the desired behavior encoded genetically would give an organism a selective advantage over organisms that were merely able to learn the desired behavior during their lifetimes, because learning a behavior is generally a less reliable process than developing a genetically encoded behavior; too many unexpected things could get in the way of learning during an organism's lifetime. Moreover, genetically encoded information can be available immediately after birth, whereas learning takes time and sometimes requires potentially fatal trial and error.

In short, the capacity to acquire a certain desired trait allows the learning organism to survive preferentially, thus giving genetic variation the possibility of independently discovering the desired trait. Without such learning, the likelihood of survival—and thus the opportunity for genetic discovery—decreases. In this indirect way, learning *can* guide evolution, even if what is learned cannot be directly transmitted genetically.

Baldwin called this mechanism "organic selection," but it was later dubbed the "Baldwin effect" (Simpson 1953), and that name has stuck. Similar mechanisms were simultaneously proposed by Lloyd Morgan (1896) and Osborn (1896).

The evolutionary biologist G. G. Simpson, in his exegesis of Baldwin's work (Simpson 1953), pointed out that it is not clear how the necessary correlation between phenotypic plasticity and genetic variation can take place. By correlation I mean that genetic variations happen to occur that produce the same adaptation that was previously learned. This kind of correlation would be easy if genetic variation were "directed" toward some particular outcome rather than random. But the randomness of genetic variation is a central principle of modern evolutionary theory, and there is no evidence that variation can be directed by acquired phenotypic traits (indeed, such direction would be a Lamarckian effect). It seems that Baldwin was assuming that, given the laws of probability, correlation between phenotypic adaptations and random genetic variation will happen, especially if the phenotypic adaptations keep the lineage alive long enough for these variations to occur. Simpson agreed that this was possible in principle and that it probably has happened, but he did not believe that there was any evidence of its being an important force in evolution.

Almost 50 years after Baldwin and his contemporaries, Waddington (1942) proposed a similar but more plausible and specific mechanism that has been called "genetic assimilation." Waddington reasoned that certain sweeping environmental changes require phenotypic adaptations that are not necessary in a normal environment. If organisms are subjected to such environmental changes, they can sometimes adapt during their lifetimes because of their inherent plasticity, thereby acquiring new physical or behavioral traits. If the genes for these traits are already in the population, although not expressed or frequent in normal environments, they can fairly quickly be expressed in the changed environments, especially if the acquired (learned) phenotypic adaptations have kept the species from dying off. (A gene is said to be "expressed" if the trait it encodes actually appears in the phenotype. Typically, many genes in an organism's chromosomes are not expressed.)

The previously acquired traits can thus become genetically expressed, and these genes will spread in the population. Waddington demonstrated that this had indeed happened in several experiments on fruit flies. Simpson's argument applies here as well: even though genetic assimilation can happen, that does not mean that it necessarily happens often or is an important force in evolution. Some in the biology and evolutionary computation communities hope that computer simulations can now offer ways to gauge the frequency and importance of such effects.

A Simple Model of the Baldwin Effect

Genetic assimilation is well known in the evolutionary biology community. Its predecessor, the Baldwin effect, is less well known, though it has recently been picked up by evolutionary computationalists because of an interesting experiment performed by Geoffrey Hinton and Steven Nowlan (1987). Hinton and Nowlan employed a GA in a computer model of the Baldwin effect. Their goal was to demonstrate this effect empirically and to measure its magnitude, using a simplified model. An extremely simple neural-network learning algorithm modeled learning, and the GA played the role of evolution, evolving a population of neural networks with varying learning capabilities. In the model, each individual is a neural network with 20 potential connections. A connection can have one of three values: "present," "absent," and "learnable." These are specified by "1," "0," and "?," respectively, where each ? connection can be set during learning to either 1 or 0. There is only one correct setting for the connections (i.e., only one correct configuration of ones and zeros), and no other setting confers any fitness on an individual. The problem to be solved is

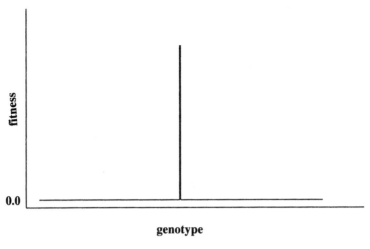

Figure 3.1 Illustration of the fitness landscape for Hinton and Nowlan's search problem. All genotypes have fitness 0 except for the one "correct" genotype, at which there is a fitness spike. (Adapted from Hinton and Nowlan 1987.)

to find this single correct set of connections. This will not be possible for those networks that have incorrect fixed connections (e.g., a 1 where there should be a 0), but those networks that have correct settings in all places except where there are question marks have the capacity to learn the correct settings.

Hinton and Nowlan used the simplest possible "learning" method: random guessing. On each learning trial, a network simply guesses 1 or 0 at random for each of its learnable connections. (The problem as stated has little to do with the usual notions of neural-network learning; Hinton and Nowlan presented this problem in terms of neural networks so as to keep in mind the possibility of extending the example to more standard learning tasks and methods.)

This is, of course, a "needle in a haystack" search problem, since there is only one correct setting in a space of 2^{20} possibilities. The fitness landscape for this problem is illustrated in figure 3.1—the single spike represents the single correct connection setting. Introducing the ability to learn indirectly smooths out the landscape, as shown in figure 3.2. Here the spike is smoothed out into a "zone of increased fitness" that includes individuals with some connections set correctly and the rest set to question marks. Once an individual is in this zone, learning makes it possible to get to the peak.

The indirect smoothing of the fitness landscape was demonstrated by Hinton and Nowlan's simulation, in which each network was represented by a string of length 20 consisting of the ones, zeros, and the question marks making up the settings on the network's connections. The initial population consisted of 1000 individuals generated at random but with

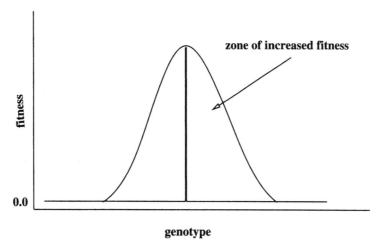

zone of increased fitness

fitness

genotype

0.0

Figure 3.2 With the possibility of learning, the fitness landscape for Hinton and Nowlan's search problem is smoother, with a zone of increased fitness containing individuals able to learn the correct connection settings. (Adapted from Hinton and Nowlan 1987.)

each individual having on average 25% zeros, 25% ones, and 50% question marks. At each generation, each individual was given 1000 learning trials. On each learning trial, the individual tried a random combination of settings for the question marks. The fitness was an inverse function of the number of trials needed to find the correct solution:

$$\text{Fitness} = 1 + \frac{19n}{1000},$$

where n is the number of trials (out of the allotted 1000) remaining after the correct solution has been found. An individual that already had all its connections set correctly was assigned the highest possible fitness (20), and an individual that never found the correct solution was assigned the lowest possible fitness (1). Hence, a tradeoff existed between efficiency and plasticity: having many question marks meant that, on average, many guesses were needed to arrive at the correct answer, but the more connections that were fixed, the more likely it was that one or more of them was fixed incorrectly, meaning that there was no possibility of finding the correct answer.

Hinton and Nowlan's GA was similar to the simple GA described in chapter 1. An individual was selected to be a parent with probability proportional to its fitness, and could be selected more than once. The individuals in the next generation were created by single-point crossovers between pairs of parents. No mutation occurred. An individual's chromosome was, of course, not affected by the learning that took place during its lifetime—parents passed on their original alleles to their offspring.

Hinton and Nowlan ran the GA for 50 generations. A plot of the mean fitness of the population versus generation for one run on each of three

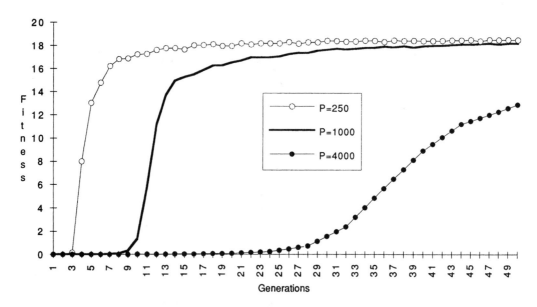

Figure 3.3 Mean fitness versus generations for one run of the GA on each of three population sizes. The solid line gives the results for population size 1000, the size used in Hinton and Nowlan's experiments; the open circles the results for population size 250; the solid circles for population size 4000. These plots are from a replication by Belew and are reprinted from Belew 1990 by permission of the publisher. © 1990 *Complex Systems*.

population sizes is given in figure 3.3. (This plot is from a replication of Hinton and Nowlan's experiments performed by Belew (1990).) The solid curve gives the results for population size 1000, the size used in Hinton and Nowlan's experiments.

Hinton and Nowlan found that without learning (i.e., with evolution alone) the mean fitness of the population never increased over time, but figure 3.3 shows that with learning the mean fitness did increase, even though what was learned by individuals was not inherited by their offspring. In this way it can be said that learning can guide evolution, even without the direct transmission of acquired traits. Hinton and Nowlan interpreted this increase as being due to the Baldwin effect: those individuals that were able to learn the correct connections quickly tended to be selected to reproduce, and crossovers among these individuals tended to increase the number of correctly fixed alleles, increasing the learning efficiency of the offspring. With this simple form of learning, evolution was able to discover individuals with all their connections fixed correctly.

Figure 3.4 shows the relative frequencies of the correct, incorrect, and undecided alleles in the population plotted over 50 generations. As can be seen, over time the frequency of fixed correct connections increased and the frequency of fixed incorrect connections decreased. But why did the frequency of undecided alleles stay so high? Hinton and Nowlan an-

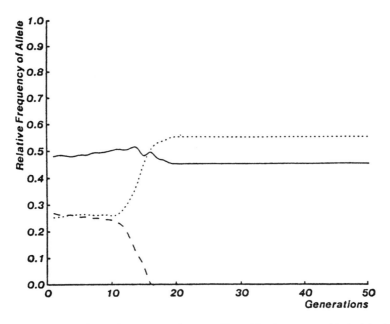

Figure 3.4 Relative frequencies of correct (dotted line), incorrect (dashed line), and undecided (solid line) alleles in the population plotted over 50 generations. (Reprinted from Hinton and Nowlan 1987 by permission of the publisher. © 1987 *Complex Systems*.)

swered that there was not much selective pressure to fix all the undecided alleles, since individuals with a small number of question marks could learn the correct answer in a small number of learning trials. If the selection pressure had been increased, the Baldwin effect would have been stronger. Figure 3.5 shows these same results over an extended run. (These results come from Belew's (1990) replication and extension of Hinton and Nowlan's original experiments.) This plot shows that the frequency of question marks goes down to about 30%. Given more time it might go down further, but under this selection regime the convergence was extremely slow.

To summarize: Learning can be a way for genetically coded partial solutions to get partial credit. A common claim for learning is that it allows an organism to respond to unpredictable aspects of the environment—aspects that change too quickly for evolution to track genetically. Although this is clearly one benefit of learning, the Baldwin effect is different: it says that learning helps organisms adapt to genetically predictable but difficult aspects of the environment, and that learning indirectly helps these adaptations become genetically encoded.

The "learning" mechanism used in Hinton and Nowlan's experiments—random guessing—is of course completely unrealistic as a model of learning. Hinton and Nowlan (1987, p. 500) pointed out that "a more sophisticated learning procedure only strengthens the argument for the

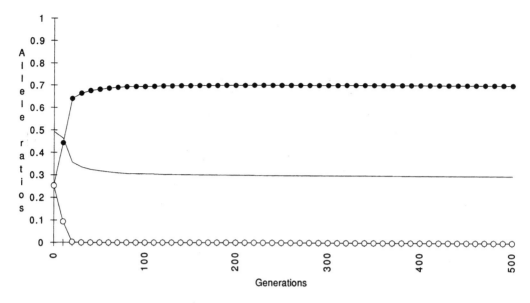

Figure 3.5 Relative frequencies of correct (solid circles), incorrect (open circles), and undecided (solid line) alleles in the population plotted over 500 generations, from Belew's replication of Hinton and Nowlan's experiments. (Reprinted from Belew 1990 by permission of the publisher. © 1990 *Complex Systems*.)

importance of the Baldwin effect." This is true insofar as a more sophisticated learning procedure would, for example, further smooth the original "needle in a haystack" fitness landscape in Hinton and Nowlan's learning task, presumably by allowing more individuals to learn the correct settings. However, if the learning procedure were too sophisticated—that is, if learning the necessary trait were too easy—there would be little selection pressure for evolution to move from the ability to learn the trait to a genetic encoding of that trait. Such tradeoffs occur in evolution and can be seen even in Hinton and Nowlan's simple model. Computer simulations such as theirs can help us to understand and to measure such tradeoffs. More detailed analyses of Hinton and Nowlan's model were performed by Belew (1990), Harvey (1993), and French and Messinger (1994).

A more important departure from biological reality in this model, and one reason why the Baldwin effect showed up so strongly, is the lack of a "phenotype." The fitness of an individual is a direct function of the alleles in its chromosome, rather than of the traits and behaviors of its phenotype. Thus, there is a direct correlation here between learned adaptations and genetic variation—in fact, they are one and the same thing. What if, as in real biology, there were a big distance between the genotypic and phenotypic levels, and learning occurred on the phenotypic level? Would the Baldwin effect show up in that case too, transferring the learned adaptations into genetically encoded traits? The next subsection describes a model that is a bit closer to this more realistic scenario.

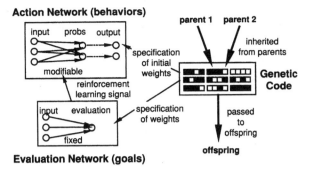

Action Network (behaviors)

Evaluation Network (goals)

Figure 3.6 A schematic illustration of the components of an agent in ERL. The agent's genotype is a bit string that encodes the weights of two neural networks: an evaluation network that maps the agent's current state to an evaluation of that state, and an action network that maps the agent's current state to an action to be taken at the next time step. The weights on the evaluation network are constant during an agent's lifetime but the weights on the action network can be modified via a reinforcement learning method that takes its positive or negative signal from the evaluation network. (The networks displayed here are simplified for clarity.) The agent's genotype is not modified by this learning procedure, and only the genotype is passed from an agent to its offspring. (Reprinted from Christopher G. Langton et al., eds., *Artificial Life: Volume II*; © 1992 Addison-Wesley Publishing Company, Inc. Reprinted by permission of the publisher.)

Evolutionary Reinforcement Learning

A second computational demonstration of the Baldwin effect was given by David Ackley and Michael Littman (1992). Their primary goal was to incorporate "reinforcement learning" (an unsupervised learning method) into an evolutionary framework and to see whether evolution could produce individuals that not only behaved appropriately but also could correctly evaluate the situations they encountered as beneficial or dangerous for future survival. In Ackley and Littman's Evolutionary Reinforcement Learning (ERL) model, individuals ("agents") move randomly on a finite two-dimensional lattice, encountering food, predators, hiding places, and other types of entities. Each agent's "state" includes the entities in its visual range, the level of its internal energy store, and other parameters.

The components making up an individual are illustrated schematically in figure 3.6. Each agent possesses two feedforward neural networks: an *evaluation network* that takes as input the agent's state at time t and produces on its single output unit an activation representing a judgment about how good that state is for the agent, and an *action network* that takes as input the agent's state at time t and produces on its two output units a code for the action the agent is to take on that time step. The only possible actions are moves from the current lattice site to one of the four neighboring sites, but actions can result in eating, being eaten, and other less radical consequences. The architectures of these two networks are common to all agents, but the weights on the links can vary between agents. The weights on a given agent's evaluation network are fixed from birth—this network represents innate goals and desires inherited from the agent's ancestors (e.g., "being near food is good"). The weights on the action network change over the agent's lifetime according to a reinforcement-learning algorithm that is a combination of back-propagation and standard reinforcement learning.

An agent's genome is a bit string encoding the permanent weights for the evaluation network and the initial weights for the action network. The network architectures are such that there are 84 possible weights, each encoded by four bits. The length of a chromosome is thus 336 bits.

Agents have an internal energy store (represented by a real number) which must be kept above a certain level to prevent death; this is accomplished by eating food that is encountered as the agent moves from site to site on the lattice. An agent must also avoid predators, or it will be killed. An agent can reproduce once it has enough energy in its internal store. Agents reproduce by copying their genomes (subject to mutation at low probability). In addition to this direct copying, two spatially nearby agents can together produce offspring via crossover. There is no explicit given ("exogenous") fitness function for evaluating a genome, as there was in Hinton and Nowlan's model and as there are in most engineering applications of GAs. Instead, the fitness of an agent (as well as the rate at which a population turns over) is "endogenous": it emerges from many actions and interactions over the course of the agent's lifetime. This feature distinguishes many GAs used in artificial-life models from those used in engineering applications.

At each time step t in an agent's life, the agent uses its evaluation network to evaluate its current state. The difference between the current evaluation and that computed at step $t - 1$ serves as a reinforcement signal judging the action the agent took at $t - 1$, and is used to modify the weights in the action network. The hope is that an agent will learn to act in ways that lead to "better" states, where "better" is defined by that particular agent's inborn evaluation network. After this learning step, the agent uses its modified action network to determine its next action.

Ackley and Littman observed many interesting phenomena in their experiments with this model. First, they wanted to see whether or not the combination of evolution and learning produced any survival advantage to a population. They measured the "performance" of the system by determining how long a population can survive before becoming extinct, and they compared the performances of ERL (evolution plus learning), E (evolution alone with no learning), L (learning alone with no evolution—i.e., no reproduction, mutation, or crossover), and two controls: F (fixed random weights) and B ("Brownian" agents that ignore any inputs and move at random). This kind of comparison is typical of the sort of experiment that can be done with a computer model; such an experiment would typically be impossible to carry out with real living systems.

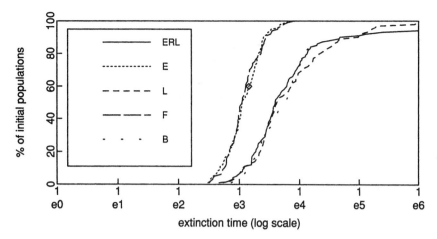

Figure 3.7 The distribution of population lifetimes for 100 runs for the ERL strategy and four variations: evolution only (E), learning only (L), fixed random weights (F), and random (Brownian) movements (B). Each plot gives the percentage of runs on which the population became extinct by a certain number of time steps. For example, the point marked with a diamond indicates that 60% of the E (evolution only) populations were extinct by ~ 1500 time steps. (Reprinted from Christopher G. Langton et al., eds., *Artificial Life: Volume II*; © 1992 Addison-Wesley Publishing Company, Inc. Reprinted by permission of the publisher.)

The comparisons were made by doing a number of runs with each variation of the model, letting each run go until either all agents had died out or a million time steps had taken place (at each time step, each agent in the population moves), and recording, for each variation of the model, the percent of runs in which the population had gone extinct at each time step. Figure 3.7 plots the results of these comparisons. The *x* axis gives a log scale of time, and the *y* axis gives the percent of populations that had gone extinct by a given time.

Figure 3.7 reveals some unexpected phenomena. Evolution alone (E) was not much better than fixed random initial weights, and, strangely, both performed considerably worse than random Brownian motion. Learning seemed to be important for keeping agents alive, and learning alone (L) was almost as successful as evolution and learning combined (ERL). However, ERL did seem to have a small advantage over the other strategies. Ackley and Littman (1992, p. 497) explained these phenomena by speculating that "it is easier to generate a good evaluation function than a good action function." That is, they hypothesize that on L runs a good evaluation network was often generated at random in the initial population, and learning was then able to produce a good action network to go along with the evaluation network. However, evolution left on its own (E) could not as easily produce a good action network. Said intuitively, it is easier to specify useful goals (encoded in the evaluation network) than useful ways of accomplishing them (encoded in the action network).

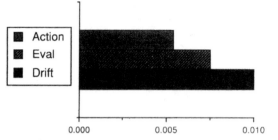

Bit substitutions per position per generation

Figure 3.8 Observed rates of change for three types of genes: "action" genes, associated with actions concerning food (here "plants"); "eval" genes associated with evaluations concerning food; and "drift" genes which did not code for anything. (Reprinted from Christopher G. Langton et al., eds., *Artificial Life: Volume II*; © 1992 Addison-Wesley Publishing Company, Inc. Reprinted by permission of the publisher.)

Ackley and Littman also wanted to understand the relative importance of evolution and learning at different stages of a run. To this end, they extended one long-lived run for almost 9 million generations. Then they used an analysis tool borrowed from biology: "functional constraints." The idea was to measure the rate of change of different parts of the genome over evolutionary time. Since mutation affected all parts of the genome equally, the parts that remained relatively fixed in the population during a certain period were assumed to be important for survival during that period ("functionally constrained"). If these parts were not important for survival, it was reasoned, otherwise fit organisms with mutations in these parts would have survived.

Ackley and Littman chose three types of genes to observe: genes associated with actions concerning food, genes associated with evaluations concerning food, and genes that did not code for anything. (Genes of the third kind were inserted into individuals so experiments like these could be done.) Figure 3.8 shows the number of bit substitutions per position per generation (i.e., rate of change) for the three types of genes. As expected, the noncoding ("drift") genes had the highest rate of change, since they had no survival value. The other two types of genes had lower rates of change, indicating that they were functionally constrained to some degree. The genes associated with evaluation had a higher rate of change than those associated with action, indicating that the action genes were more tightly functionally constrained.

A more detailed analysis revealed that during the first 600,000 time steps the evaluation genes showed the lowest rate of change, but after this the action genes were the ones remaining relatively fixed (see figure 3.9). This indicated that, early on, it was very important to maintain the goals for the learning process (encoded by the evaluation genes). In other words, early on, learning was essential for survival. However, later

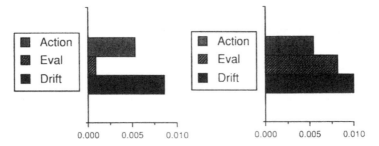

Bit substitutions per position per generation

Figure 3.9 Observed rates of change of the three types of genes before and after 600,000 time steps. (Reprinted from Christopher G. Langton et al., eds., *Artificial Life: Volume II*; © 1992 Addison-Wesley Publishing Company, Inc. Reprinted by permission of the publisher.)

in the run the evaluation genes were more variable across the population, whereas the genes encoding the initial weights of the action network remained more constant. This indicated that inherited behaviors (encoded by the action genes) were more significant than learning during this phase. Ackley and Littman interpreted this as a version of the Baldwin effect. Initially, agents must *learn* to approach food; thus, maintaining the explicit knowledge that "being near food is good" is essential to the learning process. Later, the genetic knowledge that being near food is good is superseded by the genetically encoded behavior to "approach food if near," so the evaluation knowledge is not as necessary. The initial ability to learn the behavior is what allows it to eventually become genetically encoded.

Although their model, like Hinton and Nowlan's, is biologically unrealistic in many ways, Ackley and Littman's results are to me a more convincing demonstration of the Baldwin effect because of the distance in their model between the genotype (the genes encoding the weights on neural networks) and the phenotype (the evaluations and actions produced by these neural networks). Results such as these (as well as those of Hinton and Nowlan) demonstrate the potential of computational modeling: biological phenomena can be studied with controlled computational experiments whose natural equivalent (e.g., running the experiment for thousands of generations) is impractical or impossible. And, when performed correctly, such experiments can produce new evidence for and new insights into these natural phenomena. The potential benefits of such work are not limited to understanding natural phenomena; results such as those of Ackley and Littman could be used to improve current methods for evolving neural networks to solve practical problems. For example, some researchers are investigating the benefits of adding "Lamarckian" learning to the GA, and in some cases it produces significant improvements in GA performance (see Grefenstette 1991a; Ackley and Littman 1994; Hart and Belew 1995).

3.2 MODELING SEXUAL SELECTION

One cannot help but be struck by certain seemingly "aesthetic" traits of organisms, such as the elaborate plumage of peacocks and the massive antlers of some deer. Those with some knowledge of evolution might also be struck by two strange facts: at least in mammals, it is usually the male of the species that has such traits, and they sometimes seem to be maladaptive. They require a lot of energy on the part of the organism to maintain, but they do not add much to the survival powers of the organism, and in some cases they can be positively harmful (e.g., excessively long tail feathers on birds that interfere with flying). Where did such traits come from, and why do they persist? The answer—first proposed by Darwin himself—is most likely "sexual selection." Sexual selection occurs when females (typically) of a particular species tend to select mates according to some criterion (e.g., who has the biggest, most elaborate plumage or antlers), so males having those traits are more likely to be chosen by females as mates. The offspring of such matings tend to inherit the genes encoding the sexually selected trait and those encoding the preference for the sexually selected trait. The former will be expressed only in males, and the latter only in females.

Fisher (1930) proposed that this process could result in a feedback loop between females' preference for a certain trait and the strength and frequency of that trait in males. (Here I use the more common example of a female preference for a male trait, but sexual selection has also been observed in the other direction.) As the frequency of females that prefer the trait increases, it becomes increasingly sexually advantageous for males to have it, which then causes the preference genes to increase further because of increased mating between females with the preference and males with the trait. Fisher termed this "runaway sexual selection."

Sexual selection differs from the usual notion of natural selection. The latter selects traits that help organisms survive, whereas the former selects traits only on the basis of what attracts potential mates. However, the possession of either kind of trait accomplishes the same thing: it increases the likelihood that an organism will reproduce and thus pass on the genes for the trait to its offspring.

There are many open questions about how sexual selection works, and most of them are hard to answer using traditional methods in evolutionary biology. How do particular preferences for traits (such as elaborate plumage) arise in the first place? How fast does the presence of sexual selection affect an evolving population, and in what ways? What is its relative power with respect to natural selection? Some scientists believe that questions such as these can best be answered by computer models. Here I will describe one such model, developed by Robert Collins and David Jefferson, that uses genetic algorithms. Several computer simulations of sexual selection have been reported in the population genetics literature (see, e.g., Heisler and Curtsinger 1990 or Otto 1991), but Collins and Jefferson's is one of the few to use a microanalytic method based on a genetic algorithm. (For other GA-based models, see Miller and Todd 1993, Todd and Miller 1993, and Miller 1994.) This description will give readers a feel for the kind of modeling that is being done, the kinds of questions that are being addressed, and the limits of these approaches.

Simulation and Elaboration of a Mathematical Model for Sexual Selection

Collins and Jefferson (1992) used a genetic algorithm to study an idealized mathematical model of sexual selection from the population genetics literature, formulated by Kirkpatrick (1982; see also Kirkpatrick and Ryan 1991). In this idealized model, an organism has two genes (on separate chromosomes): t ("trait") and p ("preference"). Each gene has two possible alleles, 0 and 1. The p gene encodes female preference for a particular trait T in males: if $p = 0$ the female prefers males without T, but if $p = 1$ she prefers males with T. The t gene encodes existence of T in males: if $t = 0$ the male does not have T; if $t = 1$ he does. The p gene is present but not expressed in males; likewise for the t gene in females.

The catch is that the trait T is assumed to be harmful to survival: males that have it are less likely to survive than males that do not have it. In Kirkpatrick's model, the population starts with equal numbers of males and females. At each generation a fraction of the $t = 1$ males are killed off before they can reproduce. Then each female chooses a male to mate with. A female with $p = 0$ is more likely to choose a male with $t = 0$; a female with $p = 1$ has a similar likelihood of choosing a male with $t = 1$. Kirkpatrick did not actually simulate this system; rather, he derived an equation that gives the expected frequency of females with $p = 1$ and males with $t = 1$ at equilibrium (the point in evolution at which the frequencies no longer change). Kirkpatrick believed that studying the behavior of this simple model would give insights into the equilibrium behavior of real populations with sexual selection.

It turns out that there are many values at which the frequencies of the p and t alleles are at equilibrium. Intuitively, if the frequency of $p = 1$ is high enough, the forces of natural selection and sexual selection oppose each other, since natural selection will select against males with $t = 1$ but sexual selection will select for them. For a given frequency of $p = 1$, a balance can be found so that the frequency of $t = 1$ males remains constant. Kirkpatrick's contribution was to identify what these balances must be as a function of various parameters of the model.

Like all mathematical models in population genetics, Kirkpatrick's model makes a number of assumptions that allow it to be solved analytically: each organism has only one gene of interest; the population is assumed to be infinite; each female chooses her mate by examining all the males in the population; there are no evolutionary forces apart from natural selection and sexual selection on one locus (the model does not include mutation, genetic drift, selection on other loci, or spatial restrictions on mating). In addition, the solution gives only the equilibrium dynamics of the system, not any intermediate dynamics, whereas real systems are rarely if ever at an equilibrium state. Relaxing these assumptions would make the system more realistic and perhaps more predictive of real systems, but would make analytic solution intractable.

Collins and Jefferson proposed using computer simulation as a way to study the behavior of a more realistic version of the model. Rather than the standard approach of using a computer to iterate a system of differential equations, they used a genetic algorithm in which each organism and each interaction between organisms was simulated explicitly.

The simulation was performed on a massively parallel computer (a Connection Machine 2). In Collins and Jefferson's GA the organisms were the same as in Kirkpatrick's model (that is, each individual consisted of two chromosomes, one with a p gene and one with a t gene). Females expressed only the p gene, males only the t gene. Each gene could be either 0 or 1. The population was not infinite, of course, but it was large: 131,072 individuals (equal to twice the number of processors on the Connection Machine 2). The initial population contained equal numbers of males and females, and there was a particular initial distribution of 0 and 1 alleles for t and p. At each generation a certain number of the $t = 1$ males were killed off before reproduction began; each female then chose a surviving male to mate with. In the first simulation, the choice was made by sampling a small number of surviving males throughout the population and deciding which one to mate with probabilistically as a function of the value of the female's p gene and the t genes in the males sampled. Mating consisted of recombination: the p gene from the female was paired with the t gene from the male and vice versa to produce two offspring. The two offspring were then mutated with the very small probability of 0.00001 per gene.

This simulation relaxes some of the simplifying assumptions of Kirkpatrick's analytic model: the population is large but finite; mutation is used; and each female samples only a small number of males in the population before deciding whom to mate with. Each run consisted of 500 generations. Figure 3.10 plots the frequency of $t = 1$ genes versus $p = 1$ genes in the final population for each of 51 runs—starting with various initial $t = 1$, $p = 1$ frequencies—on top of Kirkpatrick's analytic solution. As can be seen, even when the assumptions are relaxed the match between the simulation results and the analytic solution is almost perfect.

The simulation described above studied the equilibrium behavior given

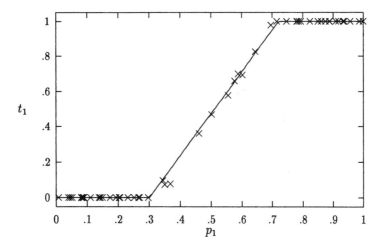

Figure 3.10 Plot of the $t = 1$ (t_1) frequency versus the $p = 1$ (p_1) frequency in the final population (generation 500) for 51 runs (diamonds) of Collins and Jefferson's experiment. The solid line is the equilibrium predicted by Kirkpatrick's analytic model. (Reprinted by permission of publisher from Collins and Jefferson 1992. © 1992 MIT Press.)

an initial population in which the allele $t = 1$ was already present in significant numbers. But how does a new male trait come about in the first place? And once it is discovered in one organism, how does it invade a population? Collins and Jefferson tried a second experiment to address these questions. Everything was the same except that in each initial population all t genes were set to 0 and the frequency of $p = 1$ was 0.7. The $t = 1$ alleles could be discovered only by mutation. Collins and Jefferson found that once $t = 1$ alleles had accumulated to approximately half the population (which took about 100 generations), they quickly took over the population (frequency > 0.9), and $p = 1$ increased from 0.7 to approximately 0.8. This indicates, in a simple model, the power of sexual selection even in the face of negative natural selection for a trait. It also shows very clearly how, above some threshold frequency, the "invasion" of the trait into the population can take place at an accelerating rate, and how the system can get caught in a feedback loop between frequency of the trait in males and preference for the trait in females in the manner of Fisher's runaway sexual selection.

Collins and Jefferson performed additional experiments in which other assumptions were relaxed. In one experiment the choice of mates not only depended on T but was also constrained by spatial distance (again more realistic than Kirkpatrick's original model, since in most populations organisms do not mate with others living far distances away); in another the organisms were diploid instead of haploid and contained "dominant" and "recessive" alleles. Both these variations are difficult to treat analytically. Collins and Jefferson found that both variations led to dynamics significantly different from those of Kirkpatrick's original model. In one

Genetic Algorithms in Scientific Models

simulation with diploid organisms, a $t = 1$ allele not initially present in large numbers in the population was unable to invade—its frequency remained close to 0 for 1000 generations. However, when mating was constrained spatially, the $t = 1$ allele was able to slowly invade the population to the point where significant sexual selection could take place.

These examples show that relaxing some of the simplifying assumptions in idealized mathematical models can dramatically change the behavior of the system. One benefit of Collins and Jefferson's simulation was to show in which ways the original analytic model does not capture the behavior of more realistic versions. It also allowed Collins and Jefferson to study the behavior and dynamics of these more realistic versions, particularly at points away from equilibrium. Another benefit of such models is that they allow scientists to systematically vary parts of the model to discover which forces are most important in changing behavior. It is clear that Collins and Jefferson's simulations do not go far enough in realism, but computer models are inching in that direction. Of course, as was pointed out earlier, the more realistic the model, the more computationally expensive it becomes and the harder it is to analyze the results. At some point, the realism of a model can override its usefulness, since studying it would be no more enlightening than studying the actual system in nature. It is the art of effective modeling to strike the proper balance between simplicity (which makes understanding possible) and generality (which ensures that the results are meaningful).

3.3 MODELING ECOSYSTEMS

In the real world, evolution takes place not in populations of independent organisms (such as our populations of evolving cellular automata described in chapter 2) but in ecologies of interacting organisms. Ecological interactions have been captured to varying degrees in some of the case studies we have considered, such as the Prisoner's Dilemma project (where the evolving strategies played against one another), the sorting networks project (where hosts and parasites were in direct competition), and the Evolutionary Reinforcement Learning (ERL) project (where the evolving agents competed indirectly for the available food). Such interactions, however, are only the faintest shadow of the complexity of interactions in real-world ecologies. A more ambitious model of evolution in an ecological setting is Echo, first conceived of and implemented by John Holland (1975, second edition, chapter 10; see also Holland 1994) and later reimplemented and extended by Terry Jones and Stephanie Forrest (Jones and Forrest 1993; see also Forrest and Jones 1994).

Like many of the other models we have looked at, Echo is meant to be as simple as possible while still capturing essential aspects of ecological systems. It is not meant to model any particular ecosystem (although more detailed versions might someday be used to do so); it is meant to capture general properties common to all ecosystems. It is intended to be a platform for controlled experiments that can reveal how changes in the model and in its parameters affect phenomena such as the relative abundance of different species, the development and stability of food webs, conditions for and times to extinction, and the evolution of symbiotic communities of organisms.

Echo's world—a two-dimensional lattice of sites—contains several different types of "resources," represented in the model by letters of the alphabet. These can be thought of as potential sources of energy for the organisms. Different types of resources appear in varying amounts at different sites.

The world is populated by "agents," similar in some ways to the agents in the ERL model. Each agent has a genotype and a phenotype. The genotype encodes a set of rules that govern the types and quantities of resources the agent needs to live and reproduce, the types and quantities of resources the agent can take up from the environment, how the agent will interact with other agents, and some physical characteristics of the agent that are visible to other agents. The phenotype is the agent's resulting behavior and physical appearance (the latter is represented as a bit pattern). As in the ERL model, each agent has an internal energy store where it hoards the resources it takes from the environment and from other agents. An agent uses up its stored energy when it moves, when it interacts with other agents, and even when it is simply sitting still (there is a "metabolic tax" for just existing). An agent can reproduce when it has enough energy stored up to create a copy of its genome. If its energy store goes below a certain threshold, the agent dies, and its remaining resources are returned to the site at which it lived.

At each time step, agents living at the same site encounter one another at random. There are three different types of interactions they can have: combat, trade, and mating. (An Echo wag once remarked that these are the three elements of a good marriage.) When two agents meet, they decide which type of interaction to have on the basis of their own internal rules and the outward physical appearance of the other agent. If they engage in combat, the outcome is decided by the rules encoded in the genomes of the agents. The loser dies, and all its stored resources are added to the winner's store.

If the two agents are less warlike and more commercial, they can agree to trade. An agent's decision to trade is again made on the basis of its internal rules and the other agent's external appearance. Agents trade any stored resources in excess of what they need to reproduce. In Echo an agent has the possibility to evolve deception—it might look on the outside as though it has something good to trade whereas it actually has nothing. This can result in other agents' getting "fleeced" unless they evolve the capacity (via internal rules) to recognize cheaters.

Finally, for more amorous agents, mating is a possibility. The decision to mate is, like combat and trade, based on an agent's internal rules and the external appearance of the potential mate. If two agents decide to mate, their chromosomes are combined via two-point crossover to form two offspring, which then replace their parents at the given site. (After reproducing, the parents die.)

If an agent lives through a time step without gaining any resources, it gives up its current site and moves on to another nearby site (picked at random), hoping for greener pastures.

The three types of interactions are meant to be idealized versions of the basic types of interactions between organisms that occur in nature. They are more extensive than the types of interactions in any of the case studies we have looked at so far. The possibilities for complex interactions, the spatial aspects of the system, and the separation between genotype and phenotype give Echo the potential to capture some very interesting and complicated ecological phenomena (including, as was mentioned above, the evolution of "deception" as a strategy for winning resources, which is seen often in real ecologies). Of course, this potential for complication means that the results of the model may be harder to understand than the results of the other models we have looked at.

Note that, as in the ERL model, the fitness of agents in Echo is endogenous. There is no explicit fitness measure; rather, the rate at which agents reproduce and the rate at which particular genes spread in the population emerge from all the different actions and interactions in the evolving population.

As yet only some preliminary experiments have been performed using Echo. Forrest and Jones (1994) have presented the results of an interesting experiment in which they looked at the relative abundance of "species" during a run of Echo. In biology, the word "species" typically means a group of individuals that can interbreed and produce viable offspring. (This definition breaks down in the case of asexual organisms; other definitions have to be used.) In Echo, it is not immediately clear how to define species—although the internal rules of an agent restrict whom it can mate with, there are no explicit boundaries around different mating groups. Forrest and Jones used similarity of genotypes as a way of grouping agents into species. The most extreme version of this is to classify each different genotype as a different species. Forrest and Jones started out by using this definition. Figure 3.11 plots the relative abundance of the 603 different genotypes that were present after 1000 time steps in one typical run of Echo. Different abundances were ranked from commonest (rank 1) to rarest (rank 603). In figure 3.11 the actual abundances arc plotted as a function of the log of the rank. For example, in this plot the most common genotype has approximately 250 instances and the least common has approximately one instance. Other runs produced very similar plots. Even though this was the simplest possible way in which to define species in

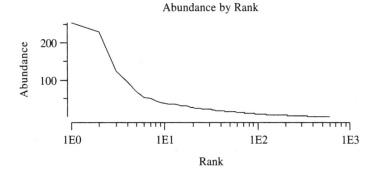

Figure 3.11 Plot of rank versus abundance for genotypes in one typical run of Echo. After 1000 time steps, the abundances of the 603 different genotypes present in the population were ranked, and their actual abundances were plotted as a function of the log of the rank. (Reprinted from R. J. Stonier and X. H. Yu, eds., *Complex Systems: Mechanism of Adaptation*, ©1994 by IOS Press. Reprinted by permission of the publisher.)

Echo, the plot in figure 3.11 is similar in shape to rank-abundance plots of data from some real ecologies. This gave Forrest and Jones some confidence that the model might be capturing something important about real-world systems. Forrest and Jones also published the results of experiments in which species were defined as groups of similar rather than identical agents—similar-shaped plots were obtained.

These experiments were intended to be a first step in "validating" Echo—that is, demonstrating that it is biologically plausible. Forrest and Jones intend to carry this process further by performing other qualitative comparisons between Echo and real ecologies. Holland has also identified some directions for future work on Echo. These include (1) studying the evolution of external physical "tags" as a mechanism for social communication, (2) extending the model to allow the evolution of "metazoans" (connected communities of agents that have internal boundaries and reproduce as a unit), (3) studying the evolutionary dynamics of schemas in the population, and (4) using the results from (3) to formulate a generalization of the Schema Theorem based on endogenous fitness (Holland 1975, second edition, chapter 10; Holland 1994). The second capacity will allow for the study of individual-agent specialization and the evolution of multi-cellularity. The fourth is a particularly important goal, since there has been very little mathematical analysis of artificial-life simulations in which fitness is endogenous.

Forrest and Jones (1994) acknowledge that there is a long way to go before Echo can be used to make precise predictions: "It will be a long time before models like Echo can be used to provide quantitative answers to many questions regarding complex adaptive systems [such as ecologies]." But they assert that models like Echo are probably best used to build intuitions about complex systems: "A more realistic goal is that these systems might be used to explore the range of possible outcomes of particular decisions and to suggest where to look in real systems for relevant features. The hope is that by using such models, people can develop deep intuitions about sensitivities and other properties of their particular worlds." This sentiment is echoed (so to speak) by Holland (1975, second edition, p. 186): "Echo is . . . designed primarily for gedanken experiments rather than precise simulations." This notion of computer models as intuition builders rather than as predictive devices—as arenas in which to perform gedanken (thought) experiments—is really what all the case studies in this chapter are about. Although the notion of gedanken experiments has a long and honorable history in science, I think the usefulness of such models has been underrated by many. Even though many scientists will dismiss a model that cannot make quantitative (and thus falsifiable) predictions, I believe that models such as those described here will soon come to play a larger role in helping us understand complex systems such as evolution. In fact, I will venture to say that we will not be able to do it without them.

3.4 MEASURING EVOLUTIONARY ACTIVITY

The words "evolution" and "adaptation" have been used throughout this book (and in most books about evolution) with little more than informal definition. But if these are phenomena of central scientific interest, it is important to define them in a more rigorous and quantitative way, and to develop methods to detect and measure them. In other words: How can we decide if an observed system is evolving? How can we measure the rate of evolution in such a system?

Mark Bedau and Norman Packard (1992) developed a measure of evolution, called "evolutionary activity," to address these questions. Bedau and Packard point out that evolution is more than "sustained change" or even "sustained complex change"; it is "the spontaneous generation of innovative functional structures." These structures are designed and continually modified by the evolutionary process; they persist because of their adaptive functionality. The goal, then, is to find a way to measure the degree to which a system is "continuously and spontaneously generating adaptations."

Bedau and Packard assert that "persistent usage of new genes is what signals genuine evolutionary activity," since evolutionary activity is meant to measure the degree to which useful new genes are discovered and persist in the population. The "use" of a gene or combination of genes is not simply its presence in a chromosome; it must be used to produce some trait or behavior. Assigning credit to particular genes for a trait or behavior is notoriously hard because of the complex interconnection of gene activities in the formation and control of an organism. However, Bedau and Packard believe that this can be usefully done in some contexts.

Bedau and Packard's first attempt at measuring evolutionary activity was in an idealized computer model, called "Strategic Bugs," in which gene use was easy to measure. Their model was similar to, though simpler than, the ERL model described above. The Strategic Bugs world is a simulated two-dimensional lattice containing only "bugs" and "food." The food supply is refreshed periodically and is distributed randomly across the lattice. Bugs survive by finding food and storing it in an internal reservoir until they have enough energy to reproduce. Bugs also use energy from their internal reservoir in order to move, and they are "taxed" energy just for surviving from time step to time step even if they do not move. A bug dies when its internal reservoir is empty. Thus, bugs must find food continually in order to survive.

Each bug's behavior is controlled by an internal lookup table that maps sensory data from the bug's local neighborhood to a vector giving the direction and distance of the bug's next foray. The sensory data come from five sites centered on the bug's current site, and the state at each site is encoded with two bits representing one of four levels of food that can be sensed (00 = least food; 01 = more food; 10 = even more food; 11 = most food). Thus, a bug's current state (input from five sites) is encoded by ten bits. The vector describing the bug's next movement is encoded by eight bits—four bits representing one of 16 possible directions (north, north-northeast, northeast, etc.) in which to move and four bits representing one of 16 possible distances to travel (0–15 steps) in that direction. Since there are 10 bits that represent sensory data, there are 2^{10} possible states the bug can be in, and a complete lookup table has $2^{10} = 1024$ entries, each of which consists of an eight-bit movement vector. Each eight-bit entry is considered to be a single "gene," and these genes make up the bug's "chromosome." One such chromosome is illustrated in figure 3.12. Crossovers can occur only at gene (lookup table entry) boundaries.

The simulation begins with a population of 50 bugs, each with a partially randomly assigned lookup table. (Most of the entries in each lookup table initially consist of the instruction "do nothing.") A time step consists of each bug's assessing its local environment and moving according to the corresponding instruction in its lookup table. When a bug encounters a site containing food, it eats the food. When it has sufficient energy in its internal reservoir (above some predefined threshold), it reproduces. A bug can reproduce asexually (in which case it passes on its chromosome to its offspring with some low probability of mutation at each gene) or sexually (in which case it mates with a spatially adjacent bug, producing offspring whose genetic material is a combination of that of the parents, possibly with some small number of mutations).

To measure evolutionary activity, Bedau and Packard kept statistics on gene use for every gene that appeared in the population. Each gene in a bug was assigned a counter, initialized to 0, which was incremented every

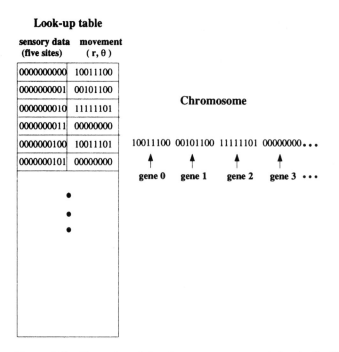

Figure 3.12 Illustration of the chromosome representation in the Strategic Bugs model. Crossovers occur only at gene (lookup-table entry) boundaries.

time the gene was used—that is, every time the specified input situation arose for the bug and the specified action was taken by the bug. When a parent passed on a gene to a child through asexual reproduction or through crossover, the value of the counter was passed on as well and remained with the gene. The only time a counter was initialized to zero was when a new gene was created through mutation. In this way, a gene's counter value reflected the usage of that gene over many generations. When a bug died, its genes (and their counters) died with it.

For each time step during a run, Bedau and Packard (1992) plotted a histogram of the number of genes in the population displaying a given usage value u (i.e., a given counter value). One such plot is shown here at the top of figure 3.13. The x axis in this plot is time steps, and the y axis gives usage values u. A vertical slice along the y axis gives the distribution of usage values over the counters in the population at a given time step, with the frequency of each usage value indicated by the grayscale. For example, the leftmost vertical column (representing the initial population) has a black region near zero, indicating that usage values near zero are most common (genes cannot have high usage after so little time). All other usage values are white, indicating that no genes had yet reached that level of usage. As time goes on, gray areas creep up the page, indicating that certain genes persisted in being used. These genes presumably were the ones that helped the bugs to survive and reproduce—the ones

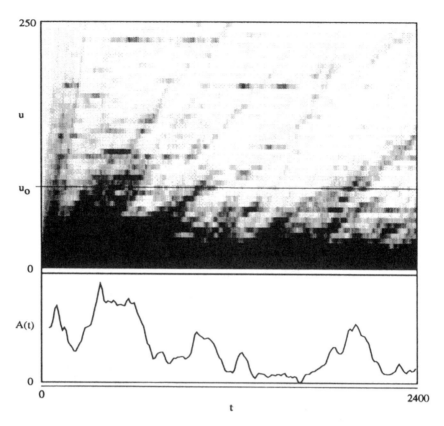

Figure 3.13 Plots of usage statistics for one run of the Strategic Bugs model. Top plot: Each vertical column is a histogram over u (usage values), with frequencies of different u values represented on a gray scale. On this scale, white represents frequency 0 and black represents the maximum frequency. These histograms are plotted over time. Bottom plot: Evolutionary activity $A(t)$ is plotted versus t for this run. Peaks in $A(t)$ correspond to the formation of new activity waves. (Reprinted from Christopher G. Langton et al. (eds.), *Artificial Life: Volume II*, ©1992 by Addison-Wesley Publishing Company, Inc. Reprinted by permission of the publisher.)

that encoded traits being selected. Bedau and Packard referred to these gray streaks as "waves of activity." New waves of activity indicated the discovery of some new set of genes that proved to be useful.

According to Bedau and Packard, the continual appearance of new waves of activity in an evolving population indicates that the population is continually finding and exploiting new genetic innovations. Bedau and Packard defined a single number, the *evolutionary activity* $A(t)$, that roughly measures the degree to which the population is acquiring new and useful genetic material at time t.

In mathematical terms, Bedau and Packard defined u_0 as the "baseline usage"—roughly the usage that genes would obtain if selection were random rather than based on fitness. As an initial attempt to compensate for these random effects, Bedau and Packard subtracted u_0 from u. They showed that, in general, the only genes that take part in activity waves are those with usage greater than u_0.

Next, Bedau and Packard defined $P(t, u)$, the "net persistence," as the proportion of genes in the population at time t that have usage u or greater. As can be seen in figure 3.13, an activity wave is occurring at time t' and usage value u' if $P(t, u)$ is changing in the neighborhood around (t', u'). Right before time t' there will be a sharp increase in $P(t, u)$, and right above usage value u' there will be a sharp decrease in $P(t, u)$. Bedau and Packard thus quantified activity waves by measuring the rate of change of $P(t, u)$ with respect to u. They measured the creation of activity waves by evaluating this rate of change right at the baseline u_0. This is how they defined $A(t)$:

$$A(t) = -\left[\frac{\partial P(t, u)}{\partial u}\right]_{u=u_0}.$$

That is, the evolutionary activity is the rate at which net persistence is dropping at $u = u_0$. In other words, $A(t)$ will be positive if new activity waves continue to be produced.

Bedau and Packard defined "evolution" in terms of $A(t)$: if $A(t)$ is positive, then evolution is occurring at time t, and the magnitude of $A(t)$ gives the "amount" of evolution that is occurring at that time. The bottom plot of figure 3.13 gives the value of $A(t)$ versus time in the given run. Peaks in $A(t)$ correspond to the formation of new activity waves. Claiming that life is a property of populations and not of individual organisms, Bedau and Packard ambitiously proposed $A(t)$ as a test for life in a system—if $A(t)$ is positive, then the system is exhibiting life at time t.

The important contribution of Bedau and Packard's 1992 paper is the attempt to define a macroscopic quantity such as evolutionary activity. In subsequent (as yet unpublished) work, they propose a macroscopic law relating mutation rate to evolutionary activity and speculate that this relation will have the same form in every evolving system (Mark Bedau and Norman Packard, personal communication). They have also used evolutionary activity to characterize differences between simulations run with different parameters (e.g., different degrees of selective pressure), and they are attempting to formulate general laws along these lines. A large part of their current work is determining the best way to measure evolutionary activity in other models of evolution—for example, they have done some preliminary work on measuring evolutionary activity in Echo (Mark Bedau, personal communication). It is clear that the notion of gene usage in the Strategic Bugs model, in which the relationship between genes and behavior is completely straightforward, is too simple. In more realistic models it will be considerably harder to define such quantities. However, the formulation of macroscopic measures of evolution and adaptation, as well as descriptions of the microscopic mechanisms by which the macroscopic quantities emerge, is, in my opinion, essential if evolutionary computation is to be made into an explanatory science and if it is to contribute significantly to real evolutionary biology.

THOUGHT EXERCISES

1. Assume that in Hinton and Nowlan's model the correct setting is the string of 20 ones. Define a "potential winner" (Belew 1990) as a string that contains only ones and question marks (i.e., that has the potential to guess the correct answer). (a) In a randomly generated population of 1000 strings, how many strings do you expect to be potential winners? (b) What is the probability that a potential winner with m ones will guess the correct string during its lifetime of 1000 guesses?

2. Write a few paragraphs explaining as clearly and succinctly as possible (a) the Baldwin effect, (b) how Hinton and Nowlan's results demonstrate it, (c) how Ackley and Littman's results demonstrate it, and (d) how Ackley and Littman's approach compares with that of Hinton and Nowlan.

3. Given the description of Echo in section 3.3, think about how Echo could be used to model the Baldwin effect. Design an experiment that might demonstrate the Baldwin effect.

4. Given the description of Echo in section 3.3, design an experiment that could be done in Echo to simulate sexual selection and to compare its strength with that of natural selection.

5. Is Bedau and Packard's "evolutionary activity" measure a good method for measuring adaptation? Why or why not?

6. Think about how Bedau and Packard's "evolutionary activity" measure could be used in Echo. What kinds of "usage" statistics could be recorded, and which of them would be valuable?

COMPUTER EXERCISES

1. Write a genetic algorithm to replicate Hinton and Nowlan's experiment. Make plots from your results similar to those in figure 3.4, and compare your plots with that figure. Do a run that goes for 2000 generations. At what frequency and at what generation do the question marks reach a steady state? Could you roughly predict this frequency ahead of time?

2. Run a GA on the fitness function $f(x) =$ the number of ones in x,

where x is a chromosome of length 20. (See computer exercise 1 in chapter 1 for suggested parameters.) Compare the performance of the GA on this problem with the performance of a modified GA with the following form of sexual selection:

a. Add a bit to each string in the initial population indicating whether the string is "male" (0) or "female" (1). (This bit should not be counted in the fitness evaluation.) Initialize the population with half females and half males.

b. Separate the two populations of males and females.

c. Choose a female with probability proportional to fitness. Then choose a male with probability proportional to fitness. Assume that females prefer males with more zeros: the probability that a female will agree to mate with a given male is a function of the number of zeros in the male (you should define the function). If the female agrees to mate, form two offspring via single-point crossover, and place the male child in the next generation's male population and the female child in the next generation's female population. If the female decides not to mate, put the male back in the male population and, keeping the same female, choose a male again with probability proportional to fitness. Continue in this way until the new male and female populations are complete. Then go to step c with the new populations.

What is the behavior of this GA? Can you explain the behavior? Experiment with different female preference functions to see how they affect the GA's behavior.

*3. Take one of the problems described in the computer exercises of chapter 1 or chapter 2 (e.g., evolving strategies to solve the Prisoner's Dilemma) and compare the performance of three different algorithms on that problem:

a. The standard GA.

b. The following Baldwinian modification: To evaluate the fitness of an individual, take the individual as a starting point and perform steepest-ascent hill climbing until a local optimum is reached (i.e., no single bit-flip yields an increase in fitness). The fitness of the original individual is the value of the local optimum. However, when forming offspring, the genetic material of the original individual is used rather than the improvements "learned" by steepest-ascent hill climbing.

c. The following Lamarckian modification: Evaluate fitness in the same way as in (b), but now with the offspring formed by the improved individuals found by steepest-ascent hill climbing (i.e., offspring inherit their parents' "acquired" traits).

How do these three variations compare in performance, in the quality of solutions found, and in the time it takes to find them?

*4. The Echo system (Jones and Forrest, 1993) is available from the Santa Fe Institute at www.santafe.edu/projects/echo/echo.html. Once Echo is up and running, do some simple experiments of your own devising. These can include, for example, experiments similar to the species-diversity experiments described in this chapter, or experiments measuring "evolutionary activity" (*à la* Bedau and Packard 1992).

4 Theoretical Foundations of Genetic Algorithms

As genetic algorithms become more widely used for practical problem solving and for scientific modeling, increasing emphasis is placed on understanding their theoretical foundations. Some major questions in this area are the following:

What laws describe the macroscopic behavior of GAs? In particular, what predictions can be made about the change in fitness over time and about the dynamics of population structures in a particular GA?

How do the low-level operators (selection, crossover, mutation) give rise to the macroscopic behavior of GAs?

On what types of problems are GAs likely to perform well?

On what types of problems are GAs likely to perform poorly?

What does it mean for a GA to "perform well" or "perform poorly"? That is, what performance criteria are appropriate for GAs?

Under what conditions (types of GAs and types of problems) will a GA outperform other search methods, such as hill climbing and other gradient methods?

A complete survey of work on the theory of GAs would fill several volumes (e.g., see the various "Foundations of Genetic Algorithms" proceedings volumes: Rawlins 1991; Whitley 1993b; Whitley and Vose 1995). In this chapter I will describe a few selected approaches of particular interest. As will become evident, there are a number of controversies in the GA theory community over some of these approaches, revealing that GA theory is by no means a closed book—indeed there are more open questions than answered ones.

4.1 SCHEMAS AND THE TWO-ARMED BANDIT PROBLEM

In chapter 1 I introduced the notion of "schema" and briefly described its relevance to genetic algorithms. John Holland's original motivation for developing GAs was to construct a theoretical framework for adaptation as seen in nature, and to apply it to the design of artificial adaptive systems. According to Holland (1975), an adaptive system must persistently identify, test, and incorporate structural properties hypothesized to give better performance in some environment. Schemas are meant to be a formalization of such structural properties. In the context of genetics, schemas correspond to constellations of genes that work together to effect some adaptation in an organism; evolution discovers and propagates such constellations. Of course, adaptation is possible only in a world in which there is structure in the environment to be discovered and exploited. Adaptation is impossible in a sufficiently random environment.

Holland's schema analysis showed that a GA, while explicitly calculating the fitnesses of the N members of a population, implicitly estimates the average fitnesses of a much larger number of schemas by implicitly calculating the observed average fitnesses of schemas with instances in the population. It does this without needing any additional memory or computation time beyond that needed to process the N members of the population. Holland called this "implicit parallelism." (The accuracy of these estimates depends, of course on the variances of the schemas in question—see below.) Holland's analysis also showed that those schemas whose fitness estimates remain above average receive increasing numbers of "trials" (instances in the population). As was described in chapter 1 above, the Schema Theorem has been interpreted to imply that, under a GA (and given certain assumptions), short, low-order schemas whose average fitness remains above the mean will receive exponentially increasing numbers of samples over time.

Holland's analysis suggests that selection increasingly focuses the search on subsets of the search space with estimated above-average fitness (defined by schemas with observed above-average fitness), whereas crossover puts high-fitness "building blocks" together on the same string in order to create strings of increasingly higher fitness. Mutation plays the role of an insurance policy, making sure genetic diversity is never irrevocably lost at any locus.

Holland frames adaptation as a tension between "exploration" (the search for new, useful adaptations) and "exploitation" (the use and propagation of these adaptations). The tension comes about since any move toward exploration—testing previously unseen schemas or schemas whose instances seen so far have low fitness—takes away from the exploitation of tried and true schemas. In any system (e.g., a population of organisms) required to face environments with some degree of unpredictability, an optimal balance between exploration and exploitation must be found. The system has to keep trying out new possibilities (or else it could "overadapt" and be inflexible in the face of novelty), but it also has to continually incorporate and use past experience as a guide for future behavior.

Holland's original GA was proposed as an "adaptive plan" for accomplishing a proper balance between exploration and exploitation in an adaptive system. (In this chapter, "GA" will generally refer to Holland's original GA, which is essentially the "simple" GA that I described in chapter 1 above.)

Holland's schema analysis demonstrated that, given certain assumptions, the GA indeed achieves a near-optimal balance. Holland's arguments for this are based on an analogy with the Two-Armed Bandit problem, whose solution is sketched below.

Holland's original theory of schemas assumed binary strings and single-point crossover. Useful schemas, as defined by Holland, are a class of high-fitness subsets of the binary strings that avoid significant disruption by single-point crossover and mutation and thus can survive to recombine with other schemas. In recent years, Holland's schema theory has been extended to different types of representations and crossover operators (see, e.g., Vose 1991).

The Two-Armed Bandit Problem

The tradeoff between exploration and exploitation can be instructively modeled in a simple scenario: the Two-Armed Bandit problem. This problem has been studied extensively in the context of statistical decision theory and adaptive control (e.g., see Bellman 1961). Holland (1975) used it as an as a mathematical model of how a GA allocates samples to schemas.

The scenario is as follows. A gambler is given N coins with which to play a slot machine having two arms. (A conventional slot machine is colloquially known as a "one-armed bandit.") The arms are labeled A_1 and A_2, and they have mean payoff (per trial) rates μ_1 and μ_2 with respective variances σ_1^2 and σ_2^2. The payoff processes from the two arms are each stationary and independent of one another, which means that the mean payoff rates do not change over time. The gambler does not know these payoff rates or their variances; she can estimate them only by playing coins on the different arms and observing the payoff obtained on each. She has no *a priori* information on which arm is likely to be better. Her goal is, of course, to maximize her total payoff during the N trials. What should her strategy be for allocating trials to each arm, given her current estimates (from payoffs received so far) of the μs and the σs? Note that the goal is not merely to guess which arm has a higher payoff rate, but to maximize payoff in the course of gaining information through allocating samples to the two arms. Such a performance criterion is called "on-line," since the payoff at every trial counts in the final evaluation of performance. This is to be contrasted with the common "off-line" performance criteria in function optimization, where the performance evaluation of an optimization method might depend only on whether or not the global optimum was discovered, or possibly on the best fitness level achieved after a given number of trials, irrespective of the fitness (payoff) of the intermediate samples.

Holland's analytic solution to the Two-Armed Bandit problem states that, as more and more information is gained through sampling, the optimal strategy is to exponentially increase the probability of sampling the better-seeming arm relative to the probability of sampling the worse-seeming arm. To apply this to schema sampling in a GA, the 3^L schemas in an L-bit search space can be viewed as the 3^L arms of a multi-armed slot machine. The observed "payoff" of a schema H is simply its observed average fitness, which the GA implicitly keeps track of via the number of samples of H in the population. Holland's (1975) claim (supported by the Schema Theorem) is that, under the GA, a near-optimal strategy for sampling schemas arises implicitly, which leads to the maximization of on-line performance.

Sketch of a Solution

The following is a sketch of Holland's solution to the Two-Armed Bandit problem. For the sake of clarity and brevity I make a number of simplifications and leave out some details that make the solution more rigorous and general. The full solution involves mathematical subtleties that go beyond the scope of this book. Interested readers should consult chapter 5 of Holland 1975, and should also see the corrections in chapter 10 of the second edition.

Let A_1 be the arm with higher average payoff μ_1, and let A_2 be the arm with lower average payoff μ_2. Let $A_h(N, N - n)$ be the arm (A_1 or A_2) with observed higher payoff, and let $A_l(N, n)$ be the arm with observed lower payoff after N trials of which $N - n$ trials were allocated to $A_h(N, N - n)$ and n trials were allocated to $A_l(N, n)$. We want to find the value $n = n^*$ that maximizes expected profits—or equivalently, minimizes expected losses—over these N trials. The losses are defined to be the trials on which the true better arm, A_1, was not sampled. Clearly the only strategy with no expected losses is to allocate all N samples to the true best, gaining an expected payoff of $N\mu_1$; however, without knowledge of which is the true better arm such an allocation cannot be made.

There are two possible sources of profit loss: (1) The observed worse arm, $A_l(N, n)$, is actually the better arm, A_1. Then the gambler has lost (expected) profits on the $N - n$ trials given to $A_h(N, N - n)$ to the tune of $(N - n)(\mu_1 - \mu_2)$. (2) The observed worse arm, $A_l(N, n)$, really is the worse arm, A_2. Then the gambler has lost (expected) profits on the n trials given to $A_l(N, n)$ to the tune of $n(\mu_1 - \mu_2)$. Let q be the probability that the observed worse arm, $A_l(N, n)$, is actually the better arm, A_1, given $N - n$ trials to $A_h(N, N - n)$ and n trials to $A_l(N, n)$:

$$q = Pr(A_l(N, n) = A_1).$$

Then the losses $L(N - n, n)$ over N trials are

$$L(N - n, n) = q(N - n)(\mu_1 - \mu_2) + (1 - q)n(\mu_1 - \mu_2). \tag{4.1}$$

The goal is to find $n = n^*$ that minimizes $L(N - n, n)$. This can be done by taking the derivative of $L(N - n, n)$ with respect to n, setting it to zero, and solving for n:

$$\frac{dL}{dn} = (\mu_1 - \mu_2)\left(1 - 2q + (N - 2n)\frac{dq}{dn}\right) = 0. \tag{4.2}$$

To solve this equation, we need to express q in terms of n so that we can find dq/dn. Recall that q is the probability that $A_l(N, n) = A_1$. Suppose $A_l(N, n)$ indeed is A_1; then A_1 was given n trials. Let S_1^n be the sum of the payoffs of the n trials given to A_1, and let S_2^{N-n} be the sum of the payoffs of the $N - n$ trials given to A_2. Then

$$q = \Pr\left(\frac{S_2^{N-n}}{N - n} > \frac{S_1^n}{n}\right); \tag{4.3}$$

that is, the probability that the *observed* average payoff of A_2 is higher than that of A_1. Equivalently,

$$q = \Pr\left(\left(\frac{S_1^n}{n} - \frac{S_2^{N-n}}{N - n}\right) < 0\right). \tag{4.4}$$

(For subtle reasons, this is actually only an approximation; see Holland 1975, chapter 5.) Since S_1^n and S_2^{N-n} are random variables, their difference is also a random variable with a well-defined distribution. $\Pr((S_1^n/n - S_2^{N-n}/(N - n)) < 0)$ is simply the area under the part of the distribution that is less than zero. The problem now is to compute this area—a tricky task. Holland originally approximated it by using the central limit theorem to assume a normal distribution. Dan Frantz (as described in chapter 10 of the second edition of Holland 1975) corrected the original approximation using the theory of large deviations rather than the central limit theorem. Here the mathematics get complicated (as is often the case for easy-to-state problems such as the Two-Armed Bandit problem). According to Frantz, the optimal allocation of trials n^* to the observed second best of the two random variables corresponding to the Two-Armed Bandit problem is approximated by

$$n^* \approx c_1 \ln\left(\frac{c_2 N^2}{\ln(c_3 N^2)}\right),$$

where $c_1, c_2,$ and c_3 are positive constants defined by Frantz. (Here ln denotes the natural logarithm.) The details of this solution are of less concern to us than its form. This can be seen by rearranging the terms and performing some algebra to get an expression for $N - n^*$, the optimal allocation of trials to the observed better arm:

$$N - n^* \approx e^{n^*/2c_1} \sqrt{\frac{\ln(c_3 N^2)}{c_2}} - n^*.$$

As n^* increases, $e^{n^*/2c_1}$ dominates everything else, so we can further approximate (letting $c = 1/2c_1$):

$$N - n^* \approx e^{cn^*}.$$

In short, the optimal allocation of trials $N - n^*$ to the observed better arm should increase exponentially with the number of trials to the observed worse arm.

Interpretation of the Solution

The Two-Armed Bandit problem is a simple model of the general problem of how to allocate resources in the face of uncertainty. This is the "exploration versus exploitation" problem faced by an adaptive system. The Schema Theorem suggests that, given a number of assumptions, the GA roughly adopts a version of the optimal strategy described above: over time, the number of trials allocated to the best observed schemas in the population increases exponentially with respect to the number of trials allocated to worse observed schemas. The GA implements this search strategy via implicit parallelism, where each of the n individuals in population can be viewed as a sample of 2^l different schemas. The number of instances of a given schema H in the population at any time is related to its observed average performance, giving (under some conditions) an exponential growth rate for highly fit schemas.

However, the correct interpretation of the Two-Armed Bandit analogy for schemas is not quite so simple. Grefenstette and Baker (1989) illustrate this with the following fitness function:

$$f(x) = \begin{cases} 2 & \text{if } x \in 111 * \cdots *, \\ 1 & \text{if } x \in 0 * \cdots *, \\ 0 & \text{otherwise.} \end{cases} \qquad (4.5)$$

(Recall that "$x \in H$" denotes "x is an instance of schema H.") Let $u(H)$ be the "static" average fitness of a schema H (the average over all instances of the schema in the search space), and let $\hat{u}(H, t)$ be the observed average fitness of H at time t (the average fitness of instances of H in the population at time t). It is easy to show that $u(1 * \cdots *) = \frac{1}{2}$ and $u(0 * \cdots *) = 1$. But under a GA, via selection, $1 * \cdots *$ will dominate the population very quickly in the form of instances of $111 * \cdots *$ since instances of the latter will be strongly selected in the population. This means that, under a GA, $\hat{u}(1 * \cdots *, t) \approx 2$ after a small number of time steps, and $1 * \cdots *$ will receive many more samples than $0 * \cdots *$ even though its static average fitness is lower.

The problem here is that in the Two-Armed Bandit each arm is an independent random variable with a fixed distribution, so the likelihood of a particular outcome does not change from play to play. But in the GA different "arms" (schemas) interact; the observed payoff for $111 * \cdots *$ has a strong (if not determining) effect on the observed payoff for $1 * \cdots *$. Unlike in the Two-Armed Bandit problem, the additional trials to $1 * \cdots *$ will not provide additional information about its true payoff rate, since they all end up being trials to $111 * \cdots *$. In short, the GA cannot be said to be sampling schemas independently to estimate their true payoffs.

Grefenstette and Baker's example shows that the GA does not play a 3^L-armed bandit with all 3^L possible schemas competing as arms. A more correct interpretation (John Holland, personal communication) is that the GA plays a 2^k-armed bandit in each order-k "schema partition," defined as a division of the search space into 2^k directly competing schemas. For example, the partition $d * \cdots *$ consists of the two schemas $0 * \cdots *$ and $1 * \cdots *$. Likewise, the partition $*d * d * \cdots *$ consists of the four schemas $*0 * 0 * \cdots *, *0 * 1 * \cdots *, *1 * 0 * \cdots *$, and $*1 * 1 * \cdots *$. The idea is that the best observed schema *within* a partition will receive exponentially more samples than the next best, and so on. Furthermore, the GA will be close to an optimal 2^k-armed bandit strategy only for partitions in which the current population's distribution of fitnesses in the competing schemas is reasonably uniform (Holland, personal communication cited in Grefenstette 1991b). Thus, the schema competition in the $d * \cdots *$ partition in Grefenstette and Baker's example will not follow a two-armed-bandit strategy.

The general idea here is that, roughly, the multi-armed-bandit strategy for competition among schemas proceeds from low-order partitions at early times to higher-order partitions at later times. The extent to which this describes the workings of actual GAs is not clear. Grefenstette (1991b) gives some further caveats concerning this description of GA behavior. In particular, he points out that, at each new generation, selection most likely produces a new set of biases in the way schemas are sampled (as in the fitness function given by equation 4.5 above). Since the Schema Theorem gives the dynamics of schema sampling over only one time step, it is difficult (if not impossible), without making unrealistic assumptions, to make any long-range prediction about how the allocation of trials to different schemas will proceed. Because of the biases introduced by selection, the static average fitnesses of schemas will not necessarily be correlated in any useful way with their observed average fitnesses.

Implications for GA Performance

In view of the solution to the Two-Armed Bandit problem, the exponential allocation of trials is clearly an appropriate strategy for problems in which "on-line" performance is important, such as real-time control problems. Less clear is its appropriateness for problems with other performance criteria, such as "Is the optimal individual reliably discovered in a reasonable time?" There have been many cases in the GA literature in which such criteria have been applied, sometimes leading to the conclusion that GAs don't work. This demonstrates the importance of understanding what a particular algorithm is good at doing before applying it to particular problems. This point was made eloquently in the context of GAs by De Jong (1993).

What is maximizing on-line performance good for? Holland's view is clear: the rough maximization of on-line performance is what goes on in adaptive systems of all kinds, and in some sense this is how "adaptation" is defined. In the realm of technology, on-line performance is important in control problems (e.g., automatically controlling machinery) and in learning problems (e.g., learning to navigate in an environment) in which each system action can lead to a gain or loss. It is also important in prediction tasks (e.g., predicting financial markets) in which gains or losses are had with each prediction. Most of the GA applications I discussed in chapter 2 had a slightly different performance criterion: to find a "reasonably good" (if not perfect) solution in a reasonable amount of time. In other words, the goal is to *satisfice* (find a solution that is good enough for one's purposes) rather than to optimize (find the best possible solution). This goal is related to maximizing on-line performance, since on-line performance will be maximized if high-fitness individuals are likely to be chosen at each step, including the last. The two-armed-bandit allocation strategy maximizes both cumulative payoff and the amount of information the gambler gets for her money as to which is the better arm. In the context of schemas, the exponential allocation strategy could be said to maximize, for a given amount of time (samples), the amount of information gained about which part of the search space is likely to provide good solutions if sampled in the future. Gaining such information is crucial to successful satisficing. For true optimization, hybrid methods such as a GA augmented by a hill climber or other kinds of gradient search have often been found to perform better than a GA alone (see, e.g., Hart and Belew 1996). GAs seem to be good at quickly finding promising regions of the search space, and hill climbers are often good at zeroing in on optimal individuals in those regions.

Although the foregoing schema analysis has suggested the types of problems for which a genetic algorithm might be useful, it does not answer more detailed questions, such as "Given a certain version of the GA, what is the expected time to find a particular fitness level?" Some approaches to such questions will be described below.

Deceiving a Genetic Algorithm

The theory of schemas has been used by some in the GA community to propose an answer to "What makes a problem hard for a GA?" As described above, the view is that competition among schemas roughly proceeds from low-order schema partitions at early times to higher-order schema partitions at later times. Bethke (1980) reasoned that it will be hard for a GA to find the optimum of a fitness function if low-order partitions contain misleading information about higher-order partitions. The following extreme example illustrates this. Call a schema H a "winner" if its static average fitness is highest in its partition. Suppose that any schema whose defined bits are all ones is a winner except for the length L schema $1111\cdots1$, and let $0000\cdots0$ be a winner. In principle, it should be hard for a GA to find $0000\cdots0$, since every lower-order partition gives misleading information about where the optimum is likely to be found. Such a fitness function is termed "fully deceptive." (The term "deceptive" was introduced by Goldberg (1987).) Fitness functions with lesser amounts of deception are also possible (i.e., some partitions give correct information about the location of the optimum). Bethke used "Walsh Transforms"—similar to Fourier transforms—to design fitness functions with various degrees of deception. For reviews of this work, see Goldberg 1989b,c and Forrest and Mitchell 1993a.

Subsequent to Bethke's work, Goldberg and his colleagues carried out a number of theoretical studies of deception in fitness functions, and deception has become a central focus of theoretical work on GAs. (See, e.g., Das and Whitley 1991; Deb and Goldberg 1993; Goldberg 1989c; Liepins and Vose 1990, 1991; Whitley 1991.)

It should be noted that the study of GA deception is generally concerned with function optimization; the deception in a fitness function is assumed to make it difficult to find a global optimum. In view of the widespread use of GAs as function optimizers, deception can be an important factor for GA practitioners to understand. However, if one takes the view that GAs are not function optimizers but rather "satisficers" or payoff maximizers, then deception may be less of a concern. As De Jong (1993, p. 15) puts it, the GA (as formulated by Holland) "is attempting to maximize *cumulative* payoff from arbitrary landscapes, deceptive or otherwise. In general, this is achieved by not investing too much effort in finding cleverly hidden peaks (the risk/reward ratio is too high)."

Limitations of "Static" Schema Analysis

A number of recent papers have questioned the relevance of schema analysis to the understanding of real GAs (e.g., Grefenstette 1993; Mason 1993; Peck and Dhawan 1993). Here I will focus on Grefenstette's critique of the "Static Building Block Hypothesis."

The following qualitative formulation of the Schema Theorem and the Building Block Hypothesis should now be familiar to the reader: The simple GA increases the number of instances of low-order, short-defining-length, high-observed-fitness schemas via the multi-armed-bandit strategy, and these schemas serve as building blocks that are combined, via crossover, into candidate solutions with increasingly higher order and higher observed fitness. The rationale for this strategy is based on the assumption that the observed and static fitnesses of schemas are correlated; some potential problems with this assumption have been pointed out in the previous sections.

Grefenstette (1993, p. 78) claims that much work on GA theory has assumed a stronger version that he calls the "Static Building Block Hypothesis" (SBBH): "Given any low-order, short-defining-length hyperplane [i.e., schema] partition, a GA is expected to converge to the hyperplane [in that partition] with the best static average fitness (the 'expected winner')." This is stronger than the original formulation, since it states that the GA will converge on the *actual* winners of each short, low-order partition competition rather than on the schemas with the best *observed* fitness. The SBBH was not what Holland (1975) proposed, and it has never been proved or even empirically validated, but it implicitly underlies the assumption that deceptive fitness functions will be difficult for a GA.

Grefenstette gives two possible reasons, related to his earlier concerns about the two-armed-bandit analogy, why the SBBH can fail:

Collateral convergence   Once the population begins to converge at some loci, the samples of some schemas are no longer uniform. For example, suppose instances of $111 * \cdots *$ are highly fit and the population has more or less converged on those bits (i.e., nearly every member of the population is an instance of that schema). Then almost all samples of, say $* * *000 * \cdots *$ will actually be samples of $111000 * \cdots *$. This may prevent the GA from making any accurate estimate of $u(* * *000 * \cdots *)$.

High fitness variance   If a schema's static average fitness has high variance, the GA may not be able to make an accurate estimate of this static average fitness. The fitness function given by equation 4.5 is an example of this: the variance of $1 * \cdots *$ is high, so the GA converges on the high-fitness subregions of it. As before, this biases all subsequent samples of this schema, preventing an accurate estimate of its static fitness.

These points bear directly on the relevance of deception to the behavior of GAs, since deceptive fitness functions are defined entirely in terms of the static average fitnesses of schemas. To illustrate the problems with this, Grefenstette gives examples of deceptive problems that are easy for GAs to optimize and of nondeceptive problems that are arbitrarily hard for GAs to optimize. He concludes that deception is neither necessary nor sufficient to cause difficulties for GAs, and that its relevance to the study of GAs remains to be demonstrated.

There is nothing to indicate that the features listed above harm search performance of GAs; they only demonstrate the danger of drawing conclusions about the expected behavior of GAs from the static average fitnesses of schemas. Instead, a more dynamic approach is needed that takes into account the biases introduced by selection at each generation. Such approaches are described in the next several sections.

4.2 ROYAL ROADS

Royal Road Functions

The Schema Theorem, by itself, addresses the positive effects of selection (allocating increasing samples of schemas with observed high performance) but only the negative aspects of crossover—that is, the extent to which it disrupts schemas. It does not address the question of how crossover works to recombine highly fit schemas, even though this is seen by many as the major source of the search power of genetic algorithms. The Building Block Hypothesis states that crossover combines short, observed high-performance schemas into increasingly fit candidate solutions, but does not give any detailed description of how this combination occurs.

To investigate schema processing and recombination in more detail, Stephanie Forrest, John Holland, and I designed a class of fitness landscapes, called Royal Road functions, that were meant to capture the essence of building blocks in an idealized form (Mitchell, Forrest, and Holland 1992; Forrest and Mitchell 1993b; Mitchell, Holland, and Forrest 1994).

The Building Block Hypothesis suggests two features of fitness landscapes that are particularly relevant to genetic algorithms: the presence of short, low-order, highly fit schemas; and the presence of intermediate "stepping stones"—intermediate-order higher-fitness schemas that result from combinations of the lower-order schemas and that, in turn, can combine to create even higher-fitness schemas.

A fitness function (Royal Road R_1) that explicitly contains these features is illustrated in figure 4.1. R_1 is defined using a list of schemas s_i. Each s_i is given with a coefficient c_i. The fitness $R_1(x)$ of a bit string x is defined as

$$R_1(x) = \sum_i c_i \delta_i(x), \quad \text{where } \delta_i(x) = \begin{cases} 1 & \text{if } x \in s_i \\ 0 & \text{otherwise.} \end{cases}$$

For example, if x is an instance of exactly two of the order-8 schemas, $R_1(x) = 16$. Likewise, $R_1(111\cdots1) = 64$.

$s_1 = 11111111$**; $c_1 = 8$
$s_2 = $********$11111111$**; $c_2 = 8$
$s_3 = $****************$11111111$**********************************; $c_3 = 8$
$s_4 = $************************$11111111$**************************; $c_4 = 8$
$s_5 = $********************************11111111******************; $c_5 = 8$
$s_6 = $**$11111111$**********; $c_6 = 8$
$s_7 = $**$11111111$**; $c_7 = 8$
$s_8 = $**$11111111$; $c_8 = 8$
$s_{opt}=$1111111111111111111111111111111111111111111111111111111111111111

Figure 4.1 An optimal string broken up into eight building blocks. The function $R_1(x)$ (where x is a bit string) is computed by summing the coefficients c_s corresponding to each of the given schemas of which x is an instance. For example, $R_1(1111111100\ldots0) = 8$, and $R_1(1111111100\ldots011111111) = 16$. Here $c_s = order(s)$.

Given the Building Block Hypothesis, one might expect that the building-block structure of R_1 will lay out a "royal road" for the GA to follow to the optimal string. One might also expect that the GA will outperform simple hill-climbing schemes, since a large number of bit positions must be optimized simultaneously in order to move from an instance of a lower-order schema (e.g., $11111111 * * \cdots *$) to an instance of a higher-order intermediate schema (e.g., $11111111 * * * * * * * *11111111 * * \cdots *$). However, as will be described below, these expectations were overturned.

Experimental Results

We ran a genetic algorithm on R_1 with a population size of 128, and with the initial population generated at random. We used a simple GA with one modification: "sigma truncation" selection was used instead of proportional selection to assign the expected number of offspring to each individual. In our scheme, each individual i's expected number of offspring is

$$1 + (F_i - \bar{F})/2\sigma,$$

where F_i is i's fitness, $\bar{F}$ is the mean fitness of the population, and σ is the standard deviation of the fitnesses in the population. The number of expected offspring of any string was cut off at 1.5—if the above formula gave a higher value, the value was reset to 1.5. This is a strict cutoff, since it implies that most individuals will reproduce only 0, 1, or 2 times. The effect of this selection scheme is to slow down convergence by restricting the effect that a single individual can have on the population, regardless of how much fitter it is than the rest of the population. The single-point crossover rate was 0.7 per pair of parents and the bitwise mutation rate was 0.005.

We compared the GA's performance on R_1 to those of three different iterated hill-climbing methods:

Steepest-ascent hill climbing (SAHC)

1. Choose a string at random. Call this string *current-hilltop*.

2. Going from left to right, systematically flip each bit in the string, one at a time, recording the fitnesses of the resulting one-bit mutants.

3. If any of the resulting one-bit mutants give a fitness increase, then set *current-hilltop* to the one-bit mutant giving the highest fitness increase. (Ties are decided at random.)

4. If there is no fitness increase, then save *current-hilltop* and go to step 1. Otherwise, go to step 2 with the new *current-hilltop*.

5. When a set number of function evaluations has been performed (here, each bit flip in step 2 is followed by a function evaluation), return the highest hilltop that was found.

Next-ascent hill climbing (NAHC)

1. Choose a string at random. Call this string *current-hilltop*.

2. For i from 1 to l (where l is the length of the string), flip bit i; if this results in a fitness increase, keep the new string, otherwise flip bit i back. As soon as a fitness increase is found, set *current-hilltop* to that increased-fitness string without evaluating any more bit flips of the original string. Go to step 2 with the new *current-hilltop*, but continue mutating the new string starting immediately after the bit position at which the previous fitness increase was found.

3. If no increases in fitness were found, save *current-hilltop* and go to step 1.

4. When a set number of function evaluations has been performed, return the highest hilltop that was found.

Random-mutation hill climbing (RMHC)

1. Choose a string at random. Call this string *best-evaluated*.

2. Choose a locus at random to flip. If the flip leads to an equal or higher fitness, then set *best-evaluated* to the resulting string.

3. Go to step 2 until an optimum string has been found or until a maximum number of evaluations have been performed.

4. Return the current value of *best-evaluated*.

(This is similar to a zero-temperature Metropolis method.)

We performed 200 runs of each algorithm, each run starting with a different random-number seed. In each run the algorithm was allowed to continue until the optimum string was discovered, and the total number of function evaluations performed was recorded. The mean and the median number of function evaluations to find the optimum string are

Table 4.1 Mean and median number of function evaluations to find the optimum string over 200 runs of the GA and of various hill-climbing algorithms on R_1. The standard error ($\sigma/\sqrt{\text{number of runs}}$) is given in parentheses.

200 runs	GA	SAHC	NAHC	RMHC
Mean	61,334 (2304)	> 256,000 (0)	> 256,000 (0)	6179 (186)
Median	54,208	> 256,000	> 256,000	5775

given in table 4.1. We compare the mean and the median number of function evaluations to find the optimum string rather than mean and median absolute run time, because in almost all GA applications (e.g., evolving neural-network architectures) the time to perform a function evaluation vastly exceeds the time required to execute other parts of the algorithm. For this reason, we consider all parts of the algorithm other than the function evaluations to take negligible time.

The results of SAHC and NAHC were as expected—whereas the GA found the optimum on R_1 in an average of 61,334 function evaluations, neither SAHC nor NAHC ever found the optimum within the maximum of 256,000 function evaluations. However, RMHC found the optimum on R_1 in an average of 6179 function evaluations—nearly a factor of 10 faster than the GA. This striking difference on landscapes originally designed to be "royal roads" for the GA underscores the need for a rigorous answer to the question posed earlier: "Under what conditions will a genetic algorithm outperform other search algorithms, such as hill climbing?"

Analysis of Random-Mutation Hill Climbing

To begin to answer this question, we analyzed the RMHC algorithm with respect to R_1. (Our analysis is similar to that given for a similar problem on page 210 of Feller 1968.) Suppose the fitness function consists of N adjacent blocks of K ones each (in R_1, $N = 8$ and $K = 8$). What is the expected time (number of function evaluations), $\mathcal{E}(K, N)$, for RMHC to find the optimum string of all ones?

Let $\mathcal{E}(K, 1)$ be the expected time to find a single block of K ones. Once it has been found, the time to discover a second block is longer, since some fraction of the function evaluations will be "wasted" on testing mutations inside the first block. These mutations will never lead to a higher or equal fitness, since once a first block is already set to all ones, any mutation to those bits will decrease the fitness. The proportion of *nonwasted* mutations is $(KN - K)/KN$; this is the proportion of mutations that occur in the $KN - K$ positions outside the first block. The expected time $\mathcal{E}(K, 2)$ to find a second block is

$$\mathcal{E}(K, 2) = \mathcal{E}(K, 1) + \mathcal{E}(K, 1)[KN/(KN - K)]$$

$$= \mathcal{E}(K, 1) + \mathcal{E}(K, 1)N/(N - 1).$$

(If the algorithm spends only $1/m$ of its time in useful mutations, it will require m times as long to accomplish what it could if no mutations were wasted.) Similarly,

$$\mathcal{E}(K, 3) = \mathcal{E}(K, 2) + \mathcal{E}(K, 1)(N/(N-2)),$$

and so on. Continuing in this manner, we derive an expression for the total expected time:

$$\mathcal{E}(K, N) = \mathcal{E}(K, 1) + \mathcal{E}(K, 1)\frac{N}{N-1} + \cdots + \mathcal{E}(K, 1)\frac{N}{N-(N-1)}$$

$$= \mathcal{E}(K, 1)N\left(1 + \frac{1}{2} + \frac{1}{3} + \cdots + \frac{1}{N}\right). \tag{4.6}$$

(The actual value is a bit larger, since $\mathcal{E}(K, 1)$ is the expected time to the first block, whereas $\mathcal{E}(K, N)$ depends on the worst time for the N blocks (Richard Palmer, personal communication).) By a well-known identity, the right side of equation 4.6 can be written as $\mathcal{E}(K, 1)N(\ln N + \gamma)$, where $\ln N$ is the natural logarithm of N and $\gamma \approx 0.5772$ is Euler's constant.

Now we only need to find $\mathcal{E}(K, 1)$. A Markov-chain analysis (not given here) yields $\mathcal{E}(K, 1)$ slightly larger than 2^K, converging slowly to 2^K from above as $K \to \infty$ (Richard Palmer, personal communication). For example, for $K = 8$, $\mathcal{E}(K, 1) = 301.2$. For $K = 8$, $N = 8$, the value of equation 4.6 is 6549. When we ran RMHC on R_1 function 200 times, the average number of function evaluations to the optimum was 6179, which agrees reasonably well with the expected value.

Hitchhiking in the Genetic Algorithm

What caused our GA to perform so badly on R_1 relative to RMHC? One reason was "hitchhiking": once an instance of a higher-order schema is discovered, its high fitness allows the schema to spread quickly in the population, with zeros in other positions in the string hitchhiking along with the ones in the schema's defined positions. This slows the discovery of schemas in the other positions, especially those that are close to the highly fit schema's defined positions. In short, hitchhiking seriously limits the implicit parallelism of the GA by restricting the schemas sampled at certain loci.

The effects of hitchhiking are strikingly illustrated in figure 4.2. The percentage of the population that is an instance of s_i is plotted versus generation for s_1–s_8 for a typical run of the GA on R_1. On this run the schemas s_2, s_4, and s_8 each had two instances in the initial population; none of the other five schemas was present initially. These schemas confer high fitness on their instances, and, as can be seen in figure 4.2, the number of instances grows very quickly. However, the original instances of s_2 and s_4 had a number of zeros in the s_3 loci, and these zeros tended to get passed on to the offspring of instances of s_2 and s_4 along with the desired blocks

Theoretical Foundations of Genetic Algorithms

of ones. (The most likely positions for hitchhikers are those close to the highly fit schema's defined positions, since they are less likely to be separated from the schema's defined positions under crossover.)

These hitchhikers prevented independent sampling in the s_3 partition; instead, most samples (strings) contained the hitchhikers. As figure 4.2 shows, an instance of s_3 was discovered early in the run and was followed by a modest increase in number of instances. However, zeros hitchhiking on instances of s_2 and s_4 then quickly drowned out the instances of s_3. The very fast increase in strings containing these hitchhikers presumably slowed the rediscovery of s_3; even when it was rediscovered, its instances again were drowned out by the instances of s_2 and s_4 that contained the hitchhikers. The same problem, to a less dramatic degree, is seen for s_1 and s_6. The effectiveness of crossover in combining building blocks is limited by early convergence to the wrong schemas in a number of partitions. This seems to be one of the major reasons for the GA's poor performance on R_1 relative to RMHC.

We observed similar effects in several variations of our original GA. Hitchhiking in GAs (which can cause serious bottlenecks) should not be too surprising: such effects are seen in real population genetics. Hitchhiking in GAs (also called "spurious correlation") has previously been discussed by Schraudolph and Belew (1992), Das and Whitley (1991), and Schaffer, Eshelman, and Offutt (1991), among others.

An Idealized Genetic Algorithm

Why would we ever expect a GA to outperform RMHC on a landscape like R_1? In principle, because of implicit parallelism and crossover. If implicit parallelism works correctly on R_1, then each of the schemas competing in the relevant partitions in R_1 should have a reasonable probability of receiving some samples at each generation—in particular, the schemas with eight adjacent ones in the defining bits should have a reasonable probability of receiving some samples. This amounts to saying that the sampling in each schema region in R_1 has to be reasonably independent of the sampling in other, nonoverlapping schema regions. In our GA this was being prevented by hitchhiking—in the run represented in figure 4.2, the samples in the s_3 region were not independent of those in the s_2 and s_4 regions.

In RMHC the successive strings examined produce far from independent samples in each schema region: each string differs from the previous string in only one bit. However, it is the constant, systematic exploration, bit by bit, never losing what has been found, that gives RMHC the edge over our GA.

Under a GA, if each partition were sampled independently and the best schema in each partition tended to be selected—most likely on differ-

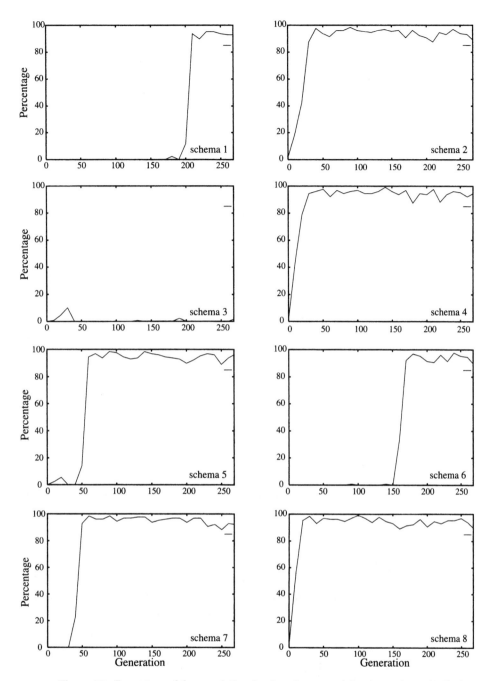

Figure 4.2 Percentage of the population that is an instance of the given schema (1–8) plotted versus generation for a typical GA run on R_1. The data are plotted every 10 generations.

ent strings—then in principle crossover should quickly combine the best schemas in different partitions to be on the same string. This is basically the "Static Building Block Hypothesis" described above. The problems encountered by our GA on R_1 illustrate very clearly the kinds of "biased sampling" problems described by Grefenstette (1991b).

Would an "idealized genetic algorithm" that actually worked according to the SBBH be faster than RMHC? If so, is there any way we could make a real genetic algorithm work more like the idealized genetic algorithm?

To answer this, we defined an idealized genetic algorithm (IGA) as follows (Mitchell, Holland, and Forrest 1994). (Note that there is no population here; the IGA works on one string at a time. Nonetheless, it captures the essential properties of a GA that satisfies the SBBH.)

On each time step, choose a new string at random, with uniform probability for each bit.

The first time a string is found that contains one or more of the desired schemas, sequester that string.

When a string containing one or more not-yet-discovered schemas is found, instantaneously cross over the new string with the sequestered string so that the sequestered string contains all the desired schemas that have been discovered so far.

How does the IGA capture the essentials of a GA that satisfies the SBBH? Since each new string is chosen completely independently, all schemas are sampled independently. Selection is modeled by sequestering strings that contain desired schemas. And crossover is modeled by instantaneous crossover between strings containing desired schemas. The IGA is, of course, unusable in practice, since it requires knowing precisely what the desired schemas are, whereas in general (as in the GA and in RMHC) an algorithm can only measure the fitness of a string and does not know ahead of time what schemas make for good fitness. But analyzing the IGA can give us a lower bound on the time any GA would take to find the optimal string of R_1. Suppose again that our desired schemas consist of N blocks of K ones each. What is the expected time (number of function evaluations) until the sequestered string contains all the desired schemas? (Here one function evaluation corresponds to the choice of one string.) Solutions have been suggested by Greg Huber and by Alex Shevoroskin (personal communications), and a detailed solution has been given by Holland (1993). Here I will sketch Huber's solution.

First consider a *single* desired schema H (i.e., $N = 1$). Let p be the probability of finding H on a random string (here $p = 1/2^K$). Let q be the probability of not finding H: $q = 1 - p$. Then the probability $\mathcal{P}_1(t)$ that H will be found by time t (that is, at any time step between 0 and t) is

$\mathcal{P}_1(t) = 1 -$ Probability that H will *not* be found by time t

$$= 1 - q^t.$$

Now consider the case with N desired schemas. Let $\mathcal{P}_N(t)$ be the probability that all N schemas have been found by time t:

$$\mathcal{P}_N(t) = (1 - q^t)^N.$$

$\mathcal{P}_N(t)$ gives the probability that all N schemas will be found *sometime* in the interval $[0, t]$. However, we do not want $\mathcal{P}_N(t)$; we want the expected time to find all N schemas. Thus, we need the probability $P_N(t)$ that the last of the N desired schemas will be found at exactly time t. This is equivalent to the probability that the last schema will not be found by time $t - 1$ but will be found by time t:

$$P_N(t) = \mathcal{P}_N(t) - \mathcal{P}_N(t - 1)$$

$$= (1 - q^t)^N - (1 - q^{t-1})^N.$$

To get the expected time $\mathcal{E}_N$ from this probability, we sum over t times the probability:

$$\mathcal{E}_N = \sum_{t=1}^{\infty} t \; P_N(t)$$

$$= \sum_{t=1}^{\infty} t \; ((1 - q^t)^N - (1 - q^{t-1})^N).$$

The expression $(1 - q^t)^N - (1 - q^{t-1})^N$ can be expanded in powers of q via the binomial theorem and becomes

$$\left[\binom{N}{1} \left(\frac{1}{q} - 1 \right) q^t \right] - \left[\binom{N}{2} \left(\frac{1}{q^2} - 1 \right) q^{2t} \right]$$

$$+ \left[\binom{N}{3} \left(\frac{1}{q^3} - 1 \right) q^{3t} \right] - \cdots - \left[\binom{N}{N} \left(\frac{1}{q^N} - 1 \right) q^{Nt} \right].$$

(N is arbitrarily assumed to be even; hence the minus sign before the last term.)

Now this entire expression must be multiplied by t and summed from 1 to ∞. We can split this infinite sum into the sum of N infinite sums, one from each of the N terms in the expression above. The infinite sum over the first term is

$$\binom{N}{1}\left(\frac{1}{q}-1\right)\sum_{t=1}^{\infty} t q^t$$

$$=\binom{N}{1}\left(\frac{1}{q}-1\right)\left(q+2q^2+3q^3+\cdots\right)$$

$$=\binom{N}{1}\left(\frac{1}{q}-1\right)q\left(1+2q+3q^2+\cdots\right)$$

$$=\binom{N}{1}\left(\frac{1}{q}-1\right)q\frac{d}{dq}\left(q+q^2+q^3+\cdots\right)$$

$$=\binom{N}{1}\left(\frac{1}{q}-1\right)q\frac{d}{dq}\left(\frac{q}{1-q}\right) \qquad \text{(using a well-known identity}$$
$$\text{for } 0\le q<1)$$

$$=\binom{N}{1}\left(\frac{1}{q}-1\right)q\left(\frac{1}{1-q}\right)^2$$

$$=\binom{N}{1}\frac{1}{1-q}.$$

Similarly, the infinite sum over the nth term of the sum can be shown to be

$$\binom{N}{n}\frac{1}{1-q^n}.$$

Recall that $q=1-p$, and $p=1/2^K$. If we substitute $1-p$ for q and assume that p is small so that $q^n=(1-p)^n\approx 1-np$, we obtain the following approximation:

$$\mathcal{E}_N\approx\frac{1}{p}\left[\frac{\binom{N}{1}}{1}-\frac{\binom{N}{2}}{2}+\frac{\binom{N}{3}}{3}-\cdots-\frac{\binom{N}{N}}{N}\right]. \tag{4.7}$$

For $N=8$, $K=8$ the approximation gives an expected time of approximately 696, which is the exact result we obtained as the mean over 200 runs of a simulation of the IGA (Mitchell, Holland, and Forrest 1994). (The standard error was 19.7.)

The sum in the brackets in equation 4.7 can be evaluated using the following identity derived from the binomial theorem and from integrating $(1+x)^N$:

$$\sum_{n=1}^{N}\binom{N}{n}\frac{x^n}{n}=\sum_{n=1}^{N}\frac{1}{n}[(1+x)^n-1].$$

Let $x=-1$. Then we can simplify equation 4.7 as follows:

$$\varepsilon_N \approx -\frac{1}{p} \sum_{n=1}^{N} \binom{N}{n} \frac{(-1)^n}{n}$$

$$= \frac{1}{p} \sum_{n=1}^{N} \frac{1}{n}$$

$$\approx \frac{1}{p} (\ln N + \gamma)$$

$$= 2^K (\ln N + \gamma).$$

Setting aside the details of this analysis, the major point is that the IGA gives an expected time that is on the order of $2^K \ln N$, whereas RMHC gives an expected time that is on the order of $2^K N \ln N$—a factor of N slower. This kind of analysis can help us understand how and when the GA will outperform hill climbing.

What makes the IGA faster than RMHC? To recap, the IGA perfectly implements implicit parallelism: each new string is completely independent of the previous one, so new samples are given independently to each schema region. In contrast, RMHC moves in the space of strings by single-bit mutations from an original string, so each new sample has all but one of the same bits as the previous sample. Thus, each new string gives a new sample to only one schema region. The IGA spends more time than RMHC constructing new samples; however, since we are counting only function evaluations, we ignore the construction time. The IGA "cheats" on each function evaluation, since it knows exactly what the desired schemas are, but in this way it gives a lower bound on the number of function evaluations that the GA will need.

Independent sampling allows for a speedup in the IGA in two ways: it allows for the possibility that multiple schemas will appear simultaneously on a given sample, and it means that there are no wasted samples as there are in RMHC (i.e., mutations in blocks that have already been set correctly). Although the comparison we have made is with RMHC, the IGA will also be significantly faster on R_1 (and similar landscapes) than any hill-climbing method that works by mutating single bits (or a small number of bits) to obtain new samples.

The hitchhiking effects described earlier also result in a loss of independent samples for the GA. The goal is to have the GA, as much as possible, approximate the IGA. Of course, the IGA works because it explicitly knows what the desired schemas are; the GA does not have this information and can only estimate what the desired schemas are by an implicit sampling procedure. But it is possible for the GA to approximate a number of the features of the IGA:

Independent samples The population has to be large enough, the selection process has to be slow enough, and the mutation rate has to be sufficiently high to make sure that no single locus is fixed at a single value in every string in the population, or even in a large majority of strings.

Sequestering desired schemas Selection has to be strong enough to preserve desired schemas that have been discovered, but it also has to be slow enough (or, equivalently, the relative fitness of the nonoverlapping desirable schemas has to be small enough) to prevent significant hitchhiking on some highly fit schemas, which can crowd out desired schemas in other parts of the string.

Instantaneous crossover The crossover rate has to be such that the time for a crossover that combines two desired schemas to occur is small with respect to the discovery time for the desired schemas.

Speedup over RMHC The string has to be long enough to make the factor of N speedup significant.

These mechanisms are not all mutually compatible (e.g., high mutation works against sequestering schemas), and thus they must be carefully balanced against one another. These balances are discussed in Holland 1993, and work on using such analyses to improve the GA is reported in Mitchell, Holland, and Forrest 1994.

4.3 EXACT MATHEMATICAL MODELS OF SIMPLE GENETIC ALGORITHMS

The theory of schemas makes predictions about the expected change in frequencies of schemas from one generation to the next, but it does not directly make predictions concerning the population composition, the speed of population convergence, or the distribution of fitnesses in the population over time. As a first step in obtaining a more detailed understanding of and making more detailed predictions about the behavior of GAs, several researchers have constructed "exact" mathematical models of simple GAs (see, e.g., Goldberg 1987; Goldberg and Segrest 1987; Davis and Principe 1991; Vose and Liepins 1991; Nix and Vose 1991; Horn 1993; Vose 1993; Whitley 1993a). These exact models capture every detail of the simple GA in mathematical operators; thus, once the model is constructed, it is possible to prove theorems about certain interesting properties of these operators. In this section I will sketch the model developed by Vose and Liepins (1991) and summarize extensions made by Nix and Vose (1991) and by Vose (1993).

Formalization of GAs

The mathematicians Michael Vose and Gunar Liepins (1991) developed a formal model based on the following simple GA: Start with a random population of binary strings of length l.

1. Calculate the fitness $f(x)$ of each string x in the population.

2. Choose (with replacement) two parents from the current population with probability proportional to each string's relative fitness in the population.

3. Cross over the two parents (at a single randomly chosen point) with probability p_c to form two offspring. (If no crossover occurs, the offspring are exact copies of the parents.) Select one of the offspring at random and discard the other.

4. Mutate each bit in the selected offspring with probability p_m, and place it in the new population.

5. Go to step 2 until a new population is complete.

6. Go to step 1.

The only difference between this and the standard simple GA is that only one offspring from each crossover survives. Thus, for population size n, a total of n recombination events take place. (This modification simplifies parts of the formalization.)

In the formal model of Vose and Liepins, each string in the search space is represented by the integer i between 0 and $2^l - 1$ encoded by the string. For example, for $l = 8$, the string 00000111 would be represented by the integer 7. The population at generation t is represented by two real-valued vectors, $\vec{p}(t)$ and $\vec{s}(t)$, each of length 2^l. The ith component of $\vec{p}(t)$ (denoted $p_i(t)$) is the proportion of the population at generation t consisting of string i, and the ith component of $\vec{s}(t)$ (denoted $s_i(t)$) is the probability that an instance of string i will be selected to be a parent at step 2 in the simple GA given above. For example, if $l = 2$ and the population consists of two copies of 11 and one copy each of 01 and 10,

$$\vec{p}(t) = (0, 0.25, 0.25, 0.5).$$

If the fitness is equal to the number of ones in the string,

$$\vec{s}(t) = (0, 0.1667, 0.1667, 0.6667).$$

(For the purpose of matrix multiplication these vectors will be assumed to be column vectors, though they will often be written as row vectors.)

The vector $\vec{p}(t)$ exactly specifies the composition of the population at generation t, and $\vec{s}(t)$ reflects the selection probabilities under the fitness function. These are connected via fitness: let F be a two-dimensional matrix such that $F_{i,j} = 0$ for $i \neq j$ and $F_{i,i} = f(i)$. That is, every entry of F is 0 except the diagonal entries (i, i), which give the fitness of the corresponding string i. Under proportional selection,

$$\vec{s}(t) = \frac{F\vec{p}(t)}{\sum_{j=0}^{2^l-1} F_{jj} p_j(t)}. \tag{4.8}$$

(This is simply the definition of proportional selection.) Thus, given $\vec{p}(t)$ and F, we can easily find $\vec{s}(t)$, and vice versa. Vose and Liepins presented most of their results in terms of $\vec{s}(t)$.

Given these preliminaries, Vose and Liepins's strategy is to define a single "operator" G such that applying G to $\vec{s}(t)$ will exactly mimic the expected effects of running the GA on the population at generation t to form the population at generation $t + 1$:

$$\vec{s}(t+1) = G\vec{s}(t). \tag{4.9}$$

Then iterating G on $\vec{s}(0)$ will give an exact description of the expected behavior of the GA. (This is quite similar to the types of models developed in population genetics by Fisher and others; see, e.g., Ewens 1979.)

To make this clearer, suppose that the GA is operating with selection alone (no crossover or mutation). Let $E(x)$ denote the expectation of x. Then, since $s_i(t)$ is the probability that i will be selected at each selection step,

$$E(\vec{p}(t+1)) = \vec{s}(t).$$

Let $\vec{x} \sim \vec{y}$ mean that $\vec{x}$ and $\vec{y}$ differ only by a scalar factor. Then, from equation 4.8, we have

$$\vec{s}(t+1) \sim F\vec{p}(t+1),$$

which means

$$E(\vec{s}(t+1)) \sim F\vec{s}(t).$$

This is the type of relation we want (i.e., of the form in equation 4.9), with $G = F$ for this case of selection alone.

These results give expectation values only; in any finite population, sampling errors will cause deviation from the expected values. In the limit of an infinite population, the expectation results are exact.

Vose and Liepins included crossover and mutation in the model by defining G as the composition of the fitness matrix F and a "recombination operator" $\mathcal{M}$ that mimics the effects of crossover and mutation. (Vose and Liepins use the term "recombination" to encompass both the crossover and mutation step. I will adopt this usage for the remainder of this section.) One way to define $\mathcal{M}$ is to find $r_{i,j}(k)$, the probability that string

k will be produced by a recombination event between string i and string j, given that i and j are selected to mate. If $r_{i,j}(k)$ were known, we could compute

$$E(p_k(t+1)) = \sum_{i,j} s_i(t)s_j(t)r_{i,j}(k).$$

In words, this means that the expected proportion of string k in generation $t+1$ is the probability that it will be produced by each given pair of parents, times those parents' probabilities of being selected, summed over all possible pairs of parents.

Defining $r_{i,j}(k)$ and $\mathcal{M}$ is somewhat tricky. Vose and Liepins first defined a simpler matrix M whose elements $M_{i,j}$ give the probability $r_{i,j}(0)$ that string 0 (i.e., the string of all zeros) will be produced by a recombination event between string i and string j, given that i and j are selected to mate. I will go through this construction in detail so readers less familiar with probability theory can see how such constructions are done. (Other readers may wish to attempt it themselves before reading the following.) Once $r_{i,j}(0)$ is defined, it can be used in a clever way to define the general case.

The expression for $r_{i,j}(0)$ is equal to the sum of two terms: the probability that crossover does not occur between i and j and the selected offspring (i or j) is mutated to all zeros (first term) and the probability that crossover does occur and the selected offspring is mutated to all zeros (second term).

If i and j are selected to mate, the probability that crossover occurs between them is p_c and the probability that it does not occur is $1 - p_c$. Likewise, the probability that mutation occurs at each bit in the selected offspring is p_m and the probability that it does not occur is $1 - p_m$. If $|i|$ is the number of ones in a string i of length l, the probability that i will be mutated to all zeros is the probability that all of the $|i|$ ones will be mutated times the probability that none of the $(l - |i|)$ zeros will be mutated:

$$p_m^{|i|}(1 - p_m)^{l-|i|}.$$

The first term in the expression for $r_{i,j}(0)$ translates to

$$\tfrac{1}{2}(1 - p_c)[p_m^{|i|}(1 - p_m)^{l-|i|} + p_m^{|j|}(1 - p_m)^{l-|j|}].$$

Recall that, in this model, only one offspring is selected for the next population. The factor $\tfrac{1}{2}$ indicates that each of the two offspring has equal probability of being selected.

For the second term, let h and k denote the two offspring produced from a crossover at point c (counted from the right-hand side of the string; see figure 4.3). Note that there are $l - 1$ possible crossover points, so the probability of choosing point c is $1/(l - 1)$. The second term can then be written as

Theoretical Foundations of Genetic Algorithms

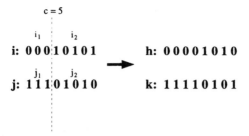

$$c = 5$$

$i_1 \qquad i_2$

i: 000|10101   **h: 00001010**

$j_1 \qquad j_2$

j: 111|01010   **k: 11110101**

Figure 4.3 Illustration of c, i_1, i_2, j_1, and j_2.

$$\frac{1}{2}\frac{p_c}{l-1}\sum_{c=1}^{l-1}[p_m^{|h|}(1-p_m)^{l-|h|} + p_m^{|k|}(1-p_m)^{l-|k|}].$$

Again, the factor $\frac{1}{2}$ indicates that one of the two offspring is selected, with equal probability for each.

To complete this, we need only the expressions for $|h|$ and $|k|$. Let i_1 be the substring of i consisting of the $l - c$ bits to the left of point c, let i_2 be the substring consisting of the c bits to the right of point c, and let j_1 and j_2 be defined likewise for string j, as illustrated in figure 4.3. Then $|h| = |i| - |i_2| + |j_2|$, and $|k| = |j| - |j_2| + |i_2|$. Vose and Liepins simplify this with a nice trick of notation. First note that

$$|i_2| = |(2^c - 1) \wedge i|,$$

where $\wedge$ denotes bitwise "and." Since $2^c - 1$ represents the string with $l - c$ zeros followed by c ones, $|(2^c - 1) \wedge i|$ returns the number of ones in the rightmost c bits of i. Likewise,

$$|j_2| = |(2^c - 1) \wedge j|.$$

Let

$$\Delta_{i,j,c} = |i_2| - |j_2| = |(2^c - 1) \wedge i| - |(2^c - 1) \wedge j|.$$

Then $|h| = |i| - \Delta_{i,j,c}$ and $|k| = |j| + \Delta_{i,j,c}$.

We can now write down a complete expression for $r_{i,j}(0)$. To simplify, let $\eta = p_m/(1 - p_m)$. Then, after some algebra, we obtain

$$r_{i,j}(0) = \frac{(1 - p_m)^l}{2}\left[\eta^{|i|}\left(1 - p_c + \frac{p_c}{l-1}\sum_{c=1}^{l-1}\eta^{-\Delta_{i,j,c}}\right)\right.$$

$$\left. + \eta^{|j|}\left(1 - p_c + \frac{p_c}{l-1}\sum_{c=1}^{l-1}\eta^{\Delta_{i,i,c}}\right)\right] \qquad (4.10)$$

This gives the flavor of how this kind of analysis is done. With a clever use of logical operators and permutations (which is beyond the scope of this discussion), Vose and Liepins were able to express the general recombination operator $\mathcal{M}$ in terms of M. (See Vose and Liepins 1991 for details.)

Let $G(\vec{x}) = F \circ \mathcal{M}(\vec{x})$ for vectors $\vec{x}$, where $\circ$ is the composition operator. Then, in the limit of an infinite population,

$$G(\vec{s}(t)) \sim \vec{s}(t+1).$$

Define G_p as

$$G_p(\vec{x}) = \mathcal{M}(F\vec{x}/|F\vec{x}|),$$

where $|\vec{v}|$ denotes the sum of the components of vector $\vec{v}$. Then, in the limit of an infinite population,

$$G_p(\vec{p}(t)) = \vec{p}(t+1).$$

G and G_p act on different representations of the population, but one can be translated into the other by a simple transformation.

Results of the Formalization

How can this formalization help us to better understand or predict the GA's behavior? Vose and Liepins, viewing G as a dynamical system, formulated a geometric picture of the GA's behavior and then used it to prove some behavioral properties. The geometric picture is that the set of all possible $\vec{s}$ vectors form a surface S on which G acts to move from point to point. The initial point is $\vec{s}(0)$, and iterating G from this point forms a trajectory on S. In analyzing the dynamics of G, the first things to determine are the fixed points of G on S—i.e., the set of $\vec{s}(t)$ such that $G(\vec{s}(t)) = \vec{s}(t)$. In other words, we want to know what points $\vec{s}(t)$ have the property that, once the GA arrives there, it will not move away.

This general problem was not solved by Vose and Liepins (1991); instead they solved the separate problems of finding the fixed points of F and $\mathcal{M}$ and analyzing their properties. It is not difficult to show that the fixed points of F (selection alone) are the populations that have completely converged to strings of equal fitness. Vose and Liepins proved that only one class of these fixed points is stable: the set of fixed points corresponding to the maximally fit strings in the search space. In other words, if the population converges to a state that does not consist entirely of maximally fit strings, a small change in the fitness distribution of the population might result in movement away from that fixed point. However, if the population is maximally fit, then under any sufficiently small change in the fitness distribution, the GA will always return to that fixed point.

Vose and Liepins then showed that $\mathcal{M}$ working alone on $\vec{s}$ has only one fixed point: the vector $\vec{s}$ consisting of equal probabilities for all strings in the search space. Likewise, $\mathcal{M}$ working on $\vec{p}$ has one fixed point: all strings present in equal proportions. This means that, in the limit of an infinite population, crossover and mutation working in the absence of selection will eventually produce maximally "mixed" populations with equal occurrences of all strings.

Vose and Liepins left open the more difficult problem of putting F and $\mathcal{M}$ together to understand the interacting effects of crossover and mutation. However, they conjectured that the formalism could shed light on the "punctuated equilibria" behavior commonly seen in genetic algorithms—relatively long periods of no improvement punctuated by quick rises in fitness. The intuition is that such punctuated equilibria arise from the combination of the "focusing" properties of F and the "diffusing" properties of $\mathcal{M}$. The periods of "stasis" correspond to periods spent near one of the unstable fixed points, and the periods of rapid improvement correspond to periods spent moving (under the diffusing force of recombination) from the vicinity of one fixed point to another. (Note that even though a fixed point is unstable, a dynamical system can stay in its vicinity for some time.) These effects have yet to be rigorously quantified under this or any other model. (The notion of focusing and mixing forces working together in a GA is discussed in less technical detail in chapter 6 of Holland 1975.)

Vose and Liepins's formalization is an excellent first step toward a more rigorous understanding of and more rigorous predictions about simple GAs. (For further work on Vose and Liepins's model see Whitley 1993a.) However, one major drawback is that the formalization and its results assume an infinite population—that is, they are phrased in terms of expectations. Assuming an infinite population is an idealization that simplifies analysis; however, the behavior of finite populations can be very different as a result of sampling error.

A Finite-Population Model

The infinite-population case involves deterministic transitions from $\vec{p}(t)$ to $\vec{p}(t+1)$ and thus from $\vec{s}(t)$ to $\vec{s}(t+1)$—in an infinite population there are no sampling errors. In contrast, modeling a finite population requires taking account of the stochastic effects of sampling.

To address the finite-population case, Nix and Vose (1991) modeled the simple GA as a Markov chain. Markov chains are stochastic processes in which the probability that the process will be in state j at time t depends only on the state i at time $t-1$. Many processes in nature can be described as Markov chains. (For an introduction to the mathematics of Markov chains see Feller 1968.)

A "state" of a finite-population GA is simply a particular finite population. The set of all states is the set of possible populations of size n. These can be enumerated in some canonical order and indexed by i. Nix and

Vose represent the ith such population as a vector $\vec{\phi}_i$ of length 2^l. The yth element of $\vec{\phi}_i$ is the number of occurrences of string y in population P_i. It is clear that under the simple GA the current population P_j depends (stochastically) only on the population at the previous generation. Thus, the GA can be modeled as a Markov chain.

To construct such a model, we need to write down the probability of going from any given population to any other under the simple GA. The set of all possible populations of size n can be represented by a giant matrix, Z, in which the columns are all possible population vectors $\vec{\phi}_i$. How many possible populations of size n are there? The answer is

$$N = \binom{n + 2^l - 1}{2^l - 1}.$$

(Deriving this is left as an exercise.) A given element $Z_{y,i}$ of Z is the number of occurrences of string y in population i.

Here is a simple example of constructing the Z matrix: Let $l = 2$ and $n = 2$. The possible populations are

$$P_0 = \left\{\begin{matrix}00\\00\end{matrix}\right\}, \quad P_1 = \left\{\begin{matrix}00\\01\end{matrix}\right\}, \quad P_2 = \left\{\begin{matrix}00\\10\end{matrix}\right\}, \quad P_3 = \left\{\begin{matrix}00\\11\end{matrix}\right\}, \quad P_4 = \left\{\begin{matrix}01\\01\end{matrix}\right\},$$

$$P_5 = \left\{\begin{matrix}01\\10\end{matrix}\right\}, \quad P_6 = \left\{\begin{matrix}01\\11\end{matrix}\right\}, \quad P_7 = \left\{\begin{matrix}10\\10\end{matrix}\right\}, \quad P_8 = \left\{\begin{matrix}10\\11\end{matrix}\right\}, \quad P_9 = \left\{\begin{matrix}11\\11\end{matrix}\right\}.$$

The array Z is

$$Z = \begin{pmatrix} 2 & 1 & 1 & 1 & 0 & 0 & 0 & 0 & 0 & 0 \\ 0 & 1 & 0 & 0 & 2 & 1 & 1 & 0 & 0 & 0 \\ 0 & 0 & 1 & 0 & 0 & 1 & 0 & 2 & 1 & 0 \\ 0 & 0 & 0 & 1 & 0 & 0 & 1 & 0 & 1 & 2 \end{pmatrix}.$$

A state for the Markov chain corresponds to a column of Z.

The next step is to set up a Markov transition matrix Q. Q is an $N \times N$ matrix, and each element $Q_{i,j}$ is the probability that population P_j will be produced from population P_i under the simple GA. Once this matrix is defined, it can be used to derive some properties of the GA's behavior.

Writing down the transition probabilities $Q_{i,j}$ is a bit complicated but instructive. Let $p_i(y)$ be the probability that string y will be generated from the selection and recombination process (i.e., steps 3 and 4) of the simple GA acting on population P_i. The number of occurrences of string y in population P_j is $Z_{y,j}$, so the probability that the correct number comes from population P_i is simply the probability that $Z_{y,j}$ occurrences of y are produced from population P_i. This is equal to the probability that y is produced on $Z_{y,j}$ different selection-and-recombination steps times the number of ways in which these $Z_{y,j}$ different selection-and-recombination steps can occur during the total n selection-and-reproduction steps. Following Nix and Vose, we will enumerate this for each possible string.

Theoretical Foundations of Genetic Algorithms

The number of ways of choosing $Z_{0,j}$ occurrences of string 0 for the $Z_{0,j}$ slots in population j is

$$\binom{n}{Z_{0,j}}.$$

Selecting string 0 $Z_{0,j}$ times leaves $n - Z_{0,j}$ positions to fill in the new population. The number of ways of placing the $Z_{1,j}$ occurrences of string 1 in the $n - Z_{0,j}$ positions is

$$\binom{n - Z_{0,j}}{Z_{1,j}}.$$

Continuing this process, we can write down an expression for all possible ways of forming population P_j from a set of n selection-and-recombination steps:

$$\binom{n}{Z_{0,j}}\binom{n - Z_{0,j}}{Z_{1,j}} \cdots \binom{n - Z_{0,j} - Z_{1,j} - \cdots - Z_{2^l-2,j}}{Z_{2^l-1,j}}$$

$$= \frac{n!}{Z_{0,j}!Z_{1,j}! \cdots Z_{2^l-1,j}!}.$$

To form this expression, we enumerated the strings in order from 0 to $2^l - 1$. It is not hard to show that performing this calculation using a different order of strings yields the same answer.

The probability that the correct number of occurrences of each string y (in population P_j) is produced (from population P_i) is

$$\prod_{y=0}^{2^l-1} [p_i(y)]^{Z_{y,j}}.$$

The probability that population P_j is produced from population P_i is the product of the previous two expressions (forming a multinomial distribution):

$$Q_{i,j} = \frac{n!}{Z_{0,j}!Z_{1,j}! \cdots Z_{2^l-1,j}!} \prod_{y=0}^{2^l-1} [p_i(y)]^{Z_{y,j}} = n! \prod_{y=0}^{2^l-1} \frac{[p_i(y)]^{Z_{y,j}}}{Z_{y,j}!}.$$

The only thing remaining to do is derive an expression for $p_i(y)$, the probability that string y will be produced from a single selection-and-recombination step acting on population P_i. To do this, we can use the matrices F and $\mathcal{M}$ defined above. $p_i(y)$ is simply the expected proportion of string y in the population produced from P_i under the simple GA. The proportion of y in P_i is $(\vec{\phi}_i/|\vec{\phi}_i|)_y$, where $|\vec{v}|$ denotes the sum of the components of vector $\vec{v}$ and $(v)_y$ denotes the yth component of vector $\vec{v}$. The probability that y will be selected at each selection step is

$$\left(\frac{F\vec{\phi_i}}{|F\vec{\phi_i}|}\right)_y,$$

and the expected proportion of string y in the next population is

$$\left[\mathcal{M}\left(\frac{F\vec{\phi_i}}{|F\vec{\phi_i}|}\right)\right]_y.$$

Since $p_i(y)$ is equivalent to the expected proportion of string y in the next population, we can finally write down a finished expression for $Q_{i,j}$:

$$Q_{i,j} = n! \prod_{y=0}^{2^l-1} \frac{\left[\mathcal{M}\left(F\vec{\phi_i}/|F\vec{\phi_i}|\right)_y\right]^{Z_{y,j}}}{Z_{y,j}!}.$$

The matrix $Q_{i,j}$ gives an exact model of the simple GA acting on finite populations.

Nix and Vose used the theory of Markov chains to prove a number of results about this model. They showed, for example, that as $n \to \infty$ the trajectories of the Markov chain converge to the iterates of G (or G_p) with probability arbitrarily close to 1. This means that for very large n the infinite-population model comes close to mimicking the behavior of the finite-population GA. They also showed that, if G_p has a single fixed point, as $n \to \infty$ the GA asymptotically spends all its time at that fixed point. If G_p has more than one fixed point, then as $n \to \infty$, the time the GA spends away from the fixed points asymptotically goes to 0. For details of the proofs of these assertions, see Nix and Vose 1991.

Vose (1993) extended both the infinite-population model and the finite-population model. He gave a geometric interpretation to these models by defining the "GA surface" on which population trajectories occur. I will not give the details of his extended model here, but the main result was a conjecture that, as $n \to \infty$, the fraction of the time the GA spends close to nonstable fixed points asymptotically goes to 0 and the time the GA spends close to stable fixed points asymptotically goes to 1. In dynamical systems terms, the GA is asymptotically most likely to be at the fixed points having the largest basins of attraction. As $n \to \infty$, the probability that the GA will be anywhere else goes to 0. Vose's conjecture implies that the short-term behavior of the GA is determined by the initial population—this determines which fixed point the GA initially approaches—but the long-term behavior is determined only by the structure of the GA surface, which determines which fixed points have the largest basins of attraction.

What are these types of formal models good for? Since they are the most detailed possible models of the simple GA, in principle they could be used to predict every aspect of the GA's behavior. However, in practice such models cannot be used to predict the GA's detailed behavior for the very reason that they are so detailed—the required matrices are intractably large. For example, even for a very modest GA with, say, $l = 8$ and $n = 8$, Nix and Vose's Markov transition matrix Q would have more than 10^{29} entries; this number grows very fast with l and n. The calculations for making detailed predictions simply cannot be done with matrices of this size.

This does not mean that such models are useless. As we have seen, there are some less detailed properties that can be derived from these models, such as properties of the fixed-point structure of the "GA surface" and properties of the asymptotic behavior of the GA with respect to these fixed points. Such properties give us some limited insight into the GA's behavior. Many of the properties discussed by Vose and his colleagues are still conjectures; there is as yet no detailed understanding of the nature of the GA surface when F and $\mathcal{M}$ are combined. Understanding this surface is a worthwhile (and still open) endeavor.

4.4 STATISTICAL-MECHANICS APPROACHES

I believe that a more useful approach to understanding and predicting GA behavior will be analogous to that of statistical mechanics in physics: rather than keep track of the huge number of individual components in the system (e.g., the exact genetic composition of each population), such approaches will aim at laws of GA behavior described by more macroscopic statistics, such as "mean fitness in the population" or "mean degree of symmetry in the chromosomes." This is in analogy with statistical mechanics' traditional goal of describing the laws of physical systems in terms of macroscopic quantities such as pressure and temperature rather than in terms of the microscopic particles (e.g., molecules) making up the system.

One approach that explicitly makes the analogy with statistical mechanics and uses techniques from that field is that of the physicists Adam Prügel-Bennett and Jonathan Shapiro. Their work is quite technical, and to understand it in full requires some background in statistical mechanics. Here, rather than go into full mathematical detail, I will sketch their work so as to convey an idea of what this kind of approach is all about.

Prügel-Bennett and Shapiro use methods from statistical mechanics to predict macroscopic features of a GA's behavior over the course of a run and to predict what parameters and representations will be the most beneficial. In their preliminary work (Prügel-Bennett and Shapiro 1994), they illustrate their methods using a simple optimization problem: finding minimal energy states in a one-dimensional "spin glass." A spin glass is a particular simple model of magnetic material. The one-dimensional version used by Prügel-Bennett and Shapiro consists of a vector of adjacent "spins," $\vec{S} = (S_1, S_2, \ldots, S_{N+1})$, where each S_i is either -1 or $+1$. Each pair of neighboring spins $(i, i+1)$ is "coupled" by a real-valued weight J_i. The total energy $E(\vec{S})$ of the spin configuration $\vec{S}$ is

$$E(\vec{S}) = -\sum_{i=1}^{N} J_i S_i S_{i+1}.$$

Setting up spin-glass models (typically, more complicated ones) and finding a spin configuration that minimizes their energy is of interest to physicists because this can help them understand the behavior of magnetic systems in nature (which are expected to be in a minimal-energy state at low temperature).

The GA is set with the problem of finding an $\vec{S}$ that minimizes the energy of a one-dimensional spin glass with given J_i's (the J_i values were selected ahead of time at random in $[-1, +1]$). A chromosome is simply a string of $N + 1$ spins (-1 or $+1$). The fitness of a chromosome is the negative of its energy. The initial population is generated by choosing such strings at random. At each generation a new population is formed by selection of parents that engage in single-point crossover to form offspring. For simplicity, mutation was not used. However, they did use an interesting form of selection. The probability p^α that an individual α would be selected to be a parent was

$$p^\alpha = \frac{e^{-\beta E^\alpha}}{Z}, \qquad Z = \sum_{\alpha=1}^{P} e^{-\beta E^\alpha},$$

with E^α the energy of individual α, P the population size, and β a variable controlling the amount of selection. This method is similar to "Boltzmann selection" with β playing the role of temperature. This selection method has some desirable properties for GAs (to be described in the next chapter), and also has useful features for Prügel-Bennett and Shapiro's analysis.

This is a rather easy problem, even with no mutation, but it serves well to illustrate Prügel-Bennett and Shapiro's approach. The goal was to predict changes in distribution of energies (the negative of fitnesses) in the population over time. Figure 4.4 plots the observed distributions at generations 0, 10, 20, 30, and 40 (going from right to left), averaged over 1000 runs, with $P = 50$, $N + 1 = 64$, and $\beta = 0.05$. Prügel-Bennett and Shapiro devised a mathematical model to predict these changes. Given $\rho_t(E)$, the energy distribution at time t, they determine first how selection changes $\rho_t(E)$ into $\rho_t^s(E)$ (the distribution after selection), and then how crossover changes $\rho_t^s(E)$ into $\rho_t^{sc}(E)$ (the distribution after selection and crossover). Schematically, the idea is to iterate

$$\rho_t(E) \xrightarrow{\text{selection}} \rho_t^s(E) \xrightarrow{\text{crossover}} \rho_t^{sc}(E) = \rho_{t+1}(E) \qquad (4.11)$$

starting from the initial distribution $\rho_0(E)$.

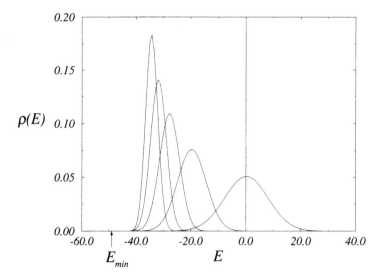

Figure 4.4 Observed energy distributions for the GA population at generations 0, 10, 20, 30, and 40. Energy E is plotted on the x axis; the proportion of individuals in the population at a given energy $\rho(E)$ is plotted on the y axis. The data were averaged over 1000 runs, with $P = 50$, $N + 1 = 64$, and $\beta = 0.05$. The minimum energy for the given spin glass is marked. (Reprinted from Prügel-Bennett and Shapiro 1994 by permission of the publisher. © 1994 American Physical Society.)

Prügel-Bennett and Shapiro began by noting that distributions such as those shown in figure 4.4 can be uniquely represented in terms of "cumulants," a statistical measure of distributions related to moments. The first cumulant, κ_1, is the mean of the distribution, the second cumulant, κ_2, is the variance, and higher cumulants describe other characteristics (e.g., "skew").

Prügel-Bennett and Shapiro used some tricks from statistical mechanics to describe the effects of selection and crossover on the cumulants. The mathematical details are quite technical. Briefly, let κ_n be the nth cumulant of the current distribution of fitnesses in the population, κ_n^S be the nth cumulant of the new distribution produced by selection alone, and κ_n^C be the nth cumulant of the new distribution produced by crossover alone. Prügel-Bennett and Shapiro constructed equations for κ_n^S using the definition of cumulant and a recent development in statistical mechanics called the Random Energy Model (Derrida 1981). For example, they show that $\kappa_1^S \approx \kappa_1 - \beta\kappa_2$ and $\kappa_2^S \approx (1 - 1/P)\kappa_2 - \beta\kappa_3$. Intuitively, selection causes the mean and the standard deviation of the distribution to be lowered (i.e., selection creates a population that has lower mean energy and is more converged), and their equation predicts precisely how much this will occur as a function of P and β. Likewise, they constructed equations for the κ_n^C:

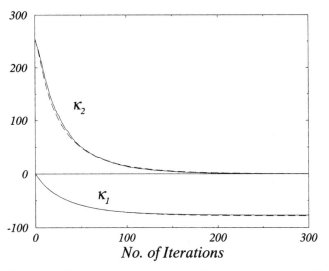

Figure 4.5 Predicted and observed evolution for κ_1 and κ_2 over 300 generations averaged over 500 runs of the GA with $P = 50$, $N + 1 = 256$, and $\beta = 0.01$. The solid lines are the results observed in the simulations, and the dashed lines (mostly obscured by the solid lines) are the predictions. (Reprinted from Prügel-Bennett and Shapiro 1994. © 1994 American Physical Society.)

$$\kappa_1^C = \kappa_1 - \kappa_1\kappa_2/(2N^2);$$

$$\kappa_2^C = \kappa_2;$$

$$\kappa_n^C = 2\kappa_n/(n + 1) \quad \text{for } n > 2.$$

These equations depend very much on the structure of the particular problem—the one-dimensional spin glass—and, in particular, how the fitness of offspring is related to that of their parents.

The equations for κ_n^S and κ_n^C can be combined as in equation 4.11 to predict the evolution of the energy distribution under the GA. The predicted evolution of κ_1 and κ_2 and their observed evolution in an actual run are plotted in figure 4.5. As can be seen, the predictions match the observations very well. The plots can be understood intuitively: the combination of crossover and selection causes the mean population energy κ_1 to fall (i.e., the mean fitness increases) and causes the variance of the population energy to fall too (i.e., the population converges). It is impressive that Prügel-Bennett and Shapiro were able to predict the course of this process so closely. Moreover, since the equations (in a different form) explicitly relate parameters such as P and β to κ_n, they can be used to determine parameter values that will produce desired ratios of minimization speed versus convergence.

The approach of Prügel-Bennett and Shapiro is not yet a general method for predicting GA behavior. Much of their analysis depends on details of the one-dimensional spin-glass problem and of their particular selection method. However, it could be a first step in developing a

Theoretical Foundations of Genetic Algorithms

more general method for using statistical-mechanics methods to predict macroscopic (rather than microscopic) properties of GA behavior and to discover the general laws governing these properties.

THOUGHT EXERCISES

1. For the fitness function defined by Equation 4.5, what are the average fitnesses of the schemas (a) $1 * * \cdots *$, (b) $11 * \cdots *$, and (c) $1 * 1 * \cdots *$?

2. How many schemas are there in a partition with k defined bits in an l-bit search space?

3. Consider the fitness function $f(x) =$ number of ones in x, where x is a chromosome of length 4. Suppose the GA has run for three generations, with the following populations:

generation 0: 1001, 1100, 0110, 0011
generation 1: 1101, 1101, 0111, 0111
generation 2: 1001, 1101, 1111, 1111

Define "on-line" performance at function evaluation step t as the average fitness of all the individuals that have been evaluated over t evaluation steps, and "off-line" performance at time t as the average value, over t evaluation steps, of the best fitness that has been seen up to each evaluation step. Give the on-line and off-line performance after the last evaluation step in each generation.

4. Design a three-bit fully deceptive fitness function. "Fully deceptive" means that the average fitness of every schema indicates that the complement of the global optimum is actually the global optimum. For example, if 111 is the global optimum, any schema containing 000 should have the highest average fitness in its partition.

5. Use a Markov-chain analysis to find an expression in terms of K for $\mathcal{E}(K, 1)$ in equation 4.6. (This is for readers with a strong background in probability theory and stochastic processes.)

6. In the analysis of the IGA, some details were left out in going from

$$\mathcal{E}_N \approx \frac{1}{p} \left[\frac{\binom{N}{1}}{1} - \frac{\binom{N}{2}}{2} + \frac{\binom{N}{3}}{3} - \cdots - \frac{\binom{N}{N}}{N} \right].$$

to

$$\mathcal{E}_N \approx (1/p)[\ln N + \gamma].$$

Show that the expression on the right-hand sides are equal.

7. Supply the missing steps in the derivation of the expression for $r_{i,j}(0)$ in equation 4.10.

8. Derive the expression for the number of possible populations of size n:

$$N = \binom{n + 2^l - 1}{2^l - 1}.$$

COMPUTER EXERCISES

1. Write a program to simulate a two-armed bandit with given μ_1, μ_2, σ_1^2, and σ_2^2 (which you should set). Test various strategies for allocating samples to the two arms, and determine which of the strategies you try maximizes the overall payoff. (Use $N > 1000$ to avoid the effects of a small number of samples.)

2. Run a GA on the fitness function defined by equation 4.5, with $l = 100$. Track the frequency of schemas $1* * * * *$, $0* * * * *$, and $111* * **$ in the population at each generation. How well do the frequencies match those expected under the Schema Theorem?

3. Replicate the experiments (described in this chapter) for the GA and RMHC on R_1. Try several variations and see how they affect the results:

Increase the population size to 1000.
Increase p_m to 0.01 and to 0.05.
Increase the string length to 128 (i.e., the GA has to discover 16 blocks of 8 ones).
Use a rank-selection scheme (see chapter 5).

4. In your run of the GA on R_1, measure and plot on-line and off-line performance versus time (number of fitness-function evaluations so far). Do the same for SAHC and RMHC.

5. Design a fitness function (in terms of schemas, as in R_1) on which you believe the GA should outperform RMHC. Test your hypothesis.

6. Simulate RMHC and the IGA to verify the analysis given in this chapter for different values of N and K.

5 Implementing a Genetic Algorithm

Most of the case studies we examined in chapters 1–3 went far beyond the simple genetic algorithm that was the main subject of the theoretical discussion in chapter 4. The case studies illustrated that when one wants to apply the GA to a particular problem, one faces a huge number of choices about how to proceed, with little theoretical guidance on how to make them.

John Holland's simple GA inspired all subsequent GAs and provided the basis for theoretical analysis of GAs. For real problem solving and modeling, however, it is clear that the simple GA is limited in its power in several respects. Not all problems should use bit-string encodings, fitness-proportionate selection is not always the best method, and the simple genetic operators are not always the most effective or appropriate ones. Furthermore, the simple GA leaves out many potentially useful ideas from real biology, several of which were proposed for use in GAs by Holland (1975) but have not been examined systematically until recently.

In this chapter I survey some implementation issues for GAs and some sophisticated GA techniques, including self-adapting GAs. Of course, this survey is by no means complete—although GA researchers speak informally of "the GA," anyone who has read the previous chapters will notice that there are actually as many different GAs as there are GA projects. Here I survey some of the more interesting approaches in order to help readers make choices about how to use GAs in their own work.

This chapter does not provide code for implementing a GA. Pascal code for a simple GA is given in Goldberg 1989a. Several GA packages are available in the public domain; information on how to get them is given in appendix B.

5.1 WHEN SHOULD A GENETIC ALGORITHM BE USED?

The GA literature describes a large number of successful applications, but there are also many cases in which GAs perform poorly. Given a particular potential application, how do we know if a GA is good method to use? There is no rigorous answer, though many researchers share the intuitions that if the space to be searched is large, is known not to be perfectly smooth and unimodal (i.e., consists of a single smooth "hill"), or is not well understood, or if the fitness function is noisy, and if the task does not require a global optimum to be found—i.e., if quickly finding a sufficiently good solution is enough—a GA will have a good chance of being competitive with or surpassing other "weak" methods (methods that do not use domain-specific knowledge in their search procedure). If a space is not large, then it can be searched exhaustively, and one can be sure that the best possible solution has been found, whereas a GA might converge on a local optimum rather than on the globally best solution. If the space is smooth or unimodal, a gradient-ascent algorithm such as steepest-ascent hill climbing will be much more efficient than a GA in exploiting the space's smoothness. If the space is well understood (as is the space for the well-known Traveling Salesman problem, for example), search methods using domain-specific heuristics can often be designed to outperform any general-purpose method such as a GA. If the fitness function is noisy (e.g., if it involves taking error-prone measurements from a real-world process such as the vision system of a robot), a one-candidate-solution-at-a-time search method such as simple hill climbing might be irrecoverably led astray by the noise, but GAs, since they work by accumulating fitness statistics over many generations, are thought to perform robustly in the presence of small amounts of noise.

These intuitions, of course, do not rigorously predict when a GA will be an effective search procedure competitive with other procedures. A GA's performance will depend very much on details such as the method for encoding candidate solutions, the operators, the parameter settings, and the particular criterion for success. The theoretical work described in the previous chapter has not yet provided very useful predictions. In this chapter I survey a number of different practical approaches to using GAs without giving theoretical justifications.

5.2 ENCODING A PROBLEM FOR A GENETIC ALGORITHM

As for any search and learning method, the way in which candidate solutions are encoded is a central, if not *the* central, factor in the success of a genetic algorithm. Most GA applications use fixed-length, fixed-order bit strings to encode candidate solutions. However, in recent years, there have been many experiments with other kinds of encodings, several of which were described in previous chapters.

Binary Encodings

Binary encodings (i.e., bit strings) are the most common encodings for a number of reasons. One is historical: in their earlier work, Holland and his students concentrated on such encodings and GA practice has tended to follow this lead. Much of the existing GA theory is based on the assumption of fixed-length, fixed-order binary encodings. Much of that theory can be extended to apply to nonbinary encodings, but such extensions are not as well developed as the original theory. In addition, heuristics about appropriate parameter settings (e.g., for crossover and mutation rates) have generally been developed in the context of binary encodings.

There have been many extensions to the basic binary encoding schema, such as gray coding (Bethke 1980; Caruana and Schaffer 1988) and Hillis's diploid binary encoding scheme. (Diploid encodings were actually first proposed in Holland 1975, and are also discussed in Goldberg 1989a.)

Holland (1975) gave a theoretical justification for using binary encodings. He compared two encodings with roughly the same information-carrying capacity, one with a small number of alleles and long strings (e.g., bit strings of length 100) and the other with a large number of alleles and short strings (e.g., decimal strings of length 30). He argued that the former allows for a higher degree of implicit parallelism than the latter, since an instance of the former contains more schemas than an instance of the latter (2^{100} versus 2^{30}). (This schema-counting argument is relevant to GA behavior only insofar as schema analysis is relevant, which, as I have mentioned, has been disputed.)

In spite of these advantages, binary encodings are unnatural and unwieldy for many problems (e.g., evolving weights for neural networks or evolving condition sets in the manner of Meyer and Packard), and they are prone to rather arbitrary orderings.

Many-Character and Real-Valued Encodings

For many applications, it is most natural to use an alphabet of many characters or real numbers to form chromosomes. Examples include Kitano's many-character representation for graph-generation grammars, Meyer and Packard's real-valued representation for condition sets, Montana and Davis's real-valued representation for neural-network weights, and Schultz-Kremer's real-valued representation for torsion angles in proteins.

Holland's schema-counting argument seems to imply that GAs should exhibit worse performance on multiple-character encodings than on binary encodings. However, this has been questioned by some (see, e.g., Antonisse 1989). Several empirical comparisons between binary encodings and multiple-character or real-valued encodings have shown better performance for the latter (see, e.g., Janikow and Michalewicz 1991; Wright 1991). But the performance depends very much on the problem and the details of the GA being used, and at present there are no rigorous guidelines for predicting which encoding will work best.

Tree Encodings

Tree encoding schemes, such as John Koza's scheme for representing computer programs, have several advantages, including the fact that they allow the search space to be open-ended (in principle, any size tree could be formed via crossover and mutation). This open-endedness also leads to some potential pitfalls. The trees can grow large in uncontrolled ways, preventing the formation of more structured, hierarchical candidate solutions. (Koza's (1992, 1994) "automatic definition of functions" is one way in which GP can be encouraged to design hierarchically structured programs.) Also, the resulting trees, being large, can be very difficult to understand and to simplify. Systematic experiments evaluating the usefulness of tree encodings and comparing them with other encodings are only just beginning in the genetic programming community. Likewise, as yet there are only very nascent attempts at extending GA theory to tree encodings (see, e.g., Tackett 1994; O'Reilly and Oppacher 1995).

These are only the most common encodings; a survey of the GA literature will turn up experiments on several others.

How is one to decide on the correct encoding for one's problem? Lawrence Davis, a researcher with much experience applying GAs to real-world problems, strongly advocates using whatever encoding is the most natural for your problem, and then devising a GA that can use that encoding (Davis 1991). Until the theory of GAs and encodings is better formulated, this might be the best philosophy; as can be seen from the examples presented in this book, most research is currently done by guessing at an appropriate encoding and then trying out a particular version of the GA on it. This is not much different from other areas of machine learning; for example, encoding a learning problem for a neural net is typically done by trial and error.

One appealing idea is to have the encoding itself adapt so that the GA can make better use of it.

5.3 ADAPTING THE ENCODING

Choosing a fixed encoding ahead of time presents a paradox to the potential GA user: for any problem that is hard enough that one would want to use a GA, one doesn't know enough about the problem ahead of time to come up with the best encoding for the GA. In fact, coming up with the best encoding is almost tantamount to solving the problem itself! An example of this was seen in the discussion on evolving cellular automata in chapter 2 above. The original lexicographic ordering of bits was arbitrary, and it probably impeded the GA from finding better solutions quickly—to find high-fitness rules, many bits spread throughout the string had to be coadapted. If these bits were close together on the string, so that they were less likely to be separated under crossover, the performance of the GA would presumably be improved. But we had no idea how best to order the bits ahead of time for this problem. This is known in the GA literature as the "linkage problem"—one wants to have functionally related loci be more likely to stay together on the string under crossover, but it is not clear how this is to be done without knowing ahead of time which loci are important in useful schemas. Faced with this problem, and having notions of evolution and adaptation already primed in the mind, many users have a revelation: "As long as I'm using a GA to solve the problem, why not have it adapt the encoding at the same time!"

A second reason for adapting the encoding is that a fixed-length representation limits the complexity of the candidate solutions. For example, in the Prisoner's Dilemma example, Axelrod fixed the memory of the evolving strategies to three games, requiring a chromosome of length 64 plus a few extra bits to encode initial conditions. But it would be interesting to know what types of strategies could evolve if the memory size were allowed to increase or decrease (requiring variable-length chromosomes). As was mentioned earlier, such an experiment was done by Lindgren (1992), in which "gene doubling" and "deletion" operators allowed the chromosome length—and thus the potential memory size—to increase and decrease over time, permitting more "open-ended" evolution. Likewise, tree encodings such as those used in genetic programming automatically allow for adaptation of the encoding, since under crossover and mutation the trees can grow or shrink. Meyer and Packard's encoding of condition sets also allowed for individuals of varying lengths, since crossovers between individuals of different lengths could cause the number of conditions in a set to increase or decrease. Other work along these lines has been done by Schaefer (1987), Harp and Samad (1991), Harvey (1992), Schraudolph and Belew (1992), and Altenberg (1994). Below I describe in detail three (of the many) approaches to adapting the encoding for a GA.

Inversion

Holland (1975) included proposals for adapting the encodings in his original proposal for GAs (also see Goldberg 1989a). Holland, acutely aware that correct linkage is essential for single-point crossover to work well, proposed an "inversion" operator specifically to deal with the linkage problem in fixed-length strings.

Inversion is a reordering operator inspired by a similar operator in real genetics. Unlike simple GAs, in real genetics the function of a gene is often independent of its position in the chromosome (though often genes in a local area work together in a regulatory network), so inverting part of the chromosome will retain much or all of the "semantics" of the original chromosome.

To use inversion in GAs, we have to find some way for the functional interpretation of an allele to be the same no matter where it appears in the string. For example, in the chromosome encoding a cellular automaton (see section 2.1), the leftmost bit under lexicographic ordering is the output bit for the neighborhood of all zeros. We would want that bit to represent that same neighborhood even if its position were changed in the string under an inversion. Holland proposed that each allele be given an index indicating its "real" position, to be used when evaluating a chromosome's fitness. For example, the string 00010101 would be encoded as

$$\{(1, 0)\ (2, 0)\ (3, 0)\ (4, 1)\ (5, 0)\ (6, 1)\ (7, 0)\ (8, 1)\},$$

with the first member of each pair giving the "real" position of the given allele. This is the same string as, say,

$$\{(1, 0)\ (2, 0)\ (6, 1)\ (5, 0)\ (4, 1)\ (3, 0)\ (7, 0)\ (8, 1)\}.$$

Inversion works by choosing two points in the string and reversing the order of the bits between them—in the example just given, bits 3–6 were reversed. This does not change the fitness of the chromosome, since to calculate the fitness the string is ordered by the indices. However, it does change the linkages: the idea behind inversion is to produce orderings in which beneficial schemas are more likely to survive. Suppose that in the original ordering the schema $00**01**$ is very important. Under the new ordering, that schema is $0010****$. Given that this is a high-fitness schema and will now tend to survive better under single-point crossover, this permutation will presumably tend to survive better than would the original string.

   The reader may have noticed a hitch in combining inversion with single-point crossover. Suppose, for example, that

$$\{(1, 0)\ (2, 0)\ (6, 1)\ (5, 0)\ (4, 1)\ (3, 0)\ (7, 0)\ (8, 1)\}$$

crosses with

$$\{(5, 1)\ (2, 0)\ (3, 1)\ (4, 1)\ (1, 1)\ (8, 1)\ (6, 0)\ (7, 0)\}$$

after the third bit. The offspring are

$$\{(1, 0)\ (2, 0)\ (6, 1)\ (4, 1)\ (1, 1)\ (8, 1)\ (6, 0)\ (7, 0)\}$$

and

$$\{(5, 1)\ (2, 0)\ (3, 1)\ (5, 0)\ (4, 1)\ (3, 0)\ (7, 0)\ (8, 1)\}.$$

The first offspring has two copies each of bits 1 and 6 and no copies of bits 3 and 5. The second offspring has two copies of bits 3 and 5 and no copies of bits 1 and 6. How can we ensure that crossover will produce offspring with a full set of loci? Holland proposed two possible solutions: (1) Permit crossover only between chromosomes with the same permutation of the loci. This would work, but it severely limits the way in which crossover can be done. (2) Employ a "master/slave" approach: choose one parent to be the master, and temporarily reorder the other parent to have the same ordering as the master. Use this ordering to produce offspring, returning the second parent to its original ordering once crossover has been performed. Both methods have been used in experiments on inversion.

Inversion was included in some early work on GAs but did not produce any stunning improvements in performance (Goldberg 1989a). More recently, forms of inversion have been incorporated with some success into GAs applied to "ordering problems" such as the DNA fragment assembly problem (Parsons, Forrest, and Burks, in press). However, the verdict on the benefits of inversion to GAs is not yet in; more systematic experimental and theoretical studies are needed. In addition, any performance benefit conferred by inversion must be weighed against the additional space (to store indices for every bit) and additional computation time (e.g., to reorder one parent before crossover) that inversion requires.

Evolving Crossover "Hot Spots"

A different approach, also inspired by nature, was taken by Schaffer and Morishima (1987). Their idea was to evolve not the order of bits in the string but rather the positions at which crossover was allowed to occur (crossover "hot spots"). Attached to each candidate solution in the population was a second string—a "crossover template"—that had a 1 at each locus at which crossover was to take place and a 0 at each locus at which crossover was not to take place. For example, 10011111:00010010 (with the chromosome preceding and the crossover template following the colon) meant that crossover should take place after the fourth and seventh loci in that string. Using an exclamation point to denote the crossover markers (each attached to the bit on its left), we can write this as 1001!111!1. Now, to perform multi-point crossover on two parents (say 1001!111!1 and 000000!00), the !s mark the crossover points, and they get inherited along with the bits to which they are attached:

Parents	1	0	0	1!	1	1	1!	1
	0	0	0	0	0	0!	0	0
Offspring	1	0	0	1!	0	0!	1!	0
	0	0	0	0	1	1	0	1

Mutation acts on both the chromosomes and the attached crossover templates. Only the candidate solution is used to determine fitness, but the hope is that selection, crossover, and mutation will not only discover good solutions but also coevolve good crossover templates. Schaffer and Morishima found that this method outperformed a version of the simple

GA on a small suite of function optimization problems. Although this method is interesting and is inspired by real genetics (in which there are crossover hot spots that have somehow coevolved with chromosomes), there has not been much further investigation into why it works and to what degree it will actually improve GA performance over a larger set of applications.

Messy GAs

The goal of "messy GAs," developed by Goldberg and his colleagues, is to improve the GA's function-optimization performance by explicitly building up increasingly longer, highly fit strings from well-tested shorter building blocks (Goldberg, Korb, and Deb 1989; Goldberg, Deb, and Korb 1990; Goldberg, Deb, Kargupta, and Harik 1993). The general idea was biologically motivated: "After all, nature did not start with strings of length 5.9×10^9 (an estimate of the number of pairs of DNA nucleotides in the human genome) or even of length two million (an estimate of the number of genes in *Homo sapiens*) and try to make man. Instead, simple life forms gave way to more complex life forms, with the building blocks learned at earlier times used and reused to good effect along the way." (Goldberg, Korb, and Deb 1989, p. 500)

Consider a particular optimization problem with candidate solutions represented as bit strings. In a messy GA each bit is tagged with its "real" locus, but in a given chromosome not all loci have to be specified ("underspecification") and some loci can be specified more than once, even with conflicting alleles ("overspecification"). For example, in a four-bit problem, the following two messy chromosomes might be found in the population:

$\{(1, 0) (2, 0) (4, 1) (4, 0)\}$

and

$\{(3, 1) (3, 0) (3, 1) (4, 0) (4, 1) (3, 1)\}$.

The first specifies no value for locus 3 and two values for locus 4. The second specifies no values for loci 1 and 2, two values for locus 4 and a whopping four values for locus 3. (The term "messy GA" is meant to be contrasted with standard "neat" fixed-length, fixed-population-size GAs.)

Given all this under- and overspecification, how is the fitness function to be evaluated? Overspecification is easy: Goldberg and his colleagues simply used a left-to-right, first-come-first-served scheme. (E.g., the chosen value for locus 4 in the first chromosome is 1.) Once overspecification has been taken care of, the specified bits in the chromosome can be thought of as a "candidate schema" rather than as a candidate solution. For example, the first chromosome above is the schema 00*1. The purpose of messy GAs is to evolve such candidate schemas, gradually building up longer and longer ones until a solution is formed. This requires a way to evaluate a candidate schema under a given fitness function. However, under most fitness functions of interest, it is difficult if not impossible to compute the "fitness" of a partial string. Many loci typically interact non-independently to determine a string's fitness, and in an underspecified string the missing loci might be crucial. Goldberg and his colleagues first proposed and then rejected an "averaging" method: for a given underspecified string, randomly generate values for the missing loci over a number of trials and take the average fitness computed with these random samples. The idea is to estimate the average fitness of the candidate schema. But, as was pointed out earlier, the variance of this average fitness will often be too high for a meaningful average to be gained from such sampling. Instead, Goldberg and his colleagues used a method they called "competitive templates." The idea was not to estimate the average fitness of the candidate schema but to see if the candidate schema yields an improvement over a local optimum. The method works by finding a local optimum at the beginning of a run by a hill-climbing technique, and then, when running the messy GA, evaluating underspecified strings by filling in missing bits from the local optimum and then applying the fitness function. A local optimum is, by definition, a string that cannot be improved by a single-bit change; thus, if a candidate schema's defined bits improve the local optimum, it is worth further exploration.

The messy GA proceeds in two phases: the "primordial phase" and the "juxtapositional phase." The purpose of the primordial phase is to enrich the population with small, promising candidate schemas, and the purpose of the juxtapositional phase is to put them together in useful ways. Goldberg and his colleagues' first method was to guess at the order k of the smallest relevant schemas and to form the initial population by completely enumerating all schemas of that order. For example, if the size of solutions is $l = 8$ and the guessed k is 3, the initial population will be

$\{(1, 0)\ (2, 0)\ (3, 0)\}$
$\{(1, 0)\ (2, 0)\ (3, 1)\}$
$\vdots$
$\{(1, 1)\ (2, 1)\ (3, 1)\}$
$\{(1, 0)\ (2, 0)\ (4, 0)\}$
$\{(1, 0)\ (2, 0)\ (4, 1)\}$
$\vdots$
$\{(6, 1)\ (7, 1)\ (8, 1)\}.$

After the initial population has been formed and the initial fitnesses evaluated (using competitive templates), the primordial phase continues by selection only (making copies of strings in proportion to their fitnesses with no crossover or mutation) and by culling the population by half at regular intervals. At some generation (a parameter of the algorithm), the primordial phase comes to an end and the juxtapositional phase is invoked. The population size stays fixed, selection continues, and two juxtapositional operators—"cut" and "splice"—are introduced. The cut operator cuts a string at a random point. For example,

$$\{(2, 0)\ (3, 0)\ (1, 1)\ (4, 1)\ (6, 0)\}$$

could be cut after the second locus to yield two strings: $\{(2, 0)\ (3, 0)\}$ and $\{(1, 1)\ (4, 1)\ (6, 0)\}$. The splice operator takes two strings and splices them together. For example,

$$\{(1, 1)\ (2, 1)\ (3, 1)\}\ \text{and}\ \{(1, 0)\ (4, 1)\ (3, 0)\}$$

could be spliced together to form

$$\{(1, 1)\ (2, 1)\ (3, 1)\ (1, 0)\ (4, 1)\ (3, 0)\}.$$

Under the messy encoding, cut and splice always produce perfectly legal strings. The hope is that the primordial phase will have produced all the building blocks needed to create an optimal string, and in sufficient numbers so that cut and splice will be likely to create that optimal string before too long. Goldberg and his colleagues did not use mutation in the experiments they reported.

Goldberg, Korb, and Deb (1989) performed a very rough mathematical analysis of this algorithm to argue why it should work better than a simple GA, and then showed empirically that it performed much better than a simple GA on a 30-bit deceptive problem. In this problem, the fitness function took a 30-bit string divided into ten adjacent segments of three bits each. Each three-bit segment received a fixed score: 111 received the highest score, but 000 received the second highest and was a local optimum (thus making the problem deceptive). The score S of each three-bit segment was as follows: $S(000) = 28$; $S(001) = 26$; $S(010) = 22$; $S(011) = 0$; $S(100) = 14$; $S(101) = 0$; $S(110) = 0$; $S(111) = 30$. The fitness of a 30-bit string was the sum of the scores of each three-bit segment. The messy GA was also tried successfully on several variants of this fitness function (all of roughly the same size).

Two immediate problems with this approach will jump out at the reader: (1) One must know (or guess) ahead of time the minimum useful schema order k, and it is not clear how one can do this *a priori* for a given fitness function. (2) Even if one could guess k, for problems of realistic size the combinatorics are intractable. For Goldberg, Korb, and Deb's (1989) $k - 3, l = 30$ problem, the primordial stage started off with a complete enumeration of the possible three-bit schemas in a 30-bit string. In general there are

$$n = 2^k \binom{l}{k}$$

such schemas, where k is the order of each schema and l is the length of the entire string. (The derivation of this formula is left as an exercise.) For $l = 30$ and $k = 3$, $n = 32, 480$, a reasonably tractable number to begin with. However, consider R_1 (defined in chapter 4), in which $l = 64$ and $k = 8$ (a very reasonably sized problem for a GA). In that case, $n \approx 10^{12}$. If each fitness evaluation took a millisecond, evaluating the initial population would take over 30 years! Since most messy-GA researchers do not have that kind of time, a new approach had to be found.

Goldberg, Deb, Kargupta, and Harik (1993) refer—a bit too calmly—to this combinatorial explosion as the "initialization bottleneck." Their proposed solution is to dispense with the complete enumeration of order-k schemas, and to replace it by a "probabilistically complete initialization." The combinatorics can be overcome in part by making the initial strings much longer than k (though shorter than l), so that implicit parallelism provides many order-k schemas on one string. Let the initial string length be denoted by l', and let the initial population size be denoted by n_g. Goldberg et al. calculate what pairs of l' and n_g values will ensure that, on average, each schema of order k will be present in the initial population. If l' is increased, n_g can be greatly decreased for the primordial stage.

The one hitch is that, as was seen in the section on Royal Road functions in chapter 4, under selection long strings containing good building blocks can be afflicted with hitchhiking bits ("parasitic bits" in the terminology of Goldberg, Korb, and Deb (1989)). To deal with this, Goldberg, Deb, Kargupta, and Harik (1993) introduce "building-block filtering," in which the longer initial strings are honed down by random deletion of bits. Their claim is that this filtering process, in conjunction with selection, is enough to overcome the problem of parasitic bits. These methods were tried on deceptive fitness functions with l up to 150 and $k = 5$, with tractable initial population sizes. With some additional changes in the juxtapositional phase, the messy GA was able to optimize these functions—functions that would be too hard for a simple GA to optimize.

Unfortunately, even with probabilistically complete initialization, the necessary initial population size still grows exponentially with k, so messy GAs will be feasible only on problems in which k is small. Goldberg and his colleagues seem to assume that most problems of interest will have small k, but this has never been demonstrated. It remains to be seen whether the promising results they have found on specially designed fitness functions will hold when messy GAs are applied to real-world problems. Goldberg, Deb, and Korb (1990, p. 442) have already announced that messy GAs are "ready for real-world applications" and recommended their "immediate application . . . to difficult, combinatorial problems of practical import." To my knowledge, they have not yet been tried on such problems.

5.4 SELECTION METHODS

After deciding on an encoding, the second decision to make in using a genetic algorithm is how to perform selection—that is, how to choose the individuals in the population that will create offspring for the next generation, and how many offspring each will create. The purpose of selection is, of course, to emphasize the fitter individuals in the population in hopes that their offspring will in turn have even higher fitness. Selection has to be balanced with variation from crossover and mutation (the "exploitation/exploration balance"): too-strong selection means that suboptimal highly fit individuals will take over the population, reducing the diversity needed for further change and progress; too-weak selection will result in too-slow evolution. As was the case for encodings, numerous selection schemes have been proposed in the GA literature. Below I will describe some of the most common methods. As was the case for encodings, these descriptions do not provide rigorous guidelines for which method should be used for which problem; this is still an open question for GAs. (For more technical comparisons of different selection methods, see Goldberg and Deb 1991, Bäck and Hoffmeister 1991, de la Maza and Tidor 1993, and Hancock 1994.)

Fitness-Proportionate Selection with "Roulette Wheel" and "Stochastic Universal" Sampling

Holland's original GA used fitness-proportionate selection, in which the "expected value" of an individual (i.e., the expected number of times an individual will be selected to reproduce) is that individual's fitness divided by the average fitness of the population. The most common method for implementing this is "roulette wheel" sampling, described in chapter 1: each individual is assigned a slice of a circular "roulette wheel," the size of the slice being proportional to the individual's fitness. The wheel is spun N times, where N is the number of individuals in the population. On each spin, the individual under the wheel's marker is selected to be in the pool of parents for the next generation. This method can be implemented as follows:

1. Sum the total expected value of individuals in the population. Call this sum T.

2. Repeat N times:

Choose a random integer r between 0 and T.

Loop through the individuals in the population, summing the expected values, until the sum is greater than or equal to r. The individual whose expected value puts the sum over this limit is the one selected.

This stochastic method statistically results in the expected number of offspring for each individual. However, with the relatively small populations typically used in GAs, the actual number of offspring allocated to an individual is often far from its expected value (an extremely unlikely series of spins of the roulette wheel could even allocate all offspring to the worst individual in the population). James Baker (1987) proposed a different sampling method—"stochastic universal sampling" (SUS)—to minimize this "spread" (the range of possible actual values, given an expected value). Rather than spin the roulette wheel N times to select N parents, SUS spins the wheel once—but with N equally spaced pointers, which are used to selected the N parents. Baker (1987) gives the following code fragment for SUS (in C):

```
ptr = Rand(); /* Returns random number uniformly distributed in [0,1] */
for (sum = i = 0; i < N; i++)
    for (sum += ExpVal(i,t); sum > ptr; ptr++)
        Select(i);
```

where i is an index over population members and where $\text{ExpVal}(i, t)$ gives the expected value of individual i at time t. Under this method, each individual i is guaranteed to reproduce at least $\lfloor \text{ExpVal}(i, t) \rfloor$ times but no more than $\lceil \text{ExpVal}(i, t) \rceil$ times. (The proof of this is left as an exercise.)

SUS does not solve the major problems with fitness-proportionate selection. Typically, early in the search the fitness variance in the population is high and a small number of individuals are much fitter than the others. Under fitness-proportionate selection, they and their descendents will multiply quickly in the population, in effect preventing the GA from doing any further exploration. This is known as "premature convergence." In other words, fitness-proportionate selection early on often puts too much emphasis on "exploitation" of highly fit strings at the expense of exploration of other regions of the search space. Later in the search, when all individuals in the population are very similar (the fitness variance is low), there are no real fitness differences for selection to exploit, and evolution grinds to a near halt. Thus, the rate of evolution depends on the variance of fitnesses in the population.

Sigma Scaling

To address such problems, GA researchers have experimented with several "scaling" methods—methods for mapping "raw" fitness values to expected values so as to make the GA less susceptible to premature convergence. One example is "sigma scaling" (Forrest 1985; it was called "sigma truncation" in Goldberg 1989a), which keeps the selection pressure (i.e., the degree to which highly fit individuals are allowed many offspring) relatively constant over the course of the run rather than depending on the fitness variances in the population. Under sigma scaling, an individual's expected value is a function of its fitness, the population mean, and the population standard deviation. A example of sigma scaling would be

$$
\text{ExpVal}(i, t) = \begin{cases} 1 + \dfrac{f(i) - \bar{f}(t)}{2\sigma(t)} & \text{if } \sigma(t) \neq 0 \\ 1.0 & \text{if } \sigma(t) = 0, \end{cases}
$$

where $\text{ExpVal}(i, t)$ is the expected value of individual i at time t, $f(i)$ is the fitness of i, $\bar{f}(t)$ is the mean fitness of the population at time t, and $\sigma(t)$ is the standard deviation of the population fitnesses at time t. This function, used in the work of Tanese (1989), gives an individual with fitness one standard deviation above the mean 1.5 expected offspring. If $\text{ExpVal}(i, t)$ was less than 0, Tanese arbitrarily reset it to 0.1, so that individuals with very low fitness had some small chance of reproducing.

At the beginning of a run, when the standard deviation of fitnesses is typically high, the fitter individuals will not be many standard deviations above the mean, and so they will not be allocated the lion's share of offspring. Likewise, later in the run, when the population is typically more converged and the standard deviation is typically lower, the fitter individuals will stand out more, allowing evolution to continue.

Elitism

"Elitism," first introduced by Kenneth De Jong (1975), is an addition to many selection methods that forces the GA to retain some number of the best individuals at each generation. Such individuals can be lost if they are not selected to reproduce or if they are destroyed by crossover or mutation. Many researchers have found that elitism significantly improves the GA's performance.

Boltzmann Selection

Sigma scaling keeps the selection pressure more constant over a run. But often different amounts of selection pressure are needed at different times in a run—for example, early on it might be good to be liberal, allowing less fit individuals to reproduce at close to the rate of fitter individuals, and having selection occur slowly while maintaining a lot of variation in the population. Later it might be good to have selection be stronger in order to strongly emphasize highly fit individuals, assuming that the early diversity with slow selection has allowed the population to find the right part of the search space.

One approach to this is "Boltzmann selection" (an approach similar to simulated annealing), in which a continuously varying "temperature" controls the rate of selection according to a preset schedule. The temperature starts out high, which means that selection pressure is low (i.e., every individual has some reasonable probability of reproducing). The temperature is gradually lowered, which gradually increases the selection pressure, thereby allowing the GA to narrow in ever more closely to the best part of the search space while maintaining the "appropriate" degree of diversity. For examples of this approach, see Goldberg 1990, de la Maza and Tidor 1991 and 1993, and Prügel-Bennett and Shapiro 1994. A typical implementation is to assign to each individual i an expected value,

$$\text{ExpVal}(i, t) = \frac{e^{f(i)/T}}{\langle e^{f(i)/T} \rangle_t},$$

where T is temperature and $\langle \rangle_t$ denotes the average over the population at time t. Experimenting with this formula will show that, as T decreases, the difference in $\text{ExpVal}(i, t)$ between high and low fitnesses increases. The desire is to have this happen gradually over the course of the search, so temperature is gradually decreased according to a predefined schedule. De la Maza and Tidor (1991) found that this method outperformed fitness-proportionate selection on a small set of test problems. They also (1993) compared some theoretical properties of the two methods.

Fitness-proportionate selection is commonly used in GAs mainly because it was part of Holland's original proposal and because it is used in the Schema Theorem, but, evidently, for many applications simple fitness-proportionate selection requires several "fixes" to make it work well. In recent years completely different approaches to selection (e.g., rank and tournament selection) have become increasingly common.

Rank Selection

Rank selection is an alternative method whose purpose is also to prevent too-quick convergence. In the version proposed by Baker (1985), the individuals in the population are ranked according to fitness, and the expected value of each individual depends on its rank rather than on its absolute fitness. There is no need to scale fitnesses in this case, since absolute differences in fitness are obscured. This discarding of absolute fitness information can have advantages (using absolute fitness can lead to convergence problems) and disadvantages (in some cases it might be important to know that one individual is far fitter than its nearest competitor). Ranking avoids giving the far largest share of offspring to a small group of highly fit individuals, and thus reduces the selection pressure when the fitness variance is high. It also keeps up selection pressure when the fitness variance is low: the ratio of expected values of individuals ranked i

and $i + 1$ will be the same whether their absolute fitness differences are high or low.

The linear ranking method proposed by Baker is as follows: Each individual in the population is ranked in increasing order of fitness, from 1 to N. The user chooses the expected value Max of the individual with rank N, with $Max \geq 0$. The expected value of each individual i in the population at time t is given by

$$\text{ExpVal}(i, t) = Min + (Max - Min)\frac{\text{rank}(i, t) - 1}{N - 1},$$ (5.1)

where Min is the expected value of the individual with rank 1. Given the constraints $Max \geq 0$ and $\sum_i \text{ExpVal}(i, t) = N$ (since population size stays constant from generation to generation), it is required that $1 \leq Max \leq 2$ and $Min = 2 - Max$. (The derivation of these requirements is left as an exercise.)

At each generation the individuals in the population are ranked and assigned expected values according to equation 5.1. Baker recommended $Max = 1.1$ and showed that this scheme compared favorably to fitness-proportionate selection on some selected test problems. Rank selection has a possible disadvantage: slowing down selection pressure means that the GA will in some cases be slower in finding highly fit individuals. However, in many cases the increased preservation of diversity that results from ranking leads to more successful search than the quick convergence that can result from fitness-proportionate selection. A variety of other ranking schemes (such as exponential rather than linear ranking) have also been tried. For any ranking method, once the expected values have assigned, the SUS method can be used to sample the population (i.e., choose parents).

As was described in chapter 2 above, a variation of rank selection with elitism was used by Meyer and Packard for evolving condition sets, and my colleagues and I used a similar scheme for evolving cellular automata. In those examples the population was ranked by fitness and the top E strings were selected to be parents. The $N - E$ offspring were merged with the E parents to create the next population. As was mentioned above, this is a form of the so-called $(\mu + \lambda)$ strategy used in the evolution strategies community. This method can be useful in cases where the fitness function is noisy (i.e., is a random variable, possibly returning different values on different calls on the same individual); the best individuals are retained so that they can be tested again and thus, over time, gain increasingly reliable fitness estimates.

Tournament Selection

The fitness-proportionate methods described above require two passes through the population at each generation: one pass to compute the mean fitness (and, for sigma scaling, the standard deviation) and one pass to compute the expected value of each individual. Rank scaling requires sorting the entire population by rank—a potentially time-consuming procedure. Tournament selection is similar to rank selection in terms of selection pressure, but it is computationally more efficient and more amenable to parallel implementation. Two individuals are chosen at random from the population. A random number r is then chosen between 0 and 1. If $r < k$ (where k is a parameter, for example 0.75), the fitter of the two individuals is selected to be a parent; otherwise the less fit individual is selected. The two are then returned to the original population and can be selected again. An analysis of this method was presented by Goldberg and Deb (1991).

Steady-State Selection

Most GAs described in the literature have been "generational"—at each generation the new population consists entirely of offspring formed by parents in the previous generation (though some of these offspring may be identical to their parents). In some schemes, such as the elitist schemes described above, successive generations overlap to some degree—some portion of the previous generation is retained in the new population. The fraction of new individuals at each generation has been called the "generation gap" (De Jong 1975). In steady-state selection, only a few individuals are replaced in each generation: usually a small number of the least fit individuals are replaced by offspring resulting from crossover and mutation of the fittest individuals. Steady-state GAs are often used in evolving rule-based systems (e.g., classifier systems; see Holland 1986) in which incremental learning (and remembering what has already been learned) is important and in which members of the population collectively (rather than individually) solve the problem at hand. Steady-state selection has been analyzed by Syswerda (1989, 1991), by Whitley (1989), and by De Jong and Sarma (1993).

5.5 GENETIC OPERATORS

The third decision to make in implementing a genetic algorithm is what genetic operators to use. This decision depends greatly on the encoding strategy. Here I will discuss crossover and mutation mostly in the context of bit-string encodings, and I will mention a number of other operators that have been proposed in the GA literature.

Crossover

It could be said that the main distinguishing feature of a GA is the use of crossover. Single-point crossover is the simplest form: a single crossover position is chosen at random and the parts of two parents after the crossover position are exchanged to form two offspring. The idea here is, of course, to recombine building blocks (schemas) on different strings. Single-point crossover has some shortcomings, though. For one thing, it cannot combine all possible schemas. For example, it cannot in general combine instances of 11*****1 and ****11** to form an instance of 11**11*1. Likewise, schemas with long defining lengths are likely to be destroyed under single-point crossover. Eshelman, Caruana, and Schaffer (1989) call this "positional bias": the schemas that can be created or destroyed by a crossover depend strongly on the location of the bits in the chromosome. Single-point crossover assumes that short, low-order schemas are the functional building blocks of strings, but one generally does not know in advance what ordering of bits will group functionally related bits together—this was the purpose of the inversion operator and other adaptive operators described above. Eshelman, Caruana, and Schaffer also point out that there may not be any way to put all functionally related bits close together on a string, since particular bits might be crucial in more than one schema. They point out further that the tendency of single-point crossover to keep short schemas intact can lead to the preservation of hitchhikers—bits that are not part of a desired schema but which, by being close on the string, hitchhike along with the beneficial schema as it reproduces. (This was seen in the "Royal Road" experiments, described above in chapter 4.) Many people have also noted that single-point crossover treats some loci preferentially: the segments exchanged between the two parents always contain the endpoints of the strings.

To reduce positional bias and this "endpoint" effect, many GA practitioners use two-point crossover, in which two positions are chosen at random and the segments between them are exchanged. Two-point crossover is less likely to disrupt schemas with large defining lengths and can combine more schemas than single-point crossover. In addition, the segments that are exchanged do not necessarily contain the endpoints of the strings. Again, there are schemas that two-point crossover cannot combine. GA practitioners have experimented with different numbers of crossover points (in one method, the number of crossover points for each pair of parents is chosen from a Poisson distribution whose mean is a function of the length of the chromosome). Some practitioners (e.g., Spears and De Jong (1991)) believe strongly in the superiority of "parameterized uniform crossover," in which an exchange happens at each bit position with probability p (typically $0.5 \leq p \leq 0.8$). Parameterized uniform crossover has no positional bias—any schemas contained at different positions in the parents can potentially be recombined in the offspring. However, this lack of positional bias can prevent coadapted alleles from ever forming in the population, since parameterized uniform crossover can be highly disruptive of any schema.

Given these (and the many other variants of crossover found in the GA literature), which one should you use? There is no simple answer; the success or failure of a particular crossover operator depends in complicated ways on the particular fitness function, encoding, and other details of the GA. It is still a very important open problem to fully understand these interactions. There are many papers in the GA literature quantifying aspects of various crossover operators (positional bias, disruption potential, ability to create different schemas in one step, and so on), but these do not give definitive guidance on when to use which type of crossover. There are also many papers in which the usefulness of different types of crossover is empirically compared, but all these studies rely on particular small suites of test functions, and different studies produce conflicting results. Again, it is hard to glean general conclusions. It is common in recent GA applications to use either two-point crossover or parameterized uniform crossover with $p \approx 0.7$–0.8.

For the most part, the comments and references above deal with crossover in the context of bit-string encodings, though some of them apply to other types of encodings as well. Some types of encodings require specially defined crossover and mutation operators—for example, the tree encoding used in genetic programming, or encodings for problems like the Traveling Salesman problem (in which the task is to find a correct ordering for a collection of objects).

Most of the comments above also assume that crossover's ability to recombine highly fit schemas is the reason it should be useful. Given some of the challenges we have seen to the relevance of schemas as a analysis tool for understanding GAs, one might ask if we should not consider the possibility that crossover is actually useful for some entirely different reason (e.g., it is in essence a "macro-mutation" operator that simply allows for large jumps in the search space). I must leave this question as an open area of GA research for interested readers to explore. (Terry Jones (1995) has performed some interesting, though preliminary, experiments attempting to tease out the different possible roles of crossover in GAs.) Its answer might also shed light on the question of why recombination is useful for real organisms (if indeed it is)—a controversial and still open question in evolutionary biology.

Mutation

A common view in the GA community, dating back to Holland's book *Adaptation in Natural and Artificial Systems*, is that crossover is the major instrument of variation and innovation in GAs, with mutation insuring the population against permanent fixation at any particular locus and thus playing more of a background role. This differs from the traditional positions of other evolutionary computation methods, such as evolutionary programming and early versions of evolution strategies, in which random mutation is the only source of variation. (Later versions of evolution strategies have included a form of crossover.)

However, the appreciation of the role of mutation is growing as the GA community attempts to understand how GAs solve complex problems. Some comparative studies have been performed on the power of mutation versus crossover; for example, Spears (1993) formally verified the intuitive idea that, while mutation and crossover have the same ability for "disruption" of existing schemas, crossover is a more robust "constructor" of new schemas. Mühlenbein (1992, p. 15), on the other hand, argues that in many cases a hill-climbing strategy will work better than a GA with crossover and that "the power of mutation has been underestimated in traditional genetic algorithms." As we saw in the Royal Road experiments in chapter 4, it is not a choice between crossover or mutation but rather the balance among crossover, mutation, and selection that is all important. The correct balance also depends on details of the fitness function and the encoding. Furthermore, crossover and mutation vary in relative usefulness over the course of a run. Precisely how all this happens still needs to be elucidated. In my opinion, the most promising prospect for producing the right balances over the course of a run is to find ways for the GA to adapt its own mutation and crossover rates during a search. Some attempts at this will be described below.

Other Operators and Mating Strategies

Though most GA applications use only crossover and mutation, many other operators and strategies for applying them have been explored in the GA literature. These include inversion and gene doubling (discussed above) and several operators for preserving diversity in the population. For example, De Jong (1975) experimented with a "crowding" operator in which a newly formed offspring replaced the existing individual most similar to itself. This prevented too many similar individuals ("crowds") from being in the population at the same time. Goldberg and Richardson (1987) accomplished a similar result using an explicit "fitness sharing" function: each individual's fitness was decreased by the presence of other population members, where the amount of decrease due to each other population member was an explicit increasing function of the similarity between the two individuals. Thus, individuals that were similar to many other individuals were punished, and individuals that were different were rewarded. Goldberg and Richardson showed that in some cases this could induce appropriate "speciation," allowing the population members to converge on several peaks in the fitness landscape rather than all converging to the same peak. Smith, Forrest, and Perelson (1993) showed that a similar effect could be obtained without the presence of an explicit sharing function.

A different way to promote diversity is to put restrictions on mating. For example, if only sufficiently similar individuals are allowed to mate, distinct "species" (mating groups) will tend to form. This approach has been studied by Deb and Goldberg (1989). Eshelman (1991) and Eshelman and Schaffer (1991) used the opposite tack: they disallowed matings between sufficiently similar individuals ("incest"). Their desire was not to form species but rather to keep the entire population as diverse as possible. Holland (1975) and Booker (1985) have suggested using "mating tags"— parts of the chromosome that identify prospective mates to one another. Only those individuals with matching tags are allowed to mate (a kind of "sexual selection" procedure). These tags would, in principle, evolve along with the rest of the chromosome to adaptively implement appropriate restrictions on mating. Finally, there have been some experiments with spatially restricted mating (see, e.g., Hillis 1992): the population evolves on a spatial lattice, and individuals are likely to mate only with individuals in their spatial neighborhoods. Hillis found that such a scheme helped preserve diversity by maintaining spatially isolated species, with innovations largely occurring at the boundaries between species.

5.6 PARAMETERS FOR GENETIC ALGORITHMS

The fourth decision to make in implementing a genetic algorithm is how to set the values for the various parameters, such as population size, crossover rate, and mutation rate. These parameters typically interact with one another nonlinearly, so they cannot be optimized one at a time. There is a great deal of discussion of parameter settings and approaches to parameter adaptation in the evolutionary computation literature—too much to survey or even list here. There are no conclusive results on what is best; most people use what has worked well in previously reported cases. Here I will review some of the experimental approaches people have taken to find the "best" parameter settings.

De Jong (1975) performed an early systematic study of how varying parameters affected the GA's on-line and off-line search performance on a small suite of test functions. Recall from chapter 4, thought exercise 3, that "on-line" performance at time t is the average fitness of all the individuals that have been evaluated over t evaluation steps. The off-line performance at time t is the average value, over t evaluation steps, of the best fitness that has been seen up to each evaluation step. De Jong's experiments indicated that the best population size was 50–100 individuals, the best single-point crossover rate was ~ 0.6 per pair of parents, and the best mutation rate was 0.001 per bit. These settings (along with De Jong's test suite) became widely used in the GA community, even though it was not clear how well the GA would perform with these settings on problems outside De Jong's test suite. Any guidance was gratefully accepted.

Somewhat later, Grefenstette (1986) noted that, since the GA could be used as an optimization procedure, it could be used to optimize the parameters for another GA! (A similar study was done by Bramlette (1991).) In Grefenstette's experiments, the "meta-level GA" evolved a population of 50 GA parameter sets for the problems in De Jong's test suite. Each individual encoded six GA parameters: population size, crossover rate, mutation rate, generation gap, scaling window (a particular scaling technique that I won't discuss here), and selection strategy (elitist or nonelitist). The fitness of an individual was a function of the on-line or off-line performance of a GA using the parameters encoded by that individual. The meta-level GA itself used De Jong's parameter settings. The fittest individual for on-line performance set the population size to 30, the crossover rate to 0.95, the mutation rate to 0.01, and the generation gap to 1, and used elitist selection. These parameters gave a small but significant improvement in on-line performance over De Jong's settings. Notice that Grefenstette's results call for a smaller population and higher crossover and mutation rates than De Jong's. The meta-level GA was not able to find a parameter set that beat De Jong's for off-line performance. This was an interesting experiment, but again, in view of the specialized test suite, it is not clear how generally these recommendations hold. Others have shown that there are many fitness functions for which these parameter settings are not optimal.

Schaffer, Caruana, Eshelman, and Das (1989) spent over a year of CPU time systematically testing a wide range of parameter combinations. The performance of a parameter set was the on-line performance of a GA with those parameters on a small set of numerical optimization problems (including some of De Jong's functions) encoded with gray coding. Schaffer et al. found that the best settings for population size, crossover rate, and mutation rate were independent of the problem in their test suite. These settings were similar to those found by Grefenstette: population size 20–30, crossover rate 0.75–0.95, and mutation rate 0.005–0.01. It may be surprising that a very small population size was better, especially in light of other studies that have argued for larger population sizes (e.g., Goldberg 1989d), but this may be due to the on-line performance measure: since each individual ever evaluated contributes to the on-line performance, there is a large cost for evaluating a large population.

Although Grefenstette and Schaffer et al. found that a particular setting of parameters worked best for on-line performance on their test suites, it seems unlikely that any general principles about parameter settings can be formulated *a priori*, in view of the variety of problem types, encodings, and performance criteria that are possible in different applications. Moreover, the optimal population size, crossover rate, and mutation rate likely change over the course of a single run. Many people feel that the most promising approach is to have the parameter values *adapt* in real time to the ongoing search. There have been several approaches to self-adaptation of GA parameters. For example, this has long been a focus of research in the evolution strategies community, in which parameters such as mutation rate are encoded as part of the chromosome. Here I will describe Lawrence Davis's approach to self-adaptation of operator rates (Davis 1989, 1991).

Davis assigns to each operator a "fitness" which is a function of how many highly fit individuals that operator has contributed to creating over the last several generations. Operators gain high fitness both for directly creating good individuals and for "setting the stage" for good individuals to be created (that is, creating the ancestors of good individuals). Davis tested this method in the context of a steady-state GA. Each operator (e.g., crossover, mutation) starts out with the same initial fitness. At each time step a single operator is chosen probabilistically (on the basis of its current fitness) to create a new individual, which replaces a low-fitness member of the population. Each individual i keeps a record of which operator created it. If i has fitness higher than the current best fitness, then i receives some credit for the operator that created it, as do i's parents, grandparents, and so on, back to a prespecified level of ancestor. The fitness of each operator over a given time interval is a function of its previous fitness and the sum of the credits received by all the individuals created by that operator during that time period. (The frequency with which operator fitnesses are updated is a parameter of the method.) In principle, the dynamically changing fitnesses of operators should keep up with their actual usefulness at different stages of the search, causing the GA to use them at appropriate rates at different times. As far as I know, this ability for the operator fitnesses to keep up with the actual usefulness of the operators has not been tested directly in any way, though Davis showed that this method improved the performance of a GA on some problems (including, it turns out, Montana and Davis's project on evolving weights for neural networks).

A big question, then, for any adaptive approach to setting parameters—including Davis's—is this: How well does the rate of adaptation of parameter settings match the rate of adaptation in the GA population? The feedback for setting parameters comes from the population's success or failure on the fitness function, but it might be difficult for this information to travel fast enough for the parameter settings to stay up to date with the population's current state. Very little work has been done on measuring these different rates of adaptation and how well they match in different parameter-adaptation experiments. This seems to me to be the most important research to be done in order to get self-adaptation methods to work well.

THOUGHT EXERCISES

1. Formulate an appropriate definition of "schema" in the context of tree encodings (à la genetic programming). Give an example of a schema in a tree encoding, and calculate the probability of disruption of that schema by crossover and by mutation.

2. Using your definition of schema in thought exercise 1, can a version of the Schema Theorem be stated for tree encodings? What (if anything) might make this difficult?

3. Derive the formula

$$n = 2^k \binom{l}{k},$$

where n is the number of schemas of order k in a search space of length l bit strings.

4. Derive the requirements for rank selection given in the subsection on rank selection: $1 \leq Max \leq 2$ and $Min = 2 - Max$.

5. Derive the expressions $\lfloor ExpVal[i] \rfloor$ and $\lceil ExpVal[i] \rceil$ for the minimum and the maximum number of times an individual will reproduce under SUS.

6. In the discussion on messy GAs, it was noted that Goldberg et al. explored a "probabilistically complete initialization" scheme in which they calculate what pairs of l' and n_g will ensure that, on average, each schema of order k will be present in the initial population. Give examples of l' and n_g that will guarantee this for $k = 5$.

COMPUTER EXERCISES

1. Implement SUS and use it on the fitness function described in computer exercise 1 in chapter 1. How does this GA differ in behavior from the original one with roulette-wheel selection? Measure the "spread" (the range of possible actual number of offspring, given an expected number of offspring) of both sampling methods.

2. Implement a GA with inversion and test it on Royal Road function R_1. Is the performance improved?

3. Design a fitness function on which you think inversion will be helpful, and compare the performance of the GA with and without inversion on that fitness function.

4. Implement Schaffer and Morishima's crossover template method and see if it improves the GA's performance on R_1. Where do the exclamation points end up?

5. Design a fitness function on which you think the crossover template method should help, and compare the performance of the GA with and without crossover templates on that fitness function.

6. Compare the performance of GAs using one-point, two-point, and uniform crossover on R_1.

7. Design a fitness function on which you think uniform crossover should perform better than one-point or two-point crossover, and test your hypothesis.

8. Compare the performance of GAs using the various selection methods described in this chapter, using R_1 as the fitness function. Which results in the best performance?

*9. Implement a meta-GA similar to the one devised by Grefenstette (described above) and use it to search for optimal parameters for a GA, using performance on R_1 as a fitness function.

*10. Implement a messy GA and try it on the 30-bit deceptive problem of Goldberg, Korb, and Deb (1989) (described in the subsection on messy GAs). Compare the messy GA's performance on this problem with that of a standard GA.

*11. Try your messy GA from the previous exercise on R_1. Compare the performance of the messy GA with that of an ordinary GA using the selection method, parameters, and crossover method that produced the best results in the computer exercises above.

*12. Implement Davis's method for self-adaptation of operator rates and try it on R_1. Does it improve the GA's performance? (For the details on how to implement Davis's method, see Davis 1989 and Davis 1991.)

6 Conclusions and Future Directions

In this book we have seen that genetic algorithms can be a powerful tool for solving problems and for simulating natural systems in a wide variety of scientific fields. In examining the accomplishments of these algorithms, we have also seen that many unanswered questions remain. It is now time to summarize what the field of genetic algorithms has achieved, and what are the most interesting and important directions for future research.

From the case studies of projects in problem-solving, scientific modeling, and theory we can draw the following conclusions:

• GAs are promising methods for solving difficult technological problems, and for machine learning. More generally, GAs are part of a new movement in computer science that is exploring biologically inspired approaches to computation. Advocates of this movement believe that in order to create the kinds of computing systems we need—systems that are adaptable, massively parallel, able to deal with complexity, able to learn, and even creative—we should copy natural systems with these qualities. Natural evolution is a particularly appealing source of inspiration.

• Genetic algorithms are also promising approaches for modeling the natural systems that inspired their design. Most models using GAs are meant to be "gedanken experiments" or "idea models" (Roughgarden et al. 1996) rather than precise simulations attempting to match real-world data. The purposes of these idea models are to make ideas precise and to test their plausibility by implementing them as computer programs (e.g., Hinton and Nowlan's model of the Baldwin effect), to understand and predict general tendencies of natural systems (e.g., Echo), and to see how these tendencies are affected by changes in details of the model (e.g., Collins and Jefferson's variations on Kirkpatrick's sexual selection model). These models can allow scientists to perform experiments that would not be possible in the real world, and to simulate phenomena that are difficult or impossible to capture and analyze in a set of equations. These models also have a largely unexplored but potentially interesting side that has not so far been mentioned here: by explicitly modeling evolution as a computer program, we explicitly cast evolution as a computational process, and thus we can think about it in this new light. For example, we can attempt to measure the "information" contained in a population and attempt to understand exactly how evolution processes that information to create structures that lead to higher fitness. Such a computational view, made concrete by GA-type computer models, will, I believe, eventually be an essential part of understanding the relationships among evolution, information theory, and the creation and adaptation of organization in biological systems (e.g., see Weber, Depew, and Smith 1988).

• Holland's *Adaptation in Natural and Artificial Systems*, in which GAs were defined, was one of the first attempts to set down a general framework for adaptation in nature and in computers. Holland's work has had considerable influence on the thinking of scientists in many fields, and it set the stage for most of the subsequent work on GA theory. However, Holland's theory is not a complete description of GA behavior. Recently a number of other approaches, such as exact mathematical models, statistical-mechanics-based models, and results from population genetics, have gained considerable attention. GA theory is not just academic; theoretical advances must be made so that we can know how best to use GAs and how to characterize the types of problems for which they are suited. I believe that theoretical advances will also filter back to the evolutionary biology community. Though it hasn't happened yet, I think there is a very good chance that proving things about these simple models will lead to new ways to think mathematically about natural evolution.

Evolutionary computation is far from being an established science with a body of knowledge that has been collected for centuries. It has been around for little more than 30 years, and only in the last decade have a reasonably large number of people been working on it. Almost all the projects discussed in this book still can be considered "work in progress." The projects described here were chosen because I find the work, or at least its general direction, worth pursuing. In each of the case studies I have tried to point out open questions and to give some ideas about what should be done next. My strong hope is that readers of this book will become excited or inspired enough to take some of this research further, or even to take genetic algorithms in new directions. Here is a brief list of some of the directions I think are the most important and promising.

Incorporating Ecological Interactions
In most GA applications the candidate solutions in the population are assigned fitnesses independent of one another and interact only by competing for selection slots via their fitnesses. However, some of the more interesting and successful applications have used more complicated "ecological" interactions among population members. Hillis's host-parasite

coevolution was a prime example; so was Axelrod's experiment in which the evolving strategies for the Prisoner's Dilemma played against one another and developed a cooperative symbiosis. These methods (along with other examples in the GA literature) are not understood very well; much more work is needed, for example, on making host-parasite coevolution a more generally applicable method and understanding how it works. In addition, other types of ecological interactions, such as individual competition for resources or symbiotic cooperation in collective problem solving, can be utilized in GAs.

Incorporating New Ideas from Genetics

Haploid crossover and mutation are only the barest bones of real-world genetic systems. I have discussed some extensions, including diploidy, inversion, gene doubling, and deletion. Other GA researchers have looked at genetics-inspired mechanisms such as dominance, translocation, sexual differentiation (Goldberg 1989a, chapter 5), and introns (Levenick 1991). These all are likely to have important roles in nature, and mechanisms inspired by them could potentially be put to excellent use in problem solving with GAs. As yet, the exploration of such mechanisms has only barely scratched the surface of their potential. Perhaps even more potentially significant is genetic regulation. In recent years a huge amount has been learned in the genetics community about how genes regulate one another—how they turn one another on and off in complicated ways so that only the appropriate genes get expressed in a given situation. It is these regulatory networks that make the genome a complex but extremely adaptive system. Capturing this kind of genetic adaptivity will be increasingly important as GAs are used in more complicated, changing environments.

Incorporating Development and Learning

Whereas in typical GA applications evolution works directly on a population of candidate solutions, in nature there is a separation between genotypes (encodings) and phenotypes (candidate solutions). There are very good reasons for such a separation. One is that, as organisms become more complex, it seems to be more efficient and tractable for the operators of evolution to work on a simpler encoding that develops into the complex organism. Another is that environments are often too unpredictable for appropriate behavior to be directly encoded into a genotype that does not change during an individual's life. In nature, the processes of development and learning help "tune" the behavioral parameters defined by the individual's genome so that the individual's behavior will become adapted for its particular environment. These reasons for separating genotype from phenotype and for incorporating development and learning have been seen in several of our case studies. Kitano pointed out that a grammatical encoding followed by a development phase allows for the evolution of more complex neural networks than is possible using a direct encoding. Incorporating development in this way has been taken further by Gruau (1992) and Belew (1993), but much more work needs to be done if we are to use GAs to evolve large, complex sytems (such as computational "brains"). The same can be said for incorporating learning into evolutionary computation—we have seen how this can have many advantages, even if what is learned is not directly transmitted to offspring—but the simulations we have seen are only early steps in understanding how to best take advantage of interactions between evolution and learning.

Adapting Encodings and Using Encodings That Permit Hierarchy and Open-Endedness

Evolution in nature not only changes the fitnesses of organisms, it also has mechanisms for changing the genetic encoding. I have discussed some re-ordering operators that occur in nature (e.g., inversion and translocation). In addition, genotypes have increased in size over evolutionary time. In chapter 5 I gave many reasons why the ability to adapt their own encodings is important for GAs. Several methods have been explored in the GA literature. In my opinion, if we want GAs eventually to be able to evolve complex structures, the most important factors will be open-endedness (the ability for evolution to increase the size and complexity of individuals to an arbitrary degree), encapsulation (the ability to protect a useful part of an encoding from genetic disruption and to make sure it acts as a single whole), and hierarchical regulation (the ability to have different parts of the genome regulate other parts, and likewise the ability to have different parts of the phenotype regulate other parts). Some explorations of open-endedness and encapsulation in genetic programming were discussed; to me these types of explorations seem to be on the right track, though the specific type of encoding used in GP may not turn out to be the most effective one for evolving complex structures.

Adapting Parameters

Natural evolution adapts its own parameters. Crossover and mutation rates are encoded (presumably in some rather complicated way) in the genomes of organisms, along with places where these operators are more likely to be applied (e.g., crossover hot spots). Likewise, population sizes in nature are not constant but are controlled by complicated ecological interactions. As was described in chapter 5, we would like to find similar ways of adapting the parameters for GAs as part of the evolutionary process. There have been several explorations of this already, but much more work needs to be done to develop more general and sophisticated techniques. As was also mentioned in chapter 5, one of the major difficulties is having the time scale of adaptation for the parameters appropriately match the time scale of adaptation of the individuals in the population. As far as I know, no theoretical work has been done on this in the GA literature. The development of such a theory is a very important future direction.

The directions listed above are important both for making GAs more sophisticated problem solvers and for using them to understand evolutionary systems in nature. The following are some important directions for GA theory:

Connections with the Mathematical Genetics Literature
The GA theory community has not paid enough attention to what has already been done in the related field of mathematical genetics, though this is changing to some degree (see, e.g., Booker 1993 and Altenberg 1995). There is much more to be learned there that is of potential interest to GA theory.

Extension of Statistical Mechanics Approaches
As I said in chapter 4, I think approaches similar to that taken by Prügel-Bennett and Shapiro are promising for better understanding the behavior of GAs. That is, rather than construct exact mathematical models that in effect take into account every individual in a population, it is more useful to understand how macroscopic population structures change as a result of evolution. Ultimately we would like to have a general theory of the evolution of such macroscopic structures that will predict the effects of changes in parameters and other details of the GA. There is much more to be mined from the field of statistical mechanics in formulating such theories.

Identifying and Overcoming Impediments to the Success of GAs
In the case studies and in the theoretical discussion we came across many potential impediments to the success of GAs, including deception, hitchhiking, symmetry breaking, overfitting, and inadequate sampling. GA researchers do not yet have anywhere near a complete understanding of the precise effects of these and other impediments on the performance of GAs, or of the precise conditions under which they come about, or of how to overcome them if that is possible.

Understanding the Role of Schemas in GAs
As readers of chapter 4 have no doubt gleaned, there is still a controversy in the GA community over the proper role of "schemas" in understanding GAs. This role must be pinned down and agreed on.

Understanding the Role of Crossover
Crossover is the primary operator distinguishing GAs from other stochastic search methods, but its role in GAs needs to be better understood.

Under what conditions does it indeed recombine building blocks to form high-fitness solutions, and under what conditions is it instead serving only as a "macro-mutation" operator, simply making larger jumps in the search space than a simple mutation operator can make? What is its role during various stages of the search? How can we quantify its ability to construct good solutions? Much theoretical work on GAs is aimed at answering these questions (e.g., the experiments on Royal Road functions described in chapter 4), but precise answers are still lacking.

Theory of GAs With Endogenous Fitness
In many of the scientific models we have looked at, "fitness" is not externally imposed but instead arises endogenously; it is reflected, for example, by the longevity and the fertility of an individual. Up to now, almost all work in GA theory has assumed exogenous rather than endogenous fitness functions. Holland (1994) has recently done some theoretical work on GA behavior with endogenous fitness in the context of Echo, using notions such a "flow-matrix" for describing the transmission of useful genetic building blocks from generation to generation. This is only a first step in theoretically analyzing such systems.

There are many open questions, and there is much important work to be done. Readers, onward!

Appendix A
Selected General References

Bäck, T. 1996. *Evolutionary Algorithms in Theory and Practice: Evolution Strategies, Evolutionary Programming, Genetic Algorithms*. Oxford.

Belew, R. K. and Booker, L. B., eds. 1991. *Proceedings of the Fourth International Conference on Genetic Algorithms*. Morgan Kaufmann.

Davis, L., ed. 1987. *Genetic Algorithms and Simulated Annealing*. Morgan Kaufmann.

Davis, L., ed. 1991. *Handbook of Genetic Algorithms*. Van Nostrand Reinhold.

Eshelman, L. J., ed. 1995. *Proceedings of the Sixth International Conference on Genetic Algorithms*. Morgan Kaufmann.

Fogel, D. B. 1995. *Evolutionary Computation: Toward a New Philosophy of Machine Intelligence*. IEEE Press.

Forrest, S., ed. 1993. *Proceedings of the Fifth International Conference on Genetic Algorithms*. Morgan Kaufmann.

Grefenstette, J. J., ed. 1985. *Proceedings of an International Conference on Genetic Algorithms and Their Applications*. Erlbaum.

Grefenstette, J. J., ed. 1987. *Genetic Algorithms and Their Applications: Proceedings of the Second International Conference on Genetic Algorithms*. Erlbaum.

Goldberg, D. E. 1989. *Genetic Algorithms in Search, Optimization, and Machine Learning*. Addison-Wesley.

Holland, J. H. 1975. *Adaptation in Natural and Artificial Systems*. University of Michigan Press. (Second edition: MIT Press, 1992.)

Michalewicz, Z. 1992. *Genetic Algorithms + Data Structures = Evolution Programs*. Springer-Verlag.

Rawlins, G., ed. 1991. *Foundations of Genetic Algorithms*. Morgan Kaufmann.

Schaffer, J. D., ed. 1989. *Proceedings of the Third International Conference on Genetic Algorithms*. Morgan Kaufmann.

Schwefel, H.-P. 1995. *Evolution and Optimum Seeking*. Wiley.

Whitley, D., ed. 1993. *Foundations of Genetic Algorithms 2*. Morgan Kaufmann.

Whitley, D., and Vose, M., eds. 1995. *Foundations of Genetic Algorithms 3*. Morgan Kaufmann.

Appendix B
Other Resources

SELECTED JOURNALS PUBLISHING WORK ON GENETIC ALGORITHMS

Annals of Mathematics and AI

Adaptive Behavior

Artificial Intelligence

Artificial Life

Biological Cybernetics

Complexity

Complex Systems

Evolutionary Computation

IEEE Transactions on Systems, Man, and Cybernetics

Machine Learning

Physica D

Theoretical Computer Science

SELECTED ANNUAL OR BIANNUAL CONFERENCES INCLUDING WORK ON GENETIC ALGORITHMS

Information on these conferences is posted on the Internet mailing list "GA-List" and at the GA-List WWW site—see below.

American Association of Artificial Intelligence

Artificial Life

Cognitive Science Society

Conference on Evolutionary Programming

European Conference on Artificial Life

Evolution Artificielle

Foundations of Genetic Algorithms

Genetic Programming Conference

IEEE Conference on Evolutionary Computation

International Conference on Genetic Algorithms

International Conference on Artificial Neural Networks and Genetic Algorithms

International Joint Conference on Artificial Intelligence

Golden West International Conference on Intelligent Systems

Machine Learning

Neural Information Processing Systems

Parallel Problem Solving from Nature

Simulation of Adaptive Behavior

World Congress on Neural Networks

INTERNET MAILING LISTS, WORLD WIDE WEB SITES, AND NEWS GROUPS WITH INFORMATION AND DISCUSSIONS ON GENETIC ALGORITHMS

ga-list (mailing list on general GA topics) (to subscribe, send an email request to ga-list-request@aic.nrl.navy.mil.)

genetic-programming (mailing list on genetic programming) (to subscribe, send an email request to genetic-programming-request @cs.stanford.edu.)

gann (mailing list on combining GAs and neural networks) (to subscribe, send a request to gann-request@cs.iastate.edu.)

GA-List WWW site: http://www.aic.nrl.navy.mil/galist (This page has many pointers to other pages related to GAs, as well as GA source code.)

ALife Online WWW site: http://alife.santafe.edu (This page has many pointers to information on GAs and artificial life.)

comp.ai.genetic (USENET news group)

comp.ai.alife (USENET news group)

ENCORE (Evolutionary Computation Repository Network—a collection of information on evolutionary computation): ftp://alife.santafe.edu/pub/USER-AREA/EC/

Bibliography

Ackley, D., and Littman, M. 1992. Interactions between learning and evolution. In C. G. Langton, C. Taylor, J. D. Farmer, and S. Rasmussen, eds., *Artificial Life II*. Addison-Wesley.

Ackley, D., and Littman, M. 1994. A case for Lamarckian evolution. In C. G. Langton, ed., *Artificial Life III*. Addison-Wesley.

Altenberg, L. 1994. The evolution of evolvability in genetic programming. In K. E. Kinnear, Jr., ed., *Advances in Genetic Programming*. MIT Press.

Altenberg, L. 1995. The Schema Theorem and Price's Theorem. In L. D. Whitley and M. D. Vose, eds., *Foundations of Genetic Algorithms 3*. Morgan Kaufmann.

Angeline, P. J., and Pollack, J. B. 1992. The evolutionary induction of subroutines. In *Proceedings of the Fourteenth Annual Conference of the Cognitive Science Society*. Erlbaum.

Antonisse, J. 1989. A new interpretation of schema notation that overturns the binary encoding constraint. In J. D. Schaffer, ed., *Proceedings of the Third International Conference on Genetic Algorithms*. Morgan Kaufmann.

Axelrod, R. 1984. *The Evolution of Cooperation*. Basic Books.

Axelrod, R. 1987. The evolution of strategies in the iterated Prisoner's Dilemma. In L. D. Davis, ed., *Genetic Algorithms and Simulated Annealing*. Morgan Kaufmann

Axelrod, R., and Dion, D. 1988. The further evolution of cooperation. *Science* 242, no. 4884: 1385–1390.

Bäck, T., and Hoffmeister, F. 1991. Extended selection mechanisms in genetic algorithms. In R. K. Belew and L. B. Booker, eds., *Proceedings of the Fourth International Conference on Genetic Algorithms*. Morgan Kaufmann.

Bäck, T., Hoffmeister, F., and Schwefel, H.-P. 1991. A survey of evolution strategies. In R. K. Belew and L. B. Booker, eds., *Proceedings of the Fourth International Conference on Genetic Algorithms*. Morgan Kaufmann.

Baker, J. E. 1985. Adaptive selection methods for genetic algorithms. In J. J. Grefenstette, ed., *Proceedings of the First International Conference on Genetic Algorithms and Their Applications*. Erlbaum.

Baker, J. E. 1987. Reducing bias and inefficiency in the selection algorithm. In J. J. Grefenstette, ed., *Genetic Algorithms and Their Applications: Proceedings of the Second International Conference on Genetic Algorithms*. Erlbaum.

Baldwin, J. M. 1896. A new factor in evolution. *American Naturalist* 30: 441–451, 536–553.

Baricelli, N. A. 1957. Symbiogenetic evolution processes realized by artificial methods. *Methodos* 9, no. 35–36: 143–182.

Baricelli, N. A. 1962. Numerical testing of evolution theories. *ACTA Biotheoretica* 16: 69–126.

Bedau, M. A., and Packard, N. H. 1992. Measurement of evolutionary activity, teleology, and life. In C. G. Langton, C. Taylor, J. D. Farmer, and S. Rasmussen, eds., *Artificial Life II*. Addison-Wesley.

Bedau, M. A., Ronneburg, F., and Zwick, M. 1992. Dynamics of diversity in an evolving population. In R. Männer and B. Manderick, eds., *Parallel Problem Solving from Nature 2*. North-Holland.

Belew, R. K. 1990. Evolution, learning, and culture: Computational metaphors for adaptive algorithms. *Complex Systems* 4: 11–49.

Belew, R. K. 1993. Interposing an ontogenic model between genetic algorithms and neural networks. In S. J. Hanson, J. D. Cowan, and C. L. Giles, eds., *Advances in Neural Information Processing (NIPS 5)*. Morgan Kaufmann.

Bellman, R. 1961. *Adaptive Control Processes: A Guided Tour*. Princeton University Press.

Berlekamp, E., Conway, J. H., and Guy, R. 1982. *Winning Ways for Your Mathematical Plays*, volume 2. Academic Press.

Bethke, A. D. 1980. Genetic Algorithms as Function Optimizers. Ph.D. thesis, University of Michigan, Ann Arbor (Dissertation Abstracts International, 41(9), 3503B, No. 8106101. University Microfilms).

Bledsoe, W. W. 1961. The use of biological concepts in the analytical study of systems. Paper presented at ORSA-TIMS National Meeting, San Francisco.

Booker, L. B. 1985. Improving the performance of genetic algorithms in classifier systems. In J. J. Grefenstette, ed., *Proceedings of the First International Conference on Genetic Algorithms and Their Applications*. Erlbaum.

Booker, L. B. 1993. Recombination distributions for genetic algorithms. In L. D. Whitley, ed., *Foundations of Genetic Algorithms 2*. Morgan Kaufmann.

Box, G. E. P. 1957. Evolutionary operation: A method for increasing industrial productivity. *Journal of the Royal Statistical Society C* 6, no. 2: 81–101.

Bramlette, M. F. 1991. Initialization, mutation and selection methods in genetic algorithms for function optimization. In R. K. Belew and L. B. Booker, eds., *Proceedings of the Fourth International Conference on Genetic Algorithms*, Morgan Kaufmann.

Bremermann, H. J. 1962. Optimization through evolution and recombination. In M. C. Yovits, G. T. Jacobi, and G. D. Goldstein, eds., *Self-Organizing Systems*. Spartan Books.

Caruana, R. A., and Schaffer, J. D. 1988. Representation and hidden bias: Gray vs. binary coding for genetic algorithms. In *Proceedings of the Fifth International Conference on Machine Learning*. Morgan Kaufmann.

Chalmers, D. J. 1990. The evolution of learning: An experiment in genetic connectionism. In D. S. Touretzky, J. L. Elman, T. J. Sejnowski, and G. E. Hinton, eds., *Proceedings of the 1990 Connectionist Models Summer School*. Morgan Kaufmann.

Collins, R. J., and Jefferson, D. R. 1992. The evolution of sexual selection and female choice. In F. J. Varela and P. Bourgine, eds., *Toward a Practice of Autonomous Systems: Proceedings of the First European Conference on Artificial Life*. MIT Press.

Cramer, N. L. 1985. A representation for the adaptive generation of simple sequential programs. In J. J. Grefenstette, ed., *Proceedings of the First International Conference on Genetic Algorithms and Their Applications*. Erlbaum.

Crutchfield, J. P., and Hanson, J. E. 1993. Turbulent pattern bases for cellular automata. *Physica D* 69: 279–301.

Crutchfield, J. P., and Mitchell, M. 1995. The evolution of emergent computation. *Proceedings of the National Academy of Science, USA,* 92, 10742–10746.

Das, R., Crutchfield, J. P., Mitchell, M., and Hanson, J. E. 1995. Evolving globally synchronized cellular automata. In L. J. Eshelman, ed., *Proceedings of the Sixth International Conference on Genetic Algorithms*. Morgan Kaufmann.

Das, R., Mitchell, M., and Crutchfield, J. P. 1994. A genetic algorithm discovers particle-based computation in cellular automata. In Y. Davidor, H.-P. Schwefel, and R. Männer, eds., *Parallel Problem Solving from Nature—PPSN III*. Springer-Verlag (Lecture Notes in Computer Science, volume 866).

Das, R., and Whitley, L. D. 1991. The only challenging problems are deceptive: Global search by solving order 1 hyperplanes. In R. K. Belew and L. B. Booker, eds., *Proceedings of the Fourth International Conference on Genetic Algorithms*. Morgan Kaufmann.

Davis, L. D. 1989. Adapting operator probabilities in genetic algorithms. In J. D. Schaffer, ed., *Proceedings of the Third International Conference on Genetic Algorithms*. Morgan Kaufmann.

Davis, L. D., ed. 1991. *Handbook of Genetic Algorithms*. Van Nostrand Reinhold.

Davis, T. E., and Principe, J. C. 1991. A simulated annealing-like convergence theory for the simple genetic algorithm. In R. K. Belew and L. B. Booker, eds., *Proceedings of the Fourth International Conference on Genetic Algorithms*. Morgan Kaufmann.

Deb, K., and Goldberg, D. E. 1989. An investigation of niche and species formation in genetic function optimization. In J. D. Schaffer, ed., *Proceedings of the Third International Conference on Genetic Algorithms*. Morgan Kaufmann.

Deb, K., and Goldberg, D. E. 1993. Analyzing deception in trap functions. In In L. D. Whitley, ed., *Foundations of Genetic Algorithms 2*. Morgan Kaufmann.

De Jong, K. A. 1975. An Analysis of the Behavior of a Class of Genetic Adaptive Systems. Ph.D. thesis, University of Michigan, Ann Arbor.

De Jong, K. A. 1993. Genetic algorithms are NOT function optimizers. In L. D. Whitley, ed., *Foundations of Genetic Algorithms 2*. Morgan Kaufmann.

De Jong, K. A., and Sarma, J. 1993. Generation gaps revisited. In L. D. Whitley, ed., *Foundations of Genetic Algorithms 2*. Morgan Kaufmann.

de la Maza, M., and Tidor, B. 1991. Boltzmann Weighted Selection Improves Performance of Genetic Algorithms. A.I. Memo 1345, MIT Artificial Intelligence Laboratory.

de la Maza, M., and Tidor, B. 1993. An analysis of selection procedures with particular attention paid to proportional and Boltzmann selection. In S. Forrest, ed., *Proceedings of the Fifth International Conference on Genetic Algorithms*. Morgan Kaufmann.

Derrida, B. 1981. Random energy model: An exactly solvable model of disordered systems. *Physical Review B* 24: 2613.

Dickerson, R. E., and Geis, I. 1969. *The Structure and Action of Proteins*. Harper & Row.

Eshelman, L. J. 1991. The CHC adaptive search algorithm: How to have safe search when engaging in nontraditional genetic recombination. In G. Rawlins, ed., *Foundations of Genetic Algorithms*. Morgan Kaufmann.

Eshelman, L. J., Caruana, R. A., and Schaffer, J. D. 1989. Biases in the crossover landscape. In J. D. Schaffer, ed., *Proceedings of the Third International Conference on Genetic Algorithms*. Morgan Kaufmann.

Eshelman, L. J., and Schaffer, J. D. 1991. Preventing premature convergence in genetic algorithms by preventing incest. In R. K. Belew and L. B. Booker, eds., *Proceedings of the Fourth International Conference on Genetic Algorithms*. Morgan Kaufmann.

Ewens, W. J. 1979. *Mathematical Population Genetics*. Springer-Verlag.

Feller, W. 1968. *An Introduction to Probability Theory and its Applications*, volume 1, third edition. Wiley.

Fisher, R. A. 1930. *The Genetical Theory of Natural Selection*. Clarendon.

Fogel, D. B., and Atmar, W., eds., 1993. *Proceedings of the Second Annual Conference on Evolutionary Programming*. Evolutionary Programming Society.

Fogel, L. J., Owens, A. J., and Walsh, M. J. 1966. *Artificial Intelligence through Simulated Evolution*. Wiley.

Fontanari, J. F., and Meir, R. 1990. The effect of learning on the evolution of asexual populations. *Complex Systems* 4: 401–414.

Forrest, S. 1985. Scaling fitnesses in the genetic algorithm. In Documentation for PRISONERS DILEMMA and NORMS Programs That Use the Genetic Algorithm. Unpublished manuscript.

Forrest, S. 1990. Emergent computation: Self-organizing, collective, and cooperative phenomena in natural and artificial computing networks. *Physica D* 42: 1–11.

Forrest, S., and Jones, T. 1994. Modeling complex adaptive systems with Echo. In R. J. Stonier and X. H. Yu, eds., *Complex Systems: Mechanism of Adaptation*. IOS Press.

Forrest, S., and Mitchell, M. 1993a. What makes a problem hard for a genetic algorithm? Some anomalous results and their explanation. *Machine Learning* 13: 285–319.

Forrest, S., and Mitchell, M. 1993b. Relative building block fitness and the building block hypothesis. In L. D. Whitley, ed., *Foundations of Genetic Algorithms 2*. Morgan Kaufmann.

Fraser, A. S. 1957a. Simulation of genetic systems by automatic digital computers: I. Introduction. *Australian Journal of Biological Science* 10: 484-491.

Fraser, A. S. 1957b. Simulation of genetic systems by automatic digital computers: II. Effects of linkage on rates of advance under selection. *Australian Journal of Biological Science* 10: 492-499.

French, R. M., and Messinger, A. 1994. Genes, phenes, and the Baldwin effect: Learning and evolution in a simulated population. In R. A. Brooks and P. Maes, eds., *Artificial Life IV*. MIT Press.

Friedman, G. J. 1959. Digital simulation of an evolutionary process. *General Systems Yearbook* 4: 171–184.

Fujiki, C., and Dickinson, J. 1987. Using the genetic algorithm to generate Lisp source code to solve the Prisoner's dilemma. In J. J. Grefenstette, ed., *Proceedings of the First International Conference on Genetic Algorithms and Their Applications*. Erlbaum.

Gacs, P., Kurdyumov, G. L., and Levin, L. A. 1978. One-dimensional uniform arrays that wash out finite islands. *Problemy Peredachi Informatsii* 14: 92–98 (in Russian).

Glover, F. 1989. Tabu search. Part I. *ORSA Journal of Computing* 1: 190–206.

Glover, F. 1990. Tabu search. Part II. *ORSA Journal of Computing* 2: 4–32.

Goldberg, D. E. 1987. Simple genetic algorithms and the minimal deceptive problem. In L. D. Davis, ed., *Genetic Algorithms and Simulated Annealing*. Morgan Kaufmann.

Goldberg, D. E. 1989a. *Genetic Algorithms in Search, Optimization, and Machine Learning*. Addison-Wesley.

Goldberg, D. E. 1989b. Genetic algorithms and Walsh functions: Part I, A gentle introduction. *Complex Systems* 3: 129–152.

Goldberg, D. E. 1989c. Genetic algorithms and Walsh functions: Part II, Deception and its analysis. *Complex Systems* 3: 153–171.

Goldberg, D. E. 1989d. Sizing populations for serial and parallel genetic algorithms. In J. D. Schaffer, ed., *Proceedings of the Third International Conference on Genetic Algorithms*. Morgan Kaufmann.

Goldberg, D. E. 1990. A note on Boltzmann tournament selection for genetic algorithms and population-oriented simulated annealing. *Complex Systems* 4: 445–460.

Goldberg, D. E., and Deb, K. 1991. A comparitive analysis of selection schemes used in genetic algorithms. In G. Rawlins, ed., *Foundations of Genetic Algorithms*. Morgan Kaufmann.

Goldberg, D. E., Deb, K., and Korb, B. 1990. Messy genetic algorithms revisited: Studies in mixed size and scale. *Complex Systems* 4: 415–444.

Goldberg, D. E., Deb, K., Kargupta, H., and Harik, G. 1993. Rapid, accurate optimization of difficult problems using fast messy genetic algorithms. In S. Forrest, ed., *Proceedings of the Fifth International Conference on Genetic Algorithms*. Morgan Kaufmann.

Goldberg, D. E., Korb, B., and Deb, K. 1989. Messy genetic algorithms: Motivation, analysis, and first results. *Complex Systems* 3: 493–530.

Goldberg, D. E., and Richardson, J. 1987. Genetic algorithms with sharing for multimodal function optimization. In J. J. Grefenstette, ed., *Genetic Algorithms and Their Applications: Proceedings of the Second International Conference on Genetic Algorithms*. Erlbaum.

Goldberg, D. E., and Segrest, P. 1987. Finite Markov chain analysis of genetic algorithms. In J. J. Grefenstette, ed., *Genetic Algorithms and Their Applications: Proceedings of the Second International Conference on Genetic Algorithms*. Erlbaum.

Gonzaga de Sá, P., and Maes, C. 1992. The Gacs-Kurdyumov-Levin automaton revisited. *Journal of Statistical Physics* 67, no. 3/4: 507–522.

Grefenstette, J. J. 1986. Optimization of control parameters for genetic algorithms. *IEEE Transactions on Systems, Man, and Cybernetics* 16, no. 1: 122–128.

Grefenstette, J. J. 1991a. Lamarckian learning in multi-agent environments. In R. K. Belew, and L. B. Booker, eds., *Proceedings of the Fourth International Conference on Genetic Algorithms*, Morgan Kaufmann.

Grefenstette, J. J. 1991b. Conditions for implicit parallelism. In G. Rawlins, ed., *Foundations of Genetic Algorithms*. Morgan Kaufmann.

Grefenstette, J. J. 1993. Deception considered harmful. In L. D. Whitley, ed., *Foundations of Genetic Algorithms 2*. Morgan Kaufmann.

Grefenstette, J. J., and Baker, J. E. 1989. How genetic algorithms work: A critical look at implicit parallelism. In J. D. Schaffer, ed., *Proceedings of the Third International Conference on Genetic Algorithms*. Morgan Kaufmann.

Gruau, F. 1992. Genetic synthesis of Boolean neural networks with a cell rewriting developmental process. In L. D. Whitley and J. D. Schaffer, eds., *COGANN-92: International Workshop on Combinations of Genetic Algorithms and Neural Networks*. IEEE Computer Society Press.

Hancock, P. J. B. 1994. An empirical comparison of selection methods in evolutionary algorithms. In T. C. Fogarty, ed., *Evolutionary Computing: AISB Workshop, Leeds, U.K., April 1994, Selected Papers*. Springer-Verlag.

Hanson, J. E., and Crutchfield, J. P. 1992. The attractor-basin portrait of a cellular automaton. *Journal of Statistical Physics* 66, no. 5/6: 1415–1462.

Harp, S. A., and Samad, T. 1991. Genetic synthesis of neural network architecture. In L. D. Davis, ed., *Handbook of Genetic Algorithms*. Van Nostrand Reinhold

Hart, W. E., and Belew, R. K. 1996. Optimization with genetic algorithm hybrids that use local search. In R. K. Belew and M. Mitchell, eds., *Adaptive Individuals in Evolving Populations: Models and Algorithms*. Addison-Wesley.

Harvey, I. 1992. Species adaptation genetic algorithms: A basis for a continuing SAGA. In F. J. Varela and P. Bourgine, eds., *Toward a Practice of Autonomous Systems: Proceedings of the First European Conference on Artificial Life*. MIT Press.

Harvey, I. 1993. The puzzle of the persistent question marks: A case study of genetic drift. In S. Forrest, ed., *Proceedings of the Fifth International Conference on Genetic Algorithms*. Morgan Kaufmann.

Heisler, I. L., and Curtsinger, J. W. 1990. Dynamics of sexual selection in diploid populations. *Evolution* 44, no. 5: 1164–1176.

Hertz, J., Krogh, A., and Palmer, R. G. 1991. *Introduction to the Theory of Neural Computation*. Addison-Wesley.

Hillis, W. D. 1990. Co-evolving parasites improve simulated evolution as an optimization procedure. *Physica D* 42: 228–234.

Hillis, W. D. 1992. Co-evolving parasites improve simulated evolution as an optimization procedure. In C. G. Langton, C. Taylor, J. D. Farmer, and S. Rasmussen, eds., *Artificial Life II*. Addison-Wesley.

Hinton, G. E., and Nowlan, S. J. 1987. How learning can guide evolution. *Complex Systems* 1: 495–502.

Holland, J. H. 1975. *Adaptation in Natural and Artificial Systems*. University of Michigan Press. (Second edition: MIT Press, 1992.)

Holland, J. H. 1986. Escaping brittleness: The possibilities of general-purpose learning algorithms applied to parallel rule-based systems. In R. S. Michalski, J. G. Carbonell, and T. M. Mitchell, eds., *Machine Learning II*. Morgan Kaufmann.

Holland, J. H. 1993. Innovation in Complex Adaptive Systems: Some Mathematical Sketches. Working Paper 93-10-062, Santa Fe Institute.

Holland, J. H. 1994. Echoing emergence: Objectives, rough definitions, and speculations for ECHO-class models. In G. Cowan, D. Pines, and D. Melzner, eds., *Complexity: Metaphors, Models, and Reality*. Addison-Wesley.

Horn, J. 1993. Finite Markov chain analysis of genetic algorithms with niching. In S. Forrest, ed., *Proceedings of the Fifth International Conference on Genetic Algorithms* Morgan Kaufmann.

Hunter, L., Searls, D., and Shavlik, J., eds. 1993. *Proceedings of the First International Conference on Intelligent Systems for Molecular Biology*. AAAI Press.

Janikow, C. Z., and Michalewicz, Z. 1991. An experimental comparison of binary and floating point representations in genetic algorithms. In R. K. Belew and L. B. Booker, eds., *Proceedings of the Fourth International Conference on Genetic Algorithms*, Morgan Kaufmann.

Jones, T. 1995. Crossover, macromutation, and population-based search. In L. J. Eshelman, ed., *Proceedings of the Sixth International Conference on Genetic Algorithms*. Morgan Kaufmann.

Jones, T., and Forrest, S. 1993. An Introduction to SFI Echo. Working Paper 93-12-074, Santa Fe Institute.

Kinnear, K. E. Jr., ed. 1994. *Advances in Genetic Programming*. MIT Press.

Kirkpatrick, M. 1982. Sexual selection and the evolution of female choice. *Evolution* 1: 1–12.

Kirkpatrick, M., and Ryan, M. 1991. The evolution of mating preferences and the paradox of the lek. *Nature* 350: 33–38.

Kirkpatrick, S., Gelatt, C. D., Jr., and Vecchi, M. P. 1983. Optimization by simulated annealing. *Science* 220: 671–680.

Kitano, H. 1990. Designing neural networks using genetic algorithms with graph generation system. *Complex Systems* 4: 461–476.

Kitano, H. 1994. Neurogenetic learning: An integrated method of designing and training neural networks using genetic algorithms. *Physica D* 75: 225–238.

Knuth, D. E. 1973. The Art of Computer Programming. Volume 3: Searching and Sorting. Addison-Wesley.

Koza, J. R. 1992. *Genetic Programming: On the Programming of Computers by Means of Natural Selection*. MIT Press.

Koza, J. R. 1994. *Genetic Programming II: Automatic Discovery of Reusable Programs*. MIT Press.

Langton, C. G. 1992. Introduction. In C. G. Langton, C. Taylor, J. D. Farmer, and S. Rasmussen, eds., *Artificial Life II*. Addison-Wesley

Lenat, D. B., and Brown, J. S. 1984. Why AM and Eurisko appear to work. *Artificial Intelligence* 23: 260–294.

Levenick, J. R. 1991. Inserting introns improves genetic algorithm success rate: Taking a cue from biology. In R. K. Belew and L. B. Booker, eds., *Proceedings of the Fourth International Conference on Genetic Algorithms*. Morgan Kaufmann.

Liepins, G. E., and Vose, M. D. 1990. Representational issues in genetic optimization. *Journal of Experimental and Theoretical Artificial Intelligence* 2: 101–115.

Liepins, G. E., and Vose, M. D. 1991. Deceptiveness and genetic algorithm dynamics. In G. Rawlins, ed., *Foundations of Genetic Algorithms*. Morgan Kaufmann.

Lindgren, K. 1992. Evolutionary phenomena in simple dynamics. In C. G. Langton, C. Taylor, J. D. Farmer, and S. Rasmussen, eds., *Artificial Life II*. Addison-Wesley.

Lloyd Morgan, C. 1896. On modification and variation. *Science* 4: 733–740.

Lucasius, C. B., and Kateman, G. 1989. In J. D. Schaffer, ed., *Proceedings of the Third International Conference on Genetic Algorithms*. Morgan Kaufmann.

Mackey, M. C., and Glass, L. 1977. *Science* 197: 297.

Martin, F. G., and Cockerham, C. C. 1960. High speed selection studies. In O. Kempthorne, ed., *Biometrical Genetics*. Pergamon.

Mason, A. J. 1993. Crossover Non-Linearity Ratios and the Genetic Algorithm: Escaping the Blinkers of Schema Processing and Intrinsic Parallelism. Report No. 535b, School of Engineering, University of Auckland (New Zealand).

Maynard Smith, J. 1987. When learning guides evolution. *Nature* 329: 761–762.

McClelland, J. L., Rumelhart, D. E., and the PDP Research Group 1986. *Parallel Distributed Processing*, Volume 2: Psychological and Biological Models. MIT Press.

Meyer, T. P. 1992. Long-Range Predictability of High-Dimensional Chaotic Dynamics. Ph.D. thesis, University of Illinois at Urbana-Champaign, Urbana.

Meyer, T. P., and Packard, N. H. 1992. Local forecasting of high-dimensional chaotic dynamics. In M. Casdagli and S. Eubank, eds., *Nonlinear Modeling and Forecasting*. Addison-Wesley.

Miller, G. F. 1994. Exploiting mate choice in evolutionary computation: Sexual selection as a process of search, optimization, and diversification. In T. C. Fogarty, ed., *Evolutionary Computing: AISB Workshop, Leeds, U.K., April 1994, Selected Papers*. Springer-Verlag.

Miller, G. F., and Todd, P. M. 1993. Evolutionary wanderlust: Sexual selection with directional mate preferences. In J.-A. Meyer, H. L. Roitblat, and S. W. Wilson, eds., *From Animals to Animats 2: Proceedings of the Second International Conference on Simulation of Adaptive Behavior*. MIT Press.

Miller, G. F., Todd, P. M., and Hegde, S. U. 1989. Designing neural networks using genetic algorithms. In J. D. Schaffer, ed., *Proceedings of the Third International Conference on Genetic Algorithms*. Morgan Kaufmann.

Mitchell, M., Crutchfield, J. P., and Hraber, P. T. 1994a. Evolving cellular automata to perform computations: Mechanisms and impediments. *Physica D* 75: 361–391.

Mitchell, M., Crutchfield, J. P., and Hraber, P. T. 1994b. Dynamics, computation, and the "edge of chaos": A re-examination. In G. Cowan, D. Pines, and D. Melzner, eds., *Complexity: Metaphors, Models, and Reality*. Addison-Wesley.

Mitchell, M., Forrest, S., and Holland, J. H. 1992. The royal road for genetic algorithms: Fitness landscapes and GA performance. In F. J. Varela and P. Bourgine, eds., *Toward a Practice of Autonomous Systems: Proceedings of the First European Conference on Artificial Life*. MIT Press.

Mitchell, M., Holland, J. H., and Forrest, S. 1994. When will a genetic algorithm outperform hill climbing? In J. D. Cowan, G. Tesauro, and J. Alspector, eds., *Advances in Neural Information Processing Systems 6*. Morgan Kaufmann.

Mitchell, M., Hraber, P. T., and Crutchfield, J. P. 1993. Revisiting the edge of chaos: Evolving cellular automata to perform computations. *Complex Systems* 7, 89–130.

Montana, D. J., and L. D. Davis 1989. Training feedforward networks using genetic algorithms. In *Proceedings of the International Joint Conference on Artificial Intelligence*. Morgan Kaufmann.

Mühlenbein, H. 1992. How genetic algorithms really work: 1. Mutation and hillclimbing. In R. Männer and B. Manderick, eds., *Parallel Problem Solving from Nature 2*. North-Holland.

Nilsson, N. J. 1989. Action networks. In J. Tenenberg et al., eds., Proceedings from the Rochester Planning Workshop: From Formal Systems to Practical Systems, Technical Report 284, Computer Science Department, University of Rochester (N.Y.).

Nix, A. E., and Vose, M. D. 1991. Modeling genetic algorithms with Markov chains. *Annals of Mathematics and Artificial Intelligence* 5: 79-88.

O'Reilly, U.-M., and Oppacher, F. 1992. An experimental perspective on genetic programming. In R. Männer and B. Manderick, eds., *Parallel Problem Solving from Nature 2*. North-Holland.

O'Reilly, U.-M, and Oppacher, F. 1994a. Program search with a hierarchical variable length representation: Genetic programming, simulated annealing, and hill climbing. In Y. Davidor, H.-P. Schwefel, and R. Männer, eds., *Parallel Problem Solving from Nature—PPSN III*. Springer-Verlag (Lecture Notes in Computer Science, Volume 866).

O'Reilly, U.-M, and Oppacher, F. 1994b. Program search with a hierarchical variable length representation: Genetic programming, simulated annealing, and hill climbing. In Y. Davidor, H.-P. Schwefel, and R. Männer, eds., *Parallel Problem Solving from Nature—PPSN III*. Springer-Verlag (Lectures Notes in Computer Science, Volume 866).

O'Reilly, U.-M., and Oppacher, F. 1995. The troubling aspects of a building block hypothesis for genetic programming. In L. D. Whitley and M. D. Vose, eds., *Foundations of Genetic Algorithms 3*. Morgan Kaufmann.

Osborne, H. F. 1896. A mode of evolution requiring neither natural selection nor the inheritance of acquired characteristics. *Transactions of the New York Academy of Science* 15: 141–142, 148.

Otto, S. P. 1991. On evolution under sexual and viability selection: A two-locus diploid model. *Evolution* 45, no. 6: 1443–1457.

Packard, N. H. 1988. Adaptation toward the edge of chaos. In J. A. S. Kelso, A. J. Mandell, M. F. Shlesinger, eds., *Dynamic Patterns in Complex Systems*. World Scientific.

Packard, N. H. 1990. A genetic learning algorithm for the analysis of complex data. *Complex Systems* 4, no. 5: 543–572.

Parsons, R., Forrest, S., and Burks, C. In press. Genetic operators for the DNA fragment assembly problem. *Machine Learning*.

Parsons, R., Forrest, S., and Burks, C. 1993. Genetic algorithms for DNA sequence assembly. In L. Hunter, D. Searls, and J. Shavlik, eds., *Proceedings of the First International Conference on Intelligent Systems for Molecular Biology*, 310–318. AAAI Press.

Peck, C. C., and Dhawan, A. P. 1993. A Review and Critique of Genetic Algorithm Theories. Technical Report TR 153/6/93/ECE, Department of Electrical and Computer Engineering, College of Engineering University of Cincinnati.

Prügel-Bennett, A., and Shapiro, J. L. 1994. An analysis of genetic algorithms using statistical mechanics. *Physical Review Letters* 72, no. 9: 1305–1309.

Radcliffe, N. J. 1991. Equivalence class analysis of genetic algorithms. *Complex Systems* 5, no. 2: 183–205.

Rawlins, G., ed. 1991. *Foundations of Genetic Algorithms*. Morgan Kaufmann.

Rechenberg, I. 1965. Cybernetic Solution Path of an Experimental Problem. Ministry of Aviation, Royal Aircraft Establishment (U.K.).

Rechenberg, I. 1973. *Evolutionsstrategie: Optimierung Technischer Systeme nach Prinzipien der Biologischen Evolution*. Frommann-Holzboog (Stuttgart).

Reed, J., Toombs, R., and Barricelli, N. A. 1967. Simulation of biological evolution and machine learning. *Journal of Theoretical Biology* 17: 319–342.

Richards, F. C., Meyer, T. P., and Packard, N. H. 1990. Extracting cellular automaton rules directly from experimental data. *Physica D* 45: 189–202.

Riolo, R. L. 1992. Survival of the fittest bits. *Scientific American*, 267, no. 1: 114–116.

Roughgarden, J., Bergman, A., Shafir, S., and Taylor, C. 1996. Adaptive computation in ecology and evolution: A guide for future research. In R. K. Belew and M. Mitchell, eds., *Adaptive Individuals in Evolving Populations: Models and Algorithms*. Addison-Wesley.

Rumelhart, D. E., Hinton, G. E., and Williams, R. J. 1986. Learning internal representations by error propagation. In D. E. Rumelhart, J. L. McClelland, and the PDP Research Group, *Parallel Distributed Processing*, Volume 1: Foundations. MIT Press.

Rumelhart, D. E., McClelland, J. L., and the PDP Research Group 1986. *Parallel Distributed Processing*, Volume 1: Foundations. MIT Press.

Schaefer, C. G. 1987. The ARGOT strategy: Adaptive representation genetic optimizer technique. In J. J. Grefenstette, ed., *Genetic Algorithms and Their Applications: Proceedings of the Second International Conference on Genetic Algorithms*. Erlbaum.

Schaffer, J. D., Caruana, R. A., Eshelman, L. J, and Das, R. 1989. A study of control parameters affecting online performance of genetic algorithms for function optimization. In J. D. Schaffer, ed., *Proceedings of the Third International Conference on Genetic Algorithms*. Morgan Kaufmann.

Schaffer, J. D., Eshelman, L. J, and Offut, D. 1991. Spurious correlations and premature convergence in genetic algorithms. In G. Rawlins, ed., *Foundations of Genetic Algorithms*. Morgan Kaufmann.

Schaffer, J. D., and Morishima, A. 1987. An adaptive crossover distribution mechanism for genetic algorithms. In J. J. Grefenstette, ed., *Genetic Algorithms and Their Applications: Proceedings of the Second International Conference on Genetic Algorithms*. Erlbaum.

Schaffer, J. D., Whitley, D., and Eshelman, L. J. 1992. Combinations of genetic algorithms and neural networks: A survey of the state of the art. In L. D. Whitley and J. D. Schaffer, eds., *COGANN-92: International Workshop on Combinations of Genetic Algorithms and Neural Networks*. IEEE Computer Society Press.

Schraudolph, N. N., and R. K. Belew 1992. Dynamic parameter encoding for genetic algorithms. *Machine Learning* 9: 9–21.

Schulze-Kremer, S. 1992. Genetic algorithms for protein tertiary structure prediction. In R. Männer and B. Manderick, eds., *Parallel Problem Solving from Nature 2*. North-Holland.

Schwefel, H.-P. 1975. Evolutionsstrategie und numerische Optimierung. Ph.D. thesis, Technische Universität Berlin.

Schwefel, H.-P. 1977. *Numerische Optimierung von Computer-Modellen mittels der Evolutionsstrategie*. Basel: Birkhäuser.

Simpson, G. G. 1953. The Baldwin effect. *Evolution* 7: 110–117.

Smith, R. E., Forrest, S., and Perelson, A. S. 1993. Population diversity in an immune system model: Implications for genetic search. In L. D. Whitley, ed., *Foundations of Genetic Algorithms 2*. Morgan Kaufmann.

Smolensky, P. 1988. On the proper treatment of connectionism. *Behavioral and Brain Sciences* 11, no. 1: 1–14.

Spears, W. M. 1993. Crossover or mutation? In L. D. Whitley, ed., *Foundations of Genetic Algorithms 2*. Morgan Kaufmann.

Spears, W. M., and De Jong, K. A. 1991. On the virtues of parameterized uniform crossover. In R. K. Belew and L. B. Booker, eds., *Proceedings of the Fourth International Conference on Genetic Algorithms*. Morgan Kaufmann.

Syswerda, G. 1989. Uniform crossover in genetic algorithms. In J. D. Schaffer, ed., *Proceedings of the Third International Conference on Genetic Algorithms*. Morgan Kaufmann.

Syswerda, G. 1991. A study of reproduction in generational and steady-state genetic algorithms. In G. Rawlins, ed., *Foundations of Genetic Algorithms*. Morgan Kaufmann.

Tackett, W.A. 1994. Recombination, Selection, and the Genetic Construction of Computer Programs. Ph.D. thesis, Department of Computer Engineering, University of Southern California.

Tanese, R. 1989. Distributed Genetic Algorithms for Function Optimization. Ph.D. thesis, Electrical Engineering and Computer Science Department, University of Michigan.

Thierens, D., and Goldberg, D. E. 1993. Mixing in genetic algorithms. In S. Forrest, ed., *Proceedings of the Fifth International Conference on Genetic Algorithms*. Morgan Kaufmann.

Todd, P. M., and Miller, G. F. 1993. Parental guidance suggested: How parental imprinting evolves through sexual selection as an adaptive learning mechanism. *Adaptive Behavior* 2, no. 1: 5–47.

Toffoli, T., and Margolus, N. 1987. *Cellular Automata Machines: A New Environment for Modeling*. MIT Press.

Urey, H. C. 1952. *The Planets: Their Origin and Development*. Yale University Press.

Vose, M. D. 1991. Generalizing the notion of schema in genetic algorithms. *Artificial Intelligence* 50: 385–396.

Vose, M. D. 1993. Modeling simple genetic algorithms. In L. D. Whitley, ed., *Foundations of Genetic Algorithms 2*. Morgan Kaufmann.

Vose, M. D., and Liepins, G. E. 1991. Punctuated equilibria in genetic search. *Complex Systems* 5: 31–44.

Waddington, C. H. 1942. Canalization of development and the inheritance of acquired characters. *Nature* 150: 563–565.

Walsh, J. L. 1923. A closed set of orthogonal functions. *American Journal of Mathematics* 55: 5–24.

Weber, B. H., Depew, D. J., and Smith, J. D, eds. 1988. *Entropy, Information, and Evolution: New Perspectives on Physical and Biological Evolution*. MIT Press.

Whitley, L. D. 1989. The *Genitor* algorithm and selection pressure: Why rank-based allocation of reproductive trials is best. In J. D. Schaffer, ed., *Proceedings of the Third International Conference on Genetic Algorithms*. Morgan Kaufmann.

Whitley, L. D. 1991. Fundamental principles of deception in genetic search. In G. Rawlins, ed., *Foundations of Genetic Algorithms* Morgan Kaufmann.

Whitley, L. D. 1993a. An executable model of a simple genetic algorithm. In L. D. Whitley, ed., *Foundations of Genetic Algorithms 2*. Morgan Kaufmann.

Whitley, L. D., ed. 1993b. *Foundations of Genetic Algorithms 2*. Morgan Kaufmann.

Whitley, L. D., and Schaffer, J. D., eds. 1992. *COGANN-92: International Workshop on Combinations of Genetic Algorithms and Neural Networks*. IEEE Computer Society Press.

Whitley, L. D., and Vose, M. D., eds. 1995. *Foundations of Genetic Algorithms 3*. Morgan Kaufmann.

Winston, P. H. 1992. *Artificial Intelligence*, third edition. Addison-Wesley.

Wolfram, S. 1986. *Theory and Applications of Cellular Automata*. World Scientific.

Wright, A. H. 1991. Genetic algorithms for real parameter optimization. In G. Rawlins, ed., *Foundations of Genetic Algorithms*. Morgan Kaufmann.

Wright, S. 1931. Evolution in Mendelian populations. *Genetics* 16: 97–159.

Index

Gacs-Kurdyumov-Levin (GKL) rule, 54
Game of Life, 44
Gamete 6, 25
Geis, Irving, 62
Gelatt, C. D., 15
Gene, 3, 5, 6
 deletion, 159, 183
 doubling, 159, 174, 183
 expression, 89
 usage, 109–113
Gene deletion, 159, 183
Gene doubling, 159, 174, 183
Gene expression, 89
Gene usage, 109–113
Generation, 11
Generation gap, 171
Generational GAs, 171
Genetic algorithms
 applications of, 15–16
 deception in, 125–127, 152
 definition 8–10
 as dynamical systems, 143–144
 in ecology, 16
 in economics, 16
 in evolution and learning, 16, 87–100
 generational, 171
 history 2–3
 idealized 132–138, 152–153
 in immunology, 16
 in machine learning, 16
 as Markov chains, 144–148
 messy 162–166, 178–179
 meta-level 176, 179
 operators, 10, 171–174
 optimization by, 6, 9, 15, 119, 124–125, 162
 vs. satisficing by, 124
 parameters 11, 175–177
 in population genetics. See Population
  genetics
 self-adaptation, 75, 158–162, 176–177, 179,
  184–185
 simple, 10–12
 in social systems, 16
 steady-state, 171
 surface, 147
 terminology, 5–6
 when to use, 155–156
Genetic assimilation, 89
Genetic hitchhiking, 131, 137
Genetic operators, 10, 171–174
Genetic programming, 36–44, 81–82
 158–159, 173, 178
Genetic regulation, 183–184

Genetics, mathematical. See Population
 genetics
Genetics, population. See Population
 genetics
Genome, 5
Genotype, 5, 6, 183
Genotype-phenotype separation, 183
Glass, Leon, 57
Glover, Fred, 15
Goldberg, David, 11, 27, 29–30, 125, 138,
 157, 159, 161–166, 168–169, 171, 174–176,
 178–179, 183
Gonzaga de Sá, Paula, 54
Gradient ascent, 156. See also Hill climbing
Gradient search, 124, 156. See also Hill
 climbing
Grammar, 73
Grammatical encoding, 72, 183–184. See also
 Encoding
Gray coding, 157, 176. See also Encoding
Gray encoding. See Gray coding
Green, Milton, 22, 26–27
Grefenstette, John, 100, 122–123, 125–127,
 134, 176, 179
Gruau, Fréderic, 76, 184
Guy, Richard, 44

Hamming distance, 7
Hancock, Peter, 166
Hanson, James, 53
Haploid chromosome, 3, 6, 23, 25
Harik, Georges, 162–166
Harp, Steven, 159
Hart, William, 100, 124
Harvey, Inman, 159
Hegde, Shailesh, 71–72, 75
Hertz, John, 66
Hierarchical regulation, 184
Hill climbing, 14–15, 124, 129, 137
 next ascent, 129
 random mutation, 32, 82, 129–131, 137, 153
 steepest ascent, 15, 32, 114, 129, 153
Hillis, W. Daniel, 21–27, 31, 35, 48, 157, 175,
 182
Hinton, Geoffrey, 66, 89–94, 99, 113, 181
History, evolutionary computation. See
 Evolutionary computation history
Hitchhiking, genetic. See Genetic
 hitchhiking
Hoffmeister, Frank, 2, 49, 166
Holland, John, 2–3, 8, 27, 29–30, 85, 104, 107–
 108, 117–121, 123–138, 155–157, 159–160,
 166, 171, 173, 175, 182, 186

Horn, Jeffrey, 138
Host-parasite coevolution, 26–27, 182–183.
 See also Coevolution
Hot spots, crossover, 161–162, 178–179
Hraber, Peter, 44–55, 82
Huber, Greg, 134
Hunter, Lawrence, 62
Hybrid methods, 124
Hyperplane, 27. *See also* Schema

Idea model, 181
Idealized genetic algorithm, 134–138,
 152–153
Immunology
 GA applications in, 16
Implicit parallelism, 30, 118, 131–132, 137,
 157
Incest, prevention of, 175
Instance, 27. *See also* Schema
Introns, 183
Inversion 3, 159–161, 174, 178, 183. *See also*
 Genetic operators, Encodings, Linkage

Janikow, Cezary, 157
Jefferson, David 101–104, 181
Jones, Terry 104–108, 173

Kargupta, Hillol, 162–166
Kateman, Gerrit, 61
Kinnear, Kenneth, 44
Kirkpatrick, Mark, 101–104, 181
Kirkpatrick, Scott, 15
Kitano, Hiroaki 72–76, 157, 183
Knuth, Donald, 21–22
Korb, Bradley, 162–166, 179
Koza, John, 36–44, 46, 158
Krogh, Anders, 66
Kurdyumov, Georgii, 54

Lamarck, Jean Baptiste, 87
Lamarckian hypothesis, 87
Lamarckian learning, 99–100, 114. *See also*
 Evolution
Landscape, fitness. *See* Fitness landscape
Langton, Christopher, 44
Learning, 183–184. *See also* Evolution
Learning and evolution, interactions, 16,
 87–100. *See also* Evolution
Learning rules. *See* Neural networks
Lenat, Douglas, 42
Levenick, James, 183
Levin, Leonid, 54
Liepins, Gunar, 125, 138–144

Life, game of, 44
Lindgren, Kristian, 21
Linear rank selection, 169–170, 178. *See also*
 Selection
Linkage, 159. *See also* Encoding, Genetic
 operators, Inversion
Littman, Michael, 95–100, 113
Locus, 5
Lucasius, Carlos, 61

McClelland, Jay, 66
Machine learning
 GA applications in, 16
Mackey, Michael, 57
Mackey-Glass equation, 57
Macro-mutation, 173, 186
Maes, Christian, 54
Many-character encoding, 157. *See also*
 Encoding
Margolus, Norman, 45
Markov chains, 144, 152
 as models of GAs, 144–148
Mason, Andrew, 125
Mathematical genetics. *See* Population
 genetics
Mating tags, 175
Mating, spatially restricted, 175. *See also*
 Crossover
Messy GAs, 162–166, 178–179
Meta-level GA, 176, 179
Meyer, Thomas, 46, 57–61, 157, 170
Michalewicz, Zbigniew, 157
Microanalytic simulation, 86–87
Miller, Geoffrey, 71–72, 75
Mitchell, Melanie, 32, 44–55, 82, 125,
 127–138
Montana, David 67–70, 75, 157
Morishima, Amy, 161–162, 178
Morgan, C. Lloyd, 88
Mühlenbein, Heinz, 174
Mutation, 3, 6, 10, 173–174. *See also* Mutation
 rate, Genetic operators, Parameters
 adaptive, 75
 rate, 11, 175–177
 real-valued, 64
 role of, 30
Mutation rate 11, 175–177
 adaptive, 177, 184–185

Nelson, Raymond, 22, 26
Neural networks, 65–79, 82, 87
 back propagation in, 66.
 back propagation vs. GA, 68–70, 83

direct encoding, 71. *See also* Encoding
evolved by GAs, 65–79
evolving architectures, 70–76
evolving learning rules, 76–79
evolving weights, 67–70
grammatical encoding, 72, 183–184. *See also* Encoding
Next ascent hill climbing, 129. *See also* Hill climbing
Nilsson, Nils, 40
Nix, Allen, 138, 144–148
Nowlan, Steven, 89–94, 99, 113, 181

Off-line performance, 119–120, 152–153, 175–176
Offutt, Daniel, 132
On-line performance, 119–120, 124, 152–153, 175–176
Open-ended evolution, 184
Oppacher, Franz, 42–43, 158
Optimization. *See* Function optimization, Genetic algorithms
Order, 27. *See also* Schema.
Ordering problems, 161, 173
O'Reilly, Una-May, 42–43, 158
Organic selection. *See* Baldwin effect
Owens, Alvin, 2–3, 35

Packard, Norman, 46, 49, 56–61, 108–113, 157, 170
Palmer, Richard, 66
Parallelism, 4
 implicit. *See* Implicit parallelism
Parameterized uniform crossover, 172. *See also* Crossover, Uniform Crossover
Parameters (for genetic algorithm), 11, 175–177
 self-adaptation of, 75, 176–177, 179, 184–185
Parasites. *See* Host-parasite coevolution
Parasitic bits. *See* Genetic hitchhiking
Parsons, Rebecca, 62, 161
Peck, Charles, 125
Perelson, Alan, 174
Performance
 off-line. *See* Off-line performance
 on-line. *See* On-line performance
Phenotype, 6, 183
Pollack, Jordan, 42
Population genetics, 7, 16, 101–102, 132, 140, 185
Population size, 11, 175–176, 184. *See also* Parameters

Positional bias, 172–173. *See also* Crossover
Prediction, 55–65
Premature convergence, 167
Principe, Jose, 138
Prisoner's Dilemma, 17–21, 31–33, 114, 183
Protein structure, 61–65
Prügel-Bennett, Adam, 148–152, 169, 185
Punctuated equilibria, 144

Radcliffe, Nicholas, 30
Random mutation hill climbing, 32, 82, 129–131, 137, 153. *See also* Hill climbing
Rank selection, 169–170, 178. *See also* Selection
Rapoport, Anatol, 18
Rawlins, Gregory, 27, 117
Real-valued encoding, 157. *See also* Encoding
Real-valued mutation, 64. *See also* Mutation
Recessive allele, 103
Rechenberg, Ingo, 2
Recombination, 3, 6. *See also* Crossover
Reed, J, 2
Reinforcement learning, 95
 evolutionary. *See* Evolutionary reinforcement learning
Representation. *See* Encoding
Richards, Fred, 46
Richardson, Jon, 174
Roughgarden, Jonathan, 181
Roulette wheel sampling, 11, 166–167. *See also* Selection
Royal Road functions, 127–138, 153, 172, 174, 178–179
Rumelhart, David, 66, 77–78
Ryan, M. 101

Samad, Tariq, 159
Sampling. *See also* Selection
 roulette-wheel, 11, 166–167
 stochastic universal, 166–167, 178
Sarma, Jayshree, 171
Satisficing, 124
Scaling, 167. *See also* Selection
 sigma, 167–168
Schaefer, Craig, 159
Schaffer, J. David, 67, 69, 72, 132, 157, 161–162, 172, 175–176, 178
Schema, 3, 27–32, 117–119, 122–127, 152–153, 178, 185. *See also* Building blocks; Hyperplane
 average fitness, 28, 31, 152
 combinatorics, 28